CONIFERS
OF CALIFORNIA

CONIFERS
OF CALIFORNIA

RONALD M. LANNER

Featuring the art of
Eugene O. Murman

Cachuma Press
Los Olivos, California

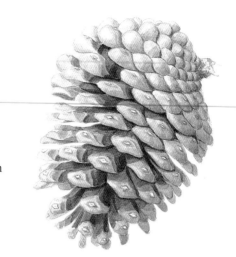

Conifers of California
Second printing, January 2002

Cachuma Press
Los Olivos, California

Text: Copyright © Ronald M. Lanner, 1999
Eugene O. Murman art: Copyright © Margo Murman
Susan Bazell art: Copyright © Susan Bazell

Editors: Marjorie Popper and John Evarts
Editorial Assistant: Darcy Shankland
Graphic Design and Production: Katey O'Neill
Cartographer: Sue Irwin
Printed in Singapore

Library of Congress Cataloging-in-Publication Data
Lanner, Ronald M.
    Conifers of California / Ronald M. Lanner: featuring the art of
  Eugene O. Murman. — 1st ed.
        p.   cm.
    Includes bibliographical references and index.
    ISBN 0-9628505-3-5. — ISBN 0-9628505-4-3
    1. Conifers—California.   I. Title.
QK494.L36   1999
585' .0974—dc21   98-52371
                                                        CIP

DEDICATION:
For William B. Critchfield (1923 - 1989), geneticist, dendrologist, scholar, who taught so many of us how to learn about California's conifers.

Front Cover: *Giant sequoias of Upper Mariposa Grove. [Yosemite N. P.]* LARRY ULRICH
Back Cover: *Western white pine above Yosemite Valley. [Yosemite N. P.]* DAVID LANNER
Half-Title Page: *Lodgepole pine in high Sierra near Cirque Crest. [Kings Canyon N. P.]* CARR CLIFTON
Title Page: *Incense-cedar, white fir, and giant sequoia at Nelder Grove. [Sierra N. F.]* BILL EVARTS

CONTENTS

CONTENTS

CONTENTS

PREFACE

California is conifer country. It has more kinds of native cone-bearing trees than any other state in the Union. It is also home to many of our most spectacular conifer species and conifer-dominated habitats. In total, California harbors 52 conifers, including 18 of this country's 39 pines, 10 of its 11 cypresses, and 7 of its 9 firs. Two members of the related yew family (taxads) are also found in California. The next highest number of conifers is claimed by Oregon, which has 32.

The conifer species in California belong to more genera than any other state can claim: they comprise 14 of the 16 conifer and taxad genera found in the nation. The pine family is represented by pines, firs, spruces, hemlocks, and Douglas-firs and the cypress family by junipers, incense-cedar, redcedar, cypresses, and false-cypresses. In addition, the baldcypress family and the yew family each have two genera in the state.

Equally impressive is the high level of endemism among California's conifers and taxads. Fourteen species grow in the wild here and nowhere

Gray pine ranges across California's arid, inland foothills. [Pinnacles N.M.] LARRY ULRICH

else, including three pines, a fir, a Douglas-fir, a sequoia, seven cypresses and a "nutmeg."

Many of California's conifers can only be described by superlatives. Sugar pine—the world's largest pine; redwood—the world's tallest tree; giant sequoia—the world's most massive tree; Great Basin bristlecone pine—the world's longest-lived tree; and the list goes on. California has more conifers that depend on fire for their regeneration than any other state or any foreign nation. It has more pines whose seeds are dis-

Douglas-fir forest is found near San Francisco. [Mt. Tamalpais S.P.]
GALEN ROWELL/MOUNTAIN LIGHT

persed by animals than any other state or nation except Mexico.

California's conifers and taxads occupy a wide variety of habitats. Redwoods along the north coast drip fog-borne moisture while single-leaf pinyons at the edge of the Mojave Desert shut their stomates to conserve precious soil water. Knobcone pines get by on serpentine out-crops within sight of ponderosas rooted in deep, red, iron-rich soils. Monterey cypresses defy the salt-laden seawinds of Point Lobos, while mountain hemlocks prostrate themselves under the weight of a wet Sierran snowpack. Few areas challenge their conifers with the extraordinary range of environmental stresses imposed by California's wildlands.

Such remarkable trees growing in such remarkable places surely deserve a book of their own. They have not had one since 1911 when the peripatetic J. Smeaton Chase wrote *Cone-Bearing Trees of the California Mountains* for fellow tree-lovers. He excluded coastal species and had little to say that went beyond the needs of field identification. But that was a long time ago, and we have learned a lot since then. It is time for a fresh look at these trees.

ACKNOWLEDGEMENTS

My publisher, John Evarts, conceived the idea of a book on California's conifers in the first place. He has my deepest gratitude for placing in me the confidence to bring his idea to fruition. Along the way I have had good advice, accurate information, or invaluable field guidance from Debbie Whitman, Anne Bradley, John Kelly, Mike Wells, Don Potter, Mark Borchert, James Shevock, Susan Dalcamo, Bro Kinloch, Bill Bigg, Calvin Bey, Harry Hutchins, Steven Vander Wall, David Hurst Thomas, Scott Stine, Tom Conkle, Sydney Smith, Beth Corbin, Sheila Logan, Mike Wickman, Linda Allen, Emily Roberson, Melody Fountain, Paul Zedler, Tom Van Devender, Dwight Willard, Greg Powers, Tom White, Kat Anderson, Bill Evarts, and Larry Ford. Keith Dixon has been an invaluable ornithological resource for many years. My thanks to old friends Herb and Rita Stein for their hospitality to Harriette and me on our trips to southern California, and to Connie Millar and Diane Delaney for the use of unpublished information on their pinyon pine isozyme studies, Bob Price for advice on nomenclatural matters, Richard J. Shaw for botanical counsel, and Angie Lopez for manuscript preparation. Robert Haller, Richard Minnich, John Sawyer, and Richard Dodd provided penetrating and most helpful technical reviews of the manuscript, and Jim Bartel made valuable comments on the cypresses. Special thanks to Hedwig and Margo Murman and the other members of the Murman family for granting Cachuma Press permission to reproduce Eugene Murman's conifer paintings, and to Katherine Donahue and Teresa Johnson of UCLA for expediting the process of photograhing the Murman art. I appreciate the assistance of Betsy Collins, Steven Jessup, Karen Messer, Bart O'Brien, Alison Sanger, Bob Schmid, and Robert Turner for collecting plant specimens for artist Susan Bazell. Finally, I thank my wife, Harriette Lanner, for her field assistance, moral and intellectual support, and good cheer on rainy days since we shared our first experience of California forests over 40 years ago.

EUGENE O. MURMAN, THE ARTIST

Eugene Otto Walter Murman was born in 1874 into a Finnish family residing in St. Petersburg, Russia. He died in March 1962 in Los Angeles, a month short of 88 years. After emigrating to the United States in 1905, Murman pursued a highly successful career as a designer of interiors, furniture, carpets, and wrought iron. But he never abandoned his boyhood love of natural history, and over the years he utilized the art training he had received in Russia and Germany in renderings of butterflies and flowers.

In 1940, a widowed Murman married Rosaleen Margaret Meek, with whom he collaborated in an ambitious attempt to paint the California flora. In the next two decades he executed more than 500 watercolors notable for their meticulous attention to botanical detail and their artistic beauty. Among them are the masterful depictions of nearly all the native California conifers that appear in this book, most of which are published here for the first time.

The reproduction of this portfolio has been facilitated by the Murman family and the History and Special Collections Division of the Louise M. Darling Biomedical Library at the University of California, Los Angeles, where the Murman originals are archived. Bill Evarts photographed the paintings. Watercolors of five species not captured by Murman were beautifully executed by California artist Susan Bazell; her name appears with the paintings she created.

THE PAINTINGS AND THEIR REPRODUCTIONS IN THIS BOOK

Eugene Murman's paintings were executed at 8 by 10 inches on watercolor board. They usually show a leafy shoot bearing a mature cone or pollen cones, dissected cone scales, seeds, needles, and needles in cross-section. Murman's sketches were life-size when feasible, sometimes indicated with his notation "x1", or, in the case of long cones, reduced to 50%, indicated by "x^1/$_2$." Small structures were sometimes drawn at two or four times their size, indicated by "x2" or "x4." The original watercolors have been photographed under studio conditions and reduced for publication by 25%.

THE NAMES OF TREES

All wild plants have common names and scientific names. Common names originate in the vernacular of all languages. They may refer to historic economic uses made of the tree (such as *canoe* cedar), the kind of habitat in which it grows (*mountain* hemlock), or some physical characteristic (*knobcone* pine). Many common names are derived from place names (*Sitka* spruce) or from the name of someone a botanist wished to honor (*Coulter* pine). These names may vary from one region to another and may change over time. They may not be botanically precise. For example, the conifer called tamarack by the Forty-niners is a pine, while the tamarack from which it derived its name is a larch. And the name larch has been applied in the Northwest to a fir!

Various attempts have been made to standardize common names. In 1895 California botanist John G. Lemmon published an impassioned appeal to "ignore senseless inappropriate names for our trees" and to insist on suitable, descriptive, distinguishing names, with only one for each species of tree. His pamphlet *Handbook of West-American Cone Bearers* expressed the hope that one day scientific names would be so familiar to all Americans that we could drop

common names entirely. That millennium has not yet arrived. In 1897 George B. Sudworth of the U.S. Division of Forestry (forerunner of the Forest Service) also advocated standardized common names. Unfortunately, many species have no distinctive name that has arisen from the vernacular. In that case, a common name does not exist, and if you want one you must invent it. This has been done on a large scale by foresters and botanists. It can lead to names that are stilted and technical and that could hardly have arisen from the vernacular if they had not been imposed by professionals. Here are some examples: *subalpine fir, bigcone Douglas-fir,* and *giant sequoia.* Over time, many such names are repeated often enough to become accepted.

The most recent effort to standardize common names of American trees was a set of guiding principles published in 1979 by U.S. Forest Service dendrologist E. L. Little, Jr. in his *Checklist of United States Trees (Native and Naturalized).* Most of the common names used in this book conform to the *Checklist,* but in some cases we differ. For example, the endemic *Pseudotsuga macrocarpa* is still often referred to by Californians as bigcone-spruce, even though it is not a spruce. The *Checklist* has it as bigcone Douglas-fir, which may be more accurate botanically, but it is an imposed name rather than an authentically vernacular one, and this has led a few southern California foresters to abbreviate it to Douglas-fir! To conform to current usage, more than one common name is given for some of the species in this book.

Scientific names are in international use among the community of plant specialists—botanists, foresters, horticulturists, and others to whom taxonomic precision is essential when referring to a particular plant. The assignment of these names, and the forms they may take, are closely prescribed by a set of highly legalistic rules published in a formal code. The rules trace back to principles established by Swedish botanist Carolus Linnaeus in 1753 and govern the procedures for describing newly discovered plants as well as for giving them names.

To the student of wildland plants the most relevant parts of that code are those that dictate the form of scientific names. Most important is the requirement that a species name is a binomial, that is, a name with two parts, which is written in Latin syntax. Here is a typical binomial: *Pinus balfouriana. Pinus* is the generic name that signifies the genus of the pines; *balfouriana* is the specific epithet that signifies the tree commonly called

foxtail pine. We can abbreviate this binomial and add its authors: *P. balfouriana* Grev. & Balf. This signifies that Robert K. Greville and John H. Balfour first described and named this tree (in 1853).

Plant scientists do not always agree on the status of a tree. For example, in *Flora of North America* most white fir in California are considered *Abies lowiana,* with some minor populations denoted as *Abies concolor,* the common fir of the Rocky Mountains. In *The Jepson Manual: Higher Plants of California,* all white fir in the state is considered to be *Abies concolor.* In this book, I refer to all but the southeastern populations as California white fir, or *Abies concolor* variety *lowiana.* I think the major populations are different enough from the Rocky Mountains trees to be separated from them at some level, but I would like to see a thorough study of the two that analyzes their differences before taking the step of calling them different species. All of those scientific names are valid because they have been published in accordance with the botanical rules. Whichever is used depends on the user's concept of the tree. That concept is an opinion, and making such decisions is less a science than an art. When practicing that art in this book, as I do in a few instances, I explain my opinions.

CONES

Conifers are plants whose sex cells are housed in cones rather than flowers. Most coniferous trees bear both male, or pollen, cones and female, or seed, cones. Pollen cones tend to develop on shaded lower branches and seed cones in the upper, more sunlit crown. This is believed to reduce the likelihood of self-pollination, which generally leads to the production of genetically less vigorous offspring.

Sexual reproduction in conifers begins when an airborne pollen grain, which contains a sperm cell, makes contact with the surface of an ovule, which contains an egg cell. This is the process of pollination. The next critical stage is fertilization, the fusion of sperm and egg nuclei, which in turn is followed by a complex set of developmental events culminating in the formation of a seed containing an embryo, or incipient seedling.

Pollen cones of the pine family are temporary, sausage-shaped structures that usually vary from ½ to almost 2 inches in length, depending on their genus and species. They emerge in the spring from buds, grow to full length, and then shed their pollen into the wind. Pollen-shed occurs when the hundreds of spirally arranged pairs of pollen sacs of a

male cone dry and split open. In years of copious production, even a small tree can fill the air with millions of microscopic, pale yellow grains, and smokelike pollen clouds may rise from the forest canopy. After releasing their pollen, male cones soon shrivel and fall to the forest floor.

Although pollen cones are short-lived, seed cones can be around for a long time. Most are formed within buds during the summer and then emerge in spring as tiny reddish or purplish conelets with their ovules exposed on

Lodgepole pine pollen cones form in clusters on lower limbs. [Yosemite N.P.] GEORGE WARD

their parted scales. Pollination occurs soon after and the conelets close up. In trees of the pine family other than pines, such as spruces and firs, fertilization occurs just weeks after pollination and mature seeds are ready to be shed in early fall from these "one-year" cones. Among all the pines of California, however, the pollinated conelets just grow a little and then overwinter on the tree. The following spring, fertilization finally occurs and the cones grow rapidly; the seeds mature in fall within these "two-year" cones.

Most cypresses and junipers have two-year cones, while most other cypress family trees, such as incense-cedar and western redcedar, have one-year cones. Giant sequoia has two-year cones, while redwood has one-year cones.

Seed cones in the pine family may vary in length from less than 1 inch up to 20 or more inches; they are sometimes very massive and woody, especially those in the genus *Pinus*. Some pine cones have sharp spines, or even claws, set upon their scales. In cones of the pine family, ovules are borne on the upper scale surface, which is where a seed forms. The cones of most conifers open by spreading their scales when the seeds mature, and seeds are then shed into the wind or removed by animals. In others, however, the seed cones may remain

Above, top: A Jeffrey pine seedcoat clings to the tips of the seedling's cotyledons, or seed leaves. [Inyo N.F.] ANDY SELTERS
Above, bottom: California juniper "berrycones" mature in one year. Some junipers need two years. [Joshua Tree N.P.] JON M. STEWART

closed for years before finally opening to release the seeds. Eventually, the empty seed cones will fall from the tree and become incorporated into the forest litter.

THE PINE FAMILY

In North America, the pine family is represented by 64 species of pines, spruces, firs, hemlocks, larches, and Douglas-firs. Thirty-two of those species are found growing wild somewhere in California, and only the larches are completely absent. Thus, for conifer enthusiasts, California indeed has much to offer.

Members of the pine family have leaves that are linear in shape and usually referred to as needles. Needles, or bundles of them in the case of pines and larches, are arranged spirally on the shoot, never oppositely. Trees of this family have seed cones made up of scales arranged spirally along an axis. Their wood is relatively soft, sometimes very resinous, and often valuable for production of lumber or paper pulp. Though the pine family is of very ancient origin, its numerous species attest to its ability to adapt to a wide range of ecological conditions.

Opposite: California's Klamath Ranges are famous for their diverse forests of pines and firs. [Trinity Alps Wilderness] DAVID MUENCH

PINES

*P*inus is by far the most diverse and complex of all the conifer genera. It contains about a hundred species that are generally agreed upon and a score of others whose status is open to argument. New species still continue to be reported from Mexico and the Far East. Virtually all pines occur in the northern hemisphere, growing in the tropics and subtropics, arctic and subarctic, and almost everywhere in between. California has more pines than any other state, and more total pine species than any foreign nation except Mexico. Thus California owes much of its forest diversity to its unique collection of pines.

Pines are an ancient line, dating back about 130 million years to the early Cretaceous. The other members of the pine family, or Pinaceae, are believed to have originated as pine offshoots. Those that appear in this book are the firs, spruces, hemlocks, and Douglas-firs. Nearly all of them, and most pines as well, have small, winged seeds adapted for dispersal by the wind, but pine's characteristic diversity has given it other options, such as dispersal by bird. Pine seed cones are often massive, and the tree's mature foliage consists of needles bound together at the base to form bundles, or fascicles. The number of needles per bundle is usually quite consistent within a species, but can be variable.

About one-third of the world's pines are classified as soft, or white, pines (subgenus *Strobus*) while the other two-thirds are hard, or yellow, pines (subgenus *Pinus*). The differences between these subgenera are described in text and tables of Appendix A on page 262. Our presentation of the pines begins with the soft pines (pages 10 to 51) and finishes with the hard pines (pages 52 to 99).

Opposite: Jeffrey pine's heavy litter of fallen needles and seed cones provides fuel for frequent light fires. [Lassen Volcanic N.P.] SCOTT T. SMITH

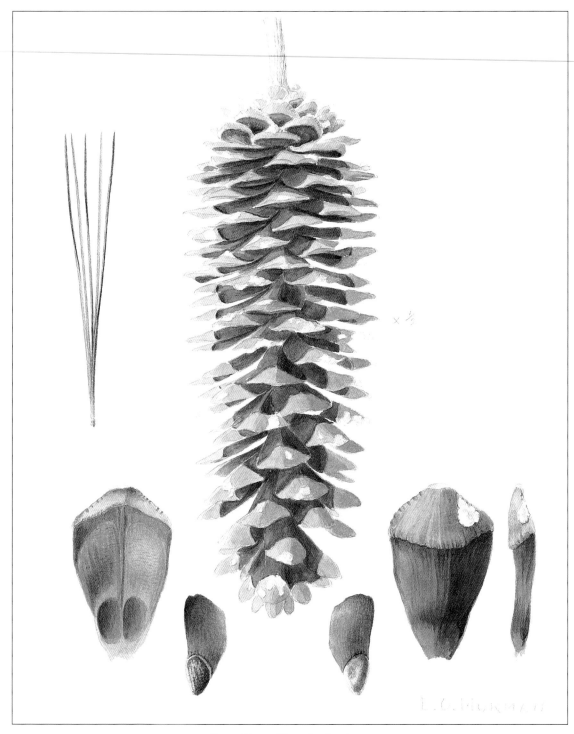

Sugar Pine • *Pinus lambertiana*

SUGAR PINE

One of my vivid memories of the westside Sierra Nevada forest is the sight of a great old sugar pine I passed twice a day while commuting between home and workplace. I could see it across a small meadow through a thin screen of young firs that lined the road. The surrounding second-growth forest, about 90 feet high, was a uniform stand of straight, narrow-crowned ponderosa pines that had seeded into abandoned grain fields in the mid-nineteenth century. My sugar pine rose above them like a giant among dwarfs, its wide spreading limbs a counterpoint to their tightly reined-in branches, its raggedly uneven crown a flamboyant dismissal of their conformity. One spring morning I jumped the roadside ditch and walked across to the big tree. The ground beneath it was strewn with hundreds of spent cones and weathered limbs that had fallen over the years. A tangle of pink-flowering azaleas bordered the tree on its meadow side. The fat trunk was covered with the thin, shiny skin of bark flakes, weathered to the dull blue-gray that adorns old members of this species. A glance up the bole disclosed the long, tapering, frondlike branches that give sugar pines the grace of tropical palms and distinguish them from the more rigid-looking conifers they grow among.

Old sugar pines are the world's largest pines. Their discoverer, David Douglas, first came upon the species on what is now Sugar Pine Mountain near Roseburg, Oregon, in September 1826. There he found a wind-thrown tree that measured 215 feet long and more than 18 feet in diameter at a point three feet up the trunk. Trees as tall as 250 feet have been recorded, but none with trunks of greater girth. In a 1902

Sugar pine is a major species of the Sierra Nevada mixed-conifer forest, where it has great scenic as well as commercial value. [Lake Tahoe] JOHN SAWYER

report, *Forest Conditions in the Northern Sierra Nevada, California,* John B. Leiberg stated that sugar pine reached heights of 150 to 275 feet, a record that must be taken seriously. Perhaps the most magnificent remaining stand of old-growth sugar pine in the Sierra Nevada is one that adjoins the South Grove of Calaveras Big Trees State Park. Here the spell woven by the huge pines is broken only when one's glance takes in a giant sequoia. Even second-growth sugar pines can be impressive. In the Plumas National Forest, I once measured a felled sugar pine only 87 years old that had risen 192 feet and had a trunk diameter of 53 inches.

Like many other five-needled white pines, the sugar pine starts life as an orderly tree, almost military in its straightness and in the rakish angle of its branches. But old trees develop those trademark horizontal sweeping limbs. A ridgeline of such disheveled-looking individual-ists silhouetted against the sky presents a wild and mysterious spectacle. Every few years, in what are called mast years, the limbs are heavy with bunches of ripening green cones, and they sag and droop until the cones dry out in the sun. It is these cones by which much of the public knows sugar pine.

The cones of sugar pine are the longest cones of any pine, and 24-inch cones, while truly exceptional, are not unknown; cones of 12 to 18 inches litter the ground wherever sugar pines grow. Their cone scales are much stiffer than those of western white pine, as well as much longer. The scales usually stick straight out from the cone axis, although some trees around the Lassen Peak area have cones with scales that bend back sharply, like those of Mexican white pines. Each cone scale harbors, in cuplike depressions at its base, two nearly black seeds, $^1/_2$ inch long, with broad wings an inch in length. When the cones dry and open in September, these huge seeds are released, whirling in the breeze as they slowly descend to the ground. Because the cones dangle on long stalks from the tips of bobbing limbs, it is hard for large seed-eating birds to make a meal of the seeds. Biologist Lloyd Tevis, Jr. once reported a Steller's jay pouncing on a cone to dislodge seed, and then catching one in midair. A more serious seed predator is the white-headed wood-pecker, which makes long, deep gashes in the green cones to empty them of their developing seed.

Sugar pine's common name is derived from the crystalline encrustations of resin that form around the edges of wounds and fire scars. The sweet resin, which contains the sugar pinitol, was used by California Indians as a laxative, per-haps the first sugar pine product to be exploited by man. White settlers later found other uses for sugar pine. When woodsmen discovered how easily straight-grained sugar pine wood could be split into shakes and shingles, they organized small parties of shake-makers who would camp in the forest for the summer. Here they reduced the trunks of great old trees to rounds 30 inches thick—like very short logs—and then split these into shakes with iron froes and mallets. Trees that lacked straight enough grain were left to rot on the ground. Ranchers contained their cattle within sugar pine "fences," which were made by felling large sugar pines so they would lie end to end. Sugar pine also provided plenty of timber for the growing towns and cities of California; the wood was used in building structures as well as for orna-mental and interior use. Its light weight, softness, and easy workability made it an apt substitute

for the familiar but distant eastern white pine. Historians claim that John Sutter's mill at Coloma, where the Gold Rush began, was built to process sugar pine logs.

Sugar pine's commercial future has been compromised by its extreme susceptibility to white pine blister rust, an introduced disease (see page 18 in the following section on western white pine). The discovery of a dominant gene that confers resistance to the disease in some sugar pines may result in the breeding of a resis-tant strain. For years the fungus that causes white pine blister rust was thought to be inca-pable of surviving in the drier southern portion of sugar pine's distribution. A new fungal strain evolved, however, and it soon spread as far

Massive old-growth sugar pines spread long, horizontal limbs, achieving a unique silhouette. [Shasta-Trinity N.F.] DAVID LANNER

Sugar pine and white fir (lower right), like most pine family trees, produce massive cone crops in periodic mast years, followed by several years of small crops. [San Bernardino Mts.] ROBERT TURNER

south as the Greenhorn Mountains in Kern County. It was also thought that old sugar pines were not susceptible to the disease, that only young trees could be infected. But then large old trees proved susceptible to another new fungal strain. White pine blister rust, in combination with timber management practices in much of California, will have the long-term effect of preventing sugar pines from becoming old and large. The species itself will be in no danger, but outside of a few parks, the towering, monumental sugar pine will be largely a thing of the past. That is not an easy thought to grasp nor a pleasant one to accept.

IDENTIFYING SUGAR PINE

At a distance: Mature trees have a dense crown of tapering, frondlike branches that arch gracefully upwards in the upper crown and spread horizontally below, carrying masses of deep green foliage supported on a long, dark, cylindrical bole. The trunks of old trees are thicker and pinker, limbs are fewer, longer, and lankier. In summer, the green cones at the tips of the branches pull them conspicuously downwards. **Standing beneath it:** The ground is littered with years' accumulations of long-stalked, cylindrical, open cones with stiff, smooth scales. Cones are usually well over one foot in length. **In the hand:** Needles are five to the bundle, about four inches long, and deep green on the outer surface with thin white lines on inner surfaces. The sheath at the base of the needle bundle disintegrates after its first year.

HABITAT

Sugar pine grows under a wide variety of conditions. Precipitation levels within its distribution vary from 20 to 90 inches annually and soil origins are of all types. It is found near sea level in the North Coast Ranges and extends up to 9,800 feet in the Transverse Ranges' San Gabriel Mountains and to 10,000 feet in the Peninsular Ranges' Sierra San Pedro Mártir, Baja

California. In the Sierra Nevada, sugar pine individuals and small groves are scattered among ponderosa pine, Douglas-fir, California white fir, incense-cedar, California black oak, and tanoak. In the Transverse and Peninsular ranges, it associates with white fir, canyon live oak, and Jeffrey pine.

DISTRIBUTION

In California it grows in the Klamath Ranges and south down the North Coast Ranges to Sonoma and Napa counties. A population is also found in the Santa Lucia Range of Monterey County. From the Cascades and Modoc Plateau it extends over the length of the Sierra Nevada, through the Transverse Ranges, and down the Peninsular Ranges as far south as the Sierra San Pedro Mártir in Baja California. Elsewhere it extends north into Oregon and east into Nevada's Peavine Mountain and Clark Range.

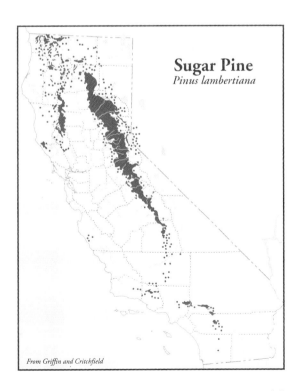

Sugar Pine
Pinus lambertiana

From Griffin and Critchfield

Western White Pine • *Pinus monticola*

WESTERN WHITE PINE

Naturalist Donald Culross Peattie considered white pines the aristocrats of the genus *Pinus*. If he was right, then western white pine must be an especial aristocrat, because from its high perches in the Sierra Nevada and Cascades it looks down even upon the great sugar pine, largest white pine of them all. Once known as mountain pine, silver pine, or little sugar pine, western white pine grows in mountain haunts where the air is cool and clear and the views panoramic. In the Sierra Nevada western white pine is not found in endlessly monotonous pure forests but is judiciously scattered among underlings—lodgepole and Jeffrey pine, mountain hemlock, and red fir. In the Klamath Ranges it sometimes forms extensive stands. Scottish botanist David Douglas thrilled to the discovery of this species on Washington's Mount St. Helens in 1825. Finding a great old veteran of lightning strikes and surface fires still brings excitement to present-day naturalists who glory in the species' seeming tenacity.

In keeping with its image as an aristocrat, western white pine will not be crowded. On the Sierra eastside it is generally widely spaced and open to the sun, not in thick clumps of mutually shading crowns. It is very intolerant of deep shade and its seedlings do not become established under a dense canopy. Young western white pines are trees of exceptional grace. Their cylindrical trunks are clothed in smooth gray bark that is easily lacerated to expose the resinous green cortex within. Whorls of gray-barked limbs emerge from the trunk at regular intervals, giving the crown a horizontally tiered "pagoda" effect. The short uppermost branches arch upwards, as in white pines everywhere. The foliage

Western white pine has also been called silver and mountain pine. [Yosemite N.P.] DAVID LANNER

is made up of short, slender, blue-green needles arranged five to the bundle. Mature trees develop blackish, checkered bark tinged with purple. Clusters of fingerlike cones hang from the branch tips; the cones open in the fall to release their winged seeds and continue to dangle in brown masses for another year.

Very old western white pines may have trunks four to six feet thick. Some get as large as a specimen in Yosemite National Park, which was reputed to have reached 120 feet in height with an eight-foot diameter trunk. But California's trees do not attain the great heights of the western white pines that grow in northern Idaho and Montana, or in the sea-level stands of Washington and British Columbia. Fire scars are common on older trees, and long-healed-over seams trace the paths of lightning discharges that followed the trunk to its roots. Large trees often lean or tilt as the ground beneath them shifts or the roots die and decay. Surviving limbs become fewer and thicker, spreading into flat, tablelike masses of silvery foliage.

John Muir characterized the "Mountain Pine" as "tossing its tough arms in the frosty air, welcoming storms and feeding on them, and

reaching the grand old age of 1,000 years." There may be some hyperbole there, as western white pine is not an especially long-lived tree and Muir offered no evidence to support his off-hand statement. Dendrologists reported a 600-year-old western white pine in British Columbia, and foresters of the Modoc National Forest counted 589 rings in a western white pine stump in the Warner Mountains.

Western white pine's closest relative is *Pinus strobus,* the eastern white pine of the eastern United States and Canada. The soft, white, fine-grained wood of western white pine is similar to that of the eastern tree. Its slender, pendulous cones are like those of its eastern cousin, though bigger and woodier. Unfortunately it is equally susceptible to the white pine blister rust, a fungal disease that has ravaged North American white pine forests throughout the twentieth century. The dreaded blister rust was introduced to North America on white pine seedlings imported from Europe at a time when such seedlings were unavailable from local growers. The causal fungus, *Cronartium ribicola,* has a life cycle requiring alternate hosts for its completion. The fungus produces spores on white pines that infect *Ribes* bushes, such as gooseberry and currants; in turn, the spores on the *Ribes* infect white pines. In Eurasia, where the fungus is native, the pines have had time to evolve resistance to the pathogen, but American white pines have only begun to do so.

Western white pine, known for its low level of genetic variability, is also susceptible to the blister rust. As a result, foresters have been breeding western white pine for increased resistance since the 1950s, and in the 1990s they began releasing resistant seedlings for planting in Idaho forests. Some earlier strategies to deal with the virulent fungus included grubbing out *Ribes* bushes to destroy the alternate host—thus interrupting the fungal life cycle—and injecting an antibiotic into diseased trees. The former approach once filled the Sierra Nevada with

Western white pine has an unusually low level of genetic variability. [Trinity Alps] ROBERT TURNER

In the hand: Cones are usually 6 to 10 inches long, moderately woody, and stiff to the touch. The cone scales are only slightly thickened at the tips and without prickles. Needles are in sheathless bundles of five, and measure two to four inches long.

HABITAT
It generally occurs from about 7,500 to 10,000 feet where the snowpack may be deep and the growing season short, but it is found as low as 400 feet in the Klamath Ranges. It grows on a variety of rock types, including granite and even serpentine.

DISTRIBUTION
In California it grows in the Sierra Nevada and Cascades from southern Tulare County to Oregon; it is also found in the Klamath and Warner mountains. Elsewhere it occurs in Oregon, Washington, British Columbia, Alberta, Idaho, and Montana, as well as in Nevada adjacent to California populations.

armies of raucous "blister busters," mostly forestry students housed by the Forest Service in tent camps during the summers. They put up thousands of miles of string lines in the woods and grubbed millions of bushes. But the bushes re-sprouted, and disease levels were unaffected. Also in the 1950s, the Forest Service developed, or thought it had, two effective antibiotics. These were injected into many Idaho white pines but proved less efficacious than their press releases had been.

IDENTIFYING WESTERN WHITE PINE
At a distance: It is usually a straight-trunked tree with neatly layered tiers of horizontal branches, except those in the upper crown, which arch upwards. Clusters of finger-shaped cones dangle from branch tips; they are either green or purple during the summer.
Standing beneath it: As the tree ages, its bark progresses from smooth and gray to blackish and checkered, to reddish and flaky.

Western White Pine
Pinus monticola

From Griffin and Critchfield

CALIFORNIA'S CONTROVERSIAL PINYON PINES

The taxonomy of California's pinyon pines has been highly controversial. In 1938 Carl B. Wolf reported that Colorado pinyon *(Pinus edulis)* grows in the New York Mountains of the Mojave Desert in southeast California. In the ensuing years, numerous other botanists followed Wolf's lead and that location became renowned as the westernmost station of the species. In the 1970s, while making studies of natural hybridization among the pinyon pines of the Southwest, I became persuaded that those two-needled pinyons were actually singleleaf pinyons in which the mutation that causes single-needleness was being suppressed. All other needle, cone, and seed characters appeared to be consistent with singleleaf pinyon *(Pinus monophylla).*

In the decade or so after these findings were published, at least four other groups of investigators came to the New York Mountains to look into the situation further. Most of them concentrated on the elevational distribution of the two-needled trees and concluded that Colorado pinyon was indeed growing on the higher ridges of the New Yorks. Then, in the mid-1990s, a group of Berkeley forest geneticists decided to settle the question once and for all. They performed a genetic analysis of the molecular structure of enzymes (isozymes) isolated from needle tissue, a powerful technique commonly used to address such problems. Their conclusion, not yet published as this is written (but cited with their permission), is that the pinyons of the New York Mountains are biochemically consistent with singleleaf pinyon, but not with Colorado pinyon. Thus, the weight of evidence indicates that Colorado pinyon does not occur in California and so it has not been included in this book. However, all research

Singleleaf pinyon and Utah juniper were a major source of fuel, posts, and charcoal in the nineteenth century. [White Mts.] DAVID LANNER

findings should be considered preliminary, and the inherently confusing nature of the New York Mountains' pinyons may someday be resolved in some other manner. Both *Flora of North America* and *The Jepson Manual* accept Colorado pinyon as a California species.

There are also differences of opinion regarding the supposed four-needled pinyon pine, Parry pinyon *(Pinus quadrifolia).* The type specimen was collected east of San Diego in 1850 by Charles Parry, botanist of the United States and Mexican Boundary Survey. Examination of that specimen disclosed that its 1848, 1849, and 1850 foliage was, respectively, 40%, 44%, and 64% four-needled, with the rest of its needles in groups of three (8% to 20%) or five (18% to 48%). Studies of needle number and several other characters in 10 Parry pinyon populations in northern Baja California, and the results of controlled crosses, convince me that Parry's type was a hybrid between singleleaf pinyon and the five-needled Sierra Juárez pinyon *(Pinus juarezensis)* I described in 1974. Another research group later confirmed that hybridization was also in progress at southern California locations I had not visited. Sierra Juárez pinyon can therefore be considered a bona fide California species and Parry pinyon a variable

Singleleaf pinyons like these hybridize with Sierra Juárez pinyon, forming the variable Parry pinyon. [Laguna Mts.] JOHN EVARTS

population of hybrids. However, *Flora of North America* and *The Jepson Manual* both retain the name *Pinus quadrifolia.*

Finally, the proposal has been made to view California's singleleaf pinyons as two separate species, *Pinus monophylla* in the north and *Pinus californiarum* in the south. Because the differences between them are minor, however, most specialists regard these tree populations merely as varieties or subspecies *monophylla* and *californiarum* of *Pinus monophylla.* The rank of variety is therefore used in the discussion of singleleaf pinyon. Neither *Flora of North America* nor *The Jepson Manual* recognize varieties or subspecies of *Pinus monophylla.*

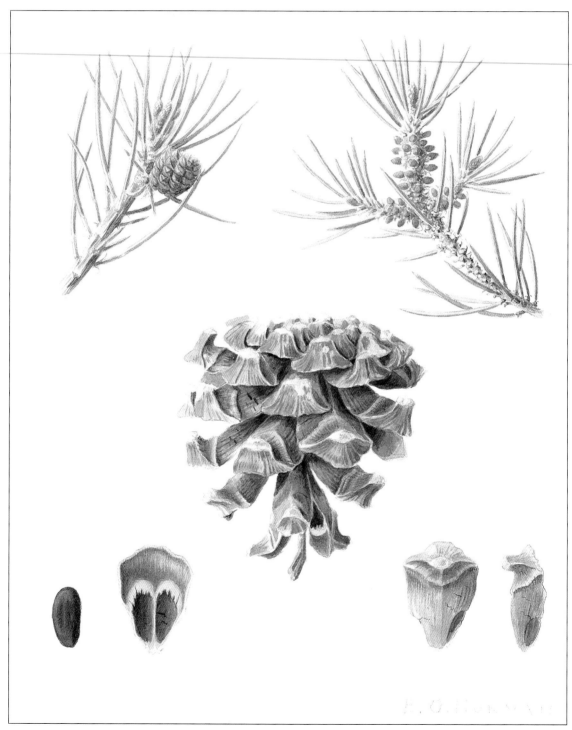

Singleleaf Pinyon • *Pinus monophylla*

SINGLELEAF PINYON

In January 1844, with his exploring party of U. S. Topographical Engineers nearly out of food on the snowy east slope of the Sierra Nevada, Brevet Captain John C. Frémont learned the meaning of providence, which he recorded in his journal:

A man was discovered running toward the camp as we were about to start this morning, who proved to be an Indian of rather advanced age—a sort of forlorn hope. . . . he brought with him in a little skin bag a few pounds of seeds of a pine tree, which today we saw for the first time. . . . we purchased them all from him.

Frémont later collaborated with botanist John Torrey in describing and naming this remarkable pine, whose seeds played a large role in fending off the possible starvation of Frémont's men.

The name pinyon is anglicized from the Spanish *piñón* and refers to the large, edible seeds of certain pines. This pine's single-needled fascicle is unique among the world's approximately 110 pines and results when only one primordial needle forms in a fascicle growing point that has space for two. Singleleaf pinyon is so ubiquitous across the Great Basin from western Utah to the eastern Sierra Nevada that it is hard to grasp that until about 11,000 years ago it was absent from this area. Populations of the species were then present in Nevada's Sheep Range to the south and in some other ranges around the Mojave Desert, however, and they were poised to expand northwards as the melting of glacial ice warmed the climate of North America. Researchers have also found evidence that singleleaf pinyon was present 35,000 years ago in Kings Canyon on the Sierra Nevada westside, where it is still found today; in addition, they have identified its remains from the McKittrick tar pits at the south end of the San Joaquin Valley, where it is not found today. Its northward migration eventually resulted in today's pinyon-juniper woodland, a low forest that, in eastern California, usually consists of singleleaf pinyon in mixture with junipers, sagebrush, rabbitbrush, and numerous other shrubs, herbs, and grasses.

Singleleaf pinyon is the major tree species on millions of acres of mountains surrounded by deserts and thus supports a great many organisms. Its inner bark, or phloem, is a major food of porcupines and the mountain pine beetle; it also sustains the fungus that causes pinyon blister rust. Dwarf mistletoes, which are green plants that live on tree limbs instead of on the ground, tap into the tree's sapstream of

water and dissolved nutrients. Pitch midges eat the never-ending supply of oozing oleoresin, and *Dianthidium* bees use the sticky resin in nest construction. There are several species of sawflies that live on singleleaf pinyon: some feed on its needles and others on its pollen. There even are gall midges that cause two-needled fascicles to develop so they can fashion protective cells in which to rear their young where the paired needles form a crotch.

Pinyon seeds, usually called pine nuts, are eaten by virtually all animals capable of cracking the thin, brittle shells and digesting their starchy contents. Pinyon mice, chipmunks, squirrels, deer, bears, and desert bighorn sheep thrive on pine nuts. Corvids such as scrub, Steller's, and pinyon Jays, and Clark's nutcrackers, harvest the nuts from their cones and bury

Since the Pleistocene, singleleaf pinyon has expanded northwards from the Mojave Desert to the eastern Sierra and the Great Basin. [White Mts.] FRANK BALTHIS

them in the soil as a winter food source. Many of the nuts buried by these birds, and probably by some chipmunks as well, are left in the ground long enough to germinate, constantly replenishing the woodland cover.

Singleleaf pinyon seeds are wingless. They are held in the opened cone for a time by a thin sheet of cone-scale tissue, thus remaining available to the animals that harvest them and cache them in the soil. Scrub and Steller's jays usually forage alone or in pairs. They carry one or a few seeds in their mouths a short distance, perhaps half a mile at the most, and bury them in the woodland soil. Pinyon jays are far more numerous in this environment and they often forage in flocks of hundreds. They can move quickly through a woodland, stripping it of most of its pine nuts. A pinyon jay can hold about 40 pine nuts in its stretchable esophagus and fly five miles before stopping to cache them in the ground. This bird is probably the major disperser and establisher of the singleleaf pinyon in California.

Singleleaf pinyon provided the staple food of many Great Basin Shoshones, Paiutes, and Washoes. The Cahuilla of the San Jacinto Mountains were also avid pine nut eaters. Much of their culture can be viewed as having been adaptive to the characteristics and behavior of the trees and their seeds.

After settlement, singleleaf pinyon became a major charcoal source, and it was used for smelting the silver ores of the Great Basin and Mojave Desert. Death Valley National Park's Wildrose Canyon contains excellent examples of the beautifully crafted beehive ovens often

In a mast year, singleleaf pinyon can produce enormous cone crops. The cones are green and photosynthetically active until September, when they dry out and open. [White Mts.] DAVID LANNER

used in this process. The environmental impact of the mining and smelting industry included the deforestation of hundreds of thousands of woodland acres, not only to supply the sacked charcoal to smelters and concentrators, but also to provide fuel for heating and cooking and for the steam engines that powered the mine hoists. The skilled Italian *carbonari* wielded sharp axes and left bare mountainsides behind them as they "coaled" their way across the Great Basin. Thanks to the corvids, however, singleleaf pinyon has made so spectacular a comeback in the places it was decimated, that today's range managers sometimes see it as a threat to the plants cattle eat rather than as a successfully reproducing natural forest tree. The response, frequently disastrous and almost always wasteful, has been the bulldozing of many thousands of acres of public lands to rid them of their pinyons and replace them with an artificial landscape of exotic grasses. This management practice destroys woodland cover, deletes its ameliorative effects on the climate of an arid region, and heavily impacts its native wildlife.

IDENTIFYING SINGLELEAF PINYON

At a distance: Short, broad-crowned trees form open woodlands in arid areas. The foliage is usually frosty gray, trunks nearly black, and branches upswept.

Standing beneath it: It bears large crops of three- to five-inch-long knobby cones that are emerald green in summer; the cones turn brown in the fall, opening and then dropping to the ground where they form a conspicuous litter.

North America's pinyon-juniper woodlands are the world's most extensive drought-adapted conifer forests, totalling over 40 million acres. [Death Valley N.P.] FRED HIRSCHMANN

In the hand: The rigid, slightly curved, single needles, which are circular in cross-section and can be rolled between the fingers, are unlike those of any other conifer. A needle cut cleanly in the middle will ooze resin droplets. Needles of variety *monophylla* of California origin will usually ooze droplets from 2 or 3 resin ducts, while those from variety *californiarum* will do so from up to 15 or more ducts. (See "Distribution" below.)

HABITAT

Singleleaf pinyon grows on dry, rocky slopes, ridges, and alluvial fans between 3,000 and 9,500 feet. It occurs in association with Utah, Sierra, or California juniper, sagebrush, rabbit-brush, canyon live oak, and Great Basin bristlecone, Jeffrey, ponderosa, or limber pine. It is occasionally found with bigcone-spruce in southern California.

DISTRIBUTION

There are two major areas of distribution in California. The northern area forms an arc that extends south from Alpine County along the east slope of the Sierra Nevada to Kern County, then south and west along the Tehachapi Mountains and western Transverse Ranges into eastern Santa Barbara County. This part of the distribution also includes ranges east of the Sierra Nevada, such as the White and Inyo mountains and the Panamint Range. The southern area of distribution extends from the San Gabriel and San Bernardino mountains south into the Peninsular Ranges and across the Mexican border, sporadically occurring as far south as Paso San Matías in Baja California.

The northern area consists of variety *monophylla* at least as far south as the San Gabriels. The southern area contains variety *californiarum* from at least the San Jacintos south; it also includes populations in the New York Mountains and nearby ranges of the eastern Mojave Desert.

The large pine nuts of singleleaf pinyon were a staple of Great Basin Indians and may have saved the lives of John Frémont's party in 1844. BILL BIGG

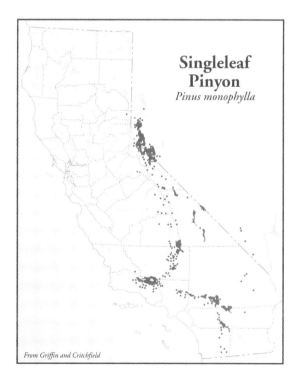

Singleleaf Pinyon
Pinus monophylla

From Griffin and Critchfield

Parry Pinyon • *Pinus* X *quadrifolia*

SIERRA JUÁREZ PINYON

AND

PARRY PINYON

All authorities agree in classifying pinyons among the soft pines, along with such species as whitebark, western white, limber, foxtail, bristlecone, and sugar pines. Unlike these others, however, pinyons have long been regarded as having a reduced needle number, down as far as one needle in the case of singleleaf pinyon. But in recent years botanists have discovered three species of five-needled pinyons in Mexico. One of these, the rare Sierra Juárez pinyon, is a native of southern California as well as Baja California. (For more information, see "California's Controversial Pinyon Pines" on pages 20 to 21.)

SIERRA JUÁREZ PINYON

Throughout its entire range, Sierra Juárez pinyon is within pollen dispersal distance of singleleaf pinyon; as a result, the two have hybridized. In fact, hybridization has been so widespread that the Sierra Juárez pinyon appears to be in the process of being bred out of existence. It can, however, still be found on Mount Laguna, east of San Diego, and just south of the border in the sierra whose name it bears.

Paleoecological research has disclosed 21,000-year-old macrofossils of Sierra Juárez pinyon from La Cataviña in central Baja California. Diligent search may well turn it up in the San Jacinto or Santa Rosa mountains as well. I first saw it just south of Mexican Route 2, about a mile west of the village of La Rumorosa. Here, pure singleleaf and Sierra Juárez pinyon trees are scattered in an open woodland with pinyons of wildly varying needle number. There are almost pure two-needled trees, mixtures of ones and twos, of twos and threes, of threes and fours, fours and fives, and threes, fours, and fives! Trees intermediate in needle number between singleleaf and Sierra Juárez pinyons are also intermediate in such characters as leaf resin canal number, twig hairiness, and stomate

position. The woodland forms a classic "hybrid swarm," a population of parent species, hybrids, and the "backcross" offspring of parent species and their hybrids.

PARRY PINYON

Parry pinyon was named *Pinus quadrifolia* in the nineteenth century because it has *some* four-needled fascicles, which is most unusual for a pine. But botanical descriptions of this presumed species were so inconsistent over the years that anything with one to five needles seemed to qualify. That variability can now be attributed to hybridization between singleleaf and Sierra Juárez pinyon, and trees neither purely one or the other can be collectively termed Parry pinyon, *Pinus* X *quadrifolia*.

IDENTIFYING SIERRA JUÁREZ AND PARRY PINYONS

At a distance: They are short trees with pyramidal to rounded crowns, dark trunks, and bluish green foliage. They grow in open to dense woodlands.

Standing beneath it: The ground is littered with open brown cones about two inches long and two to three inches wide. The foliage is shiny, the needles slightly curved.

In the hand: Needle counts are definitive. If needles are entirely or almost entirely five to the fascicle (use 95% as the cut-off point), it is Sierra Juárez pinyon. If the admixture of less-than-five-needled

Sierra Juárez pinyons, like this tree in the Laguna Mts., have at least 95% of their needles in fives. Trees with an admixture of needles in threes and fours are hybrid Parry pinyons. [Cleveland N.F.] ROBERT TURNER

Parry pinyon is one of California's more drought-tolerant pines. Much of its population grows on desert-facing slopes of the Peninsular Ranges. [Laguna Mts.] JOHN EVARTS

fascicles is greater than 5%, it is Parry pinyon. The needle-bundle sheath scales roll up to form scrolls at the base of the needles, as do those of singleleaf pinyon.

HABITAT

They are found in open to dense woodlands or in chaparral, with California juniper, interior live oak, chamise, agave, and cholla cactus, on dry, rocky, often granitic slopes and ridges from 3,400 to 6,400 feet.

DISTRIBUTION

Their range forms a narrow strip in the Peninsular Ranges that extends from the San

Jacinto and Santa Rosa mountains south through the Laguna Mountains and into Baja California to the southern end of the Sierra San Pedro Mártir.

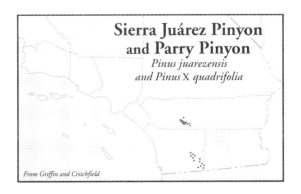

Sierra Juárez Pinyon and Parry Pinyon
Pinus juarezensis and Pinus X quadrifolia

From Griffin and Critchfield

Whitebark Pine • *Pinus albicaulis*

WHITEBARK PINE

The cones [of this pine] were so rare, that, though constantly among the trees and on the lookout myself, I had for two weeks an offer, open to all our party, of a dollar for a good cone; and no one was able to claim the reward. Fragments of cones, recent or of other years, were under every tree . . . torn up by the little pine squirrels.

These words were written by a frustrated John S. Newberry, M.D., about his 1855 encounter with a "summit pine," its trunk "white as milk." Newberry was the botanist accompanying Lieutenant R. S. Williamson, Corps of Topographical Engineers, in his explorations for a feasible railroad route from the Sacramento Valley to the Columbia River. It might have appeased Newberry to know that his difficulty in finding intact cones was in part a squirrel problem, but was mainly due to whitebark pine's curious mutualistic relationship with Clark's nut-cracker. In fact, had he known about this relationship, the lack of "good" cones would then have made sense to him.

Whitebark pine cones develop at the ends of upswept branches. Throughout the summer of their maturity, they form their large, wing-less seeds beneath a cover of pulpy, deep-purple scales with thick, swollen tips. Then, in early fall, the cones dry out and turn brownish in color. But the scales do not part, as in other pines, to allow the seeds to exit. Instead, most of them merely loosen. If they part at all, they do so only enough to expose their seeds, but not enough to let them fall out when branches sway in the wind. All this is good news for Clark's

Narrow-crowned lodgepole pines grow on this island because the wind blew their seeds here. Broad-crowned whitebark pines are here because Clark's nutcracker planted their seeds. [Kings Canyon N.P.] CARR CLIFTON

nutcrackers, who live almost exclusively on a diet of pine nuts.

The positioning of the cones at the tips of ascending limbs makes them highly visible to nutcrackers, and gives the birds firm perches from which to harvest seeds. The cones' bright color, and the twinkling of sunlight in their beads of resin, also make the cones conspicuous. The pulpy scales are easy to riddle, which allows seed removal early in the season. In addition, the tendency of the cone to remain closed insures that seeds will not be lost on the ground.

Despite their formidable appearance, the cone scales of whitebark pine are fragile. They lack the tough fibers—found in most other pine cones—that shrink as they dry, pulling the scale back and opening the cone. The absence of these fibers also makes the scales brittle, and as a result, they are easy for a nutcracker to break off with a swipe of its bill. When a scale is broken

off, the one or two seeds thus exposed remain firmly held in the cone's core. This placement prevents the seeds from falling to the ground and eases the nutcracker's task of harvesting large numbers of fat-laden, protein-rich pine nuts. After grasping a seed, the nutcracker points its quivering bill skywards, briefly, as the seed drops below the floor of its mouth into a pouch lying beneath the tongue. The bird continues the harvest, one seed at a time, pausing to change cones or to change trees; it may also pause to wipe its pitch-smeared bill on a branch or to shell and swallow an occasional seed. Perhaps 100 seeds will be pouched, swelling the bird's throat and increasing its weight by a fourth. Then, black and white feathers glinting in the sun, the nutcracker flies off in search of a caching area.

When it caches its seeds, a nutcracker may select a spot at the base of the tree where it has

The "krummholz" form of whitebark pine is not genetic, but is due to the cold, windy, short growing seasons of high elevations. Cones and seeds seldom mature here. [John Muir Wilderness] CARR CLIFTON

been feeding or it may fly to some other location, up to several miles away. Cautiously, the bird hops to the ground and clears away litter with its bill; bringing seeds up from the pouch one at a time, it pushes them an inch or so into the soil. A cache may have 1 to 15 or more seeds in it; the average is usually 3 to 4. During the long mountain winter, these caches will provide for the survival of the nutcracker that made them.

Research has shown that nutcrackers rely on their memory to find their caches. Considering the great numbers of seeds they conceal beneath the soil, that is indeed a prodigious accomplishment. In a 1990 study made in Tioga Pass in the Sierra Nevada, each adult nutcracker was estimated to have cached 89,000 seeds and each juvenile about 34,000 seeds. In years when the whitebark pines produce a large seed crop, nutcrackers will harvest and cache many more seeds than they and their future offspring can possibly

Clark's nutcracker, seen here foraging in a limber pine, is the essential seed-disperser for this species and for whitebark pine. RON LANNER

Whitebark pine is the only North American member of the stone pine group. The other four live in the Alps and eastwards across Siberia to Korea and Japan. [John Muir Wilderness] FRED HIRSCHMANN

consume. Seeds not recovered from caches and not discovered by hungry squirrels or other predators are then free to germinate and produce a new generation of pines. In fact, there is no other known reliable means for whitebark pine to regenerate itself. Whitebark pine appears to be completely dependent on Clark's nutcracker for its posterity. Because most seed caches are multi-seeded, the majority of trees that grow from them are members of stem clumps. Even mature whitebark pines frequently grow not as single-stemmed trees, but in clusters of two, three, four, or more.

IDENTIFYING WHITEBARK PINE

At a distance: Whitebark pine ranges in habit from a wind-pruned treeline shrub *(krummholz)* to a 60-foot-high forest tree. Narrow-crowned trees in the forest, as well as broader trees in meadows, frequently grow in stem clumps and have forked, strongly upswept limbs.

Standing beneath it: The mature trunks have chalky-white bark. Seed cones are purple most of their last year, while pollen cones are in crimson clusters. Loose cone scales and cores litter the ground.

In the hand: Needles are in sheathless bundles

Whitebark pines arise from seeds cached in the soil by Clark's nutcrackers. Caches average three seeds each. Multiple germinations from multi-seeded caches result in tree clumps. [Inyo N.F.] JIM STIMSON

of five, 1 1/2 to 3 1/2 inches long, attached to pliable, smooth, gray-barked branchlets.

HABITAT

Whitebark pine grows on high ridges, slopes, cirques, and meadows with lodgepole or western white pine, red fir, or mountain hemlock. It is usually found between 9,000 and 11,000 feet in the southern Sierra—to about 12,000 feet as *krummholz*—and from 8,000 to 9,500 feet in the Klamath Ranges and on Mount Shasta.

DISTRIBUTION

In California it ranges from Mount Whitney north along the Sierra crest to Lake Tahoe. It is scattered in the Cascades, including Mount Shasta and Lassen Peak. It also grows in the Warner Mountains and Klamath Ranges. Elsewhere, it extends up the Cascades, along the Coast Mountains of British Columbia, down the northern Rockies to southwest Wyoming, and into several ranges of northern Nevada.

Whitebark Pine
Pinus albicaulis

From Griffin and Critchfield

Limber Pine • *Pinus flexilis*

LIMBER PINE

Limber pine is really a cordilleran species spread along the Rocky Mountain backbone from Arizona and New Mexico to Alberta and British Columbia. It also scatters widely across the Great Basin, softening the harsh tops of most of Nevada's mountains with a fringe of aromatic, gray-green foliage. Finally, limber pine extends into California by way of desert ranges before reaching the White-Inyo chain and the southeastern flank of the Sierra Nevada.

The best specimens of limber pine look a lot like whitebark pine at its best. Both have straight, vertical trunks that are often clumped and acutely forked with steeply ascending branches that display clusters of resinous cones at their tips. This resemblance is no coincidence, for both species are "bird pines," caught up with Clark's nutcracker in a mutualistic relationship revolving around their nutritious seeds. (See pages 33 to 36 in whitebark pine for details of this symbiosis.) Since the nutcracker causes the regeneration of trees whose nuts it chooses to cache, traits that facilitate the harvest are likely to be passed on to future generations of pines. Among those facilitative traits are upswept branches with clearly displayed cones bearing wingless seeds. Limber and whitebark pines probably exhibit these traits because avian seed harvesters have selected for them. But the outward similarity of the two species does not mean they are very closely related. Although both are members of the soft pine subgenus, DNA and isozyme data show they are not similar.

Whitebark pine traces its ancestry to an Asian stone pine progenitor that arrived on this continent in a nutcracker's pouch over what is now the Bering Strait. Then both Asian pine and Asian nutcracker

Conifers outside the forest, such as this lone limber pine, have a high probability of producing self-pollinated seeds. The resulting seedlings often lack vigor and are unlikely to survive. [White Mts.] ROBERT TURNER

evolved into North American species. Limber pine, however, took form in Mexico under the selective pressure of jays that preferentially harvested and cached the largest and least-winged seeds they could find among limber pine's forbears. With climatic shifts, limber pine moved north, eventually encountering Clark's nutcracker. Since then, the nutcrackers have selected for similar traits in the two pines, causing them to evolve convergently in matters of tree form.

The southernmost timberline in California is on Mount San Gorgonio in the San Bernardino Mountains just 60 miles east of Los Angeles. Here limber pine mingles with lodgepole pine, growing to 50 feet or higher. At elevations exceeding about 10,800 feet, a progressive dwarfing of the pines begins; it ends with stunted, wind-beaten, waist-high cushions of *krummholz* near 11,500 feet. Heavy accumulations of wet snow break and batter these beleaguered little trees, but many limber pines in this locale have lived for over 900 years. Some huge, distorted limber pines on nearby Lake Peak are reported to be 2,000 years old.

Limber pine seldom impresses one as tall timber, but nineteenth-century Nevadans used this tree to build much of the infrastructure of an industrialized society. Known then as "white pine" because of its relationship to eastern white pine, limber pine found its way into homes, saloons, hotels, and other edifices of the developing Great Basin.

IDENTIFYING LIMBER PINE

At a distance: Under favorable conditions it is upright, of medium height and displays forked, upswept branches. Its trunks are often in clumps of two or more and never chalky white in color (like whitebark pine).

Standing beneath it: Seed cones are bright green (never purple) in summer, ripening to yellow brown. Pollen cones are in bright yellow clusters on lower limbs. The ground is littered with weathering, open cones.

In the hand: Needles are in sheathless bundles of five, to three inches long, attached to flexible (therefore *flexilis*) gray-barked branchlets. Cones lack bristles or spines, are strongly woody, and measure up to five inches long.

HABITAT

It forms open woodland variously with Great Basin bristlecone, foxtail, Jeffrey, lodgepole, or singleleaf pinyon pine, or with white fir on dry, high-elevation sites that are moderated by late-season snowmelt.

DISTRIBUTION

In the Sierra Nevada it grows from Mono Pass south to the vicinity of Walker Pass. It also occurs in California's highest Great Basin and desert ranges, including the Sweetwaters, Whites, Inyos, and Panamints. In the Transverse Ranges, it grows near Reyes Peak, in the Mount Pinos area, and in the San Gabriel and San Bernardino mountains, while in the Peninsular Ranges it is found in the San Jacinto and Santa Rosa mountains. It is most common from about 8,000 feet to treeline, near 11,000 to 11,500 feet.

Limber pine attains great ages on harsh, barren sites where there are few fires, competitors, or pests. [Mt. Baden Powell] GEORGE WUERTHNER

Limber Pine
Pinus flexilis

From Griffin and Critchfield

Foxtail Pine • *Pinus balfouriana*

FOXTAIL PINE

Foxtail pine is unique among North America's conifers in consisting of two major populations separated by a gap of about 300 miles. There is disagreement on how long the two have been separated—whether it is hundreds of thousands or millions of years—but there has been time for them to diverge in several of their characteristics and be treated as two subspecies. The southern population (ssp. *austrina*) is concentrated near Kings Canyon and Sequoia national parks in the Sierra Nevada. The northern population (ssp. *balfouriana*) is found in the Klamath Ranges. Despite their differences, some of which are listed below as identifying characteristics, the two subspecies are still closely enough related to be fully reproductively compatible and have been experimentally hybridized.

Experimental crosses have also been very successful between the southern subspecies of foxtail pine and Great Basin bristlecone pine from the White Mountains. Such high "crossability" suggests that natural hybrids ought to be found in the White Mountains. After all, only 20 miles of Owens Valley separates the species here, a distance easily negotiated by airborne pollen carried on westerly winds. Yet no such hybrids have ever been found.

Taxonomists place foxtail pine, Rocky Mountain bristlecone, and Great Basin bristlecone in the pine subsection *Balfourianae*. This hardy group of pines is adapted to harsh environmental conditions tolerable to few other conifers. They differ from the other five-needled soft pines (see table on page 262) in having cone scales with thickenings (apophyses) on the dorsal surface and bearing a prickle or spine, seeds with long

It is speculated that foxtail pines of the southern population may live 2,500 years. [Sequoia N.P.] ANDY SELTERS

Foxtail pine in the Klamath Ranges is usually straight and full-crowned, and it suffers less from cambial die-back than the southern population. Dendrologists estimate that trees here can live 1,500 years, though no tree nearly that old has yet been documented. In the Sierra Nevada, old foxtails look quite a bit like some of the bristlecones of the White and Inyo mountains. Leaders die back, leaving spike-tops; trunks twist and turn as cambial die-back results in bare trunkwood traversed by narrow strips of bark. Researchers speculate that the southern subspecies may attain maximum ages of 2,500 to 3,000 years, but really old trees have yet to be discovered. This is a species in need of more attention than it has received.

detachable wings, and branches that routinely (about half) originate *within* the needle fascicles. Foxtail pine, the first-described of the three, and therefore the subsection's common-name namesake, is a California endemic though its northern population grows close to the Oregon border.

Foxtail pine was discovered in the Scott Mountains by Scotsman John Jeffrey in 1852. He named it in honor of his benefactor, Professor John Balfour, who headed the committee that financed Jeffrey's North American travels. The needles of this new pine were found to be short, densely set, and retained well down the shoot. There was less branching of shoots than might be expected, so the whole had the appearance of what some called "foxtails" and what John Muir later termed "bottle-brush tassels." The foxtail habit is more characteristic of the northern than the southern subspecies, but both are named for it.

IDENTIFYING FOXTAIL PINE
At a distance: Northern foxtails are erect, with full crowns of deep green to blue-green foliage and intact leaders and pendulous branches. Southern foxtails are often tilted or distorted, with strongly tapering trunks topped by a dead

Conifers continue to photosynthesize all winter long. [Sequoia N.P.] JOHN DITTLI

The pines of subsection Balfourianae, *including foxtail pine, are all western American, are of ancient origin, and may have given rise to the pinyon pine group. [Sequoia N.P.]* DAVID LANNER

leader; ragged crowns of upswept branches bearing yellowish foliage are common.

Standing beneath it: Bark of mature northern foxtails is usually gray with ridges and furrows and fully encircles the trunk. Bark of mature southern foxtails is bright reddish brown to orange, in blocky plates, and often present on old trunks as narrow strips.

In the hand: Both populations have needles in sheathless fascicles of five, sharply tipped, and 1 to 1 1/2 inches long. Cones are three to five inches long, deep purple in summer, with thickened scale tips bearing very short bristles.

HABITAT

Northern foxtail usually grows on south-facing slopes underlain by gabbro, serpentine, granodiorite, limestone, or schist. It occurs alone or with Brewer spruce, lodgepole pine, or western white pine at 6,000 to 8,000 feet. Southern foxtail is typically found amid granite boulders or outcrops with red fir, whitebark pine, or lodgepole pine at 9,000 to 11,300 feet.

DISTRIBUTION

Northern populations are in the Klamath Ranges, including the Marble, Salmon, Scott, Eddy, and Yolla Bolly mountains and Trinity Alps. Southern foxtails grow in the Sierra Nevada, mainly within Kings Canyon and Sequoia national parks and adjacent areas of Inyo and Tulare counties to the east and south.

Foxtail Pine
Pinus balfouriana

From Griffin and Critchfield

45

Great Basin Bristlecone Pine • *Pinus longaeva*

GREAT BASIN BRISTLECONE PINE

In the March 1958 *National Geographic* dendrochronologist Edmund Schulman announced to the world his unprecedented discovery of trees that exceeded 4,000 years of age. They were Great Basin bristlecone pines growing high atop the White Mountains of eastern California. Ironically, Schulman did not live to see his article in print, nor to enjoy the fame it brought him and his remarkable trees. But today, thousands of reverent visitors come each year to see the ancient bristlecone pines—Earth's oldest living things—in the Inyo National Forest where Schulman studied them.

In the White Mountains, Great Basin bristlecone usually grows between 10,000 and 11,500 feet, but it can range in elevation from 8,500 feet to its upper limit at 11,650 feet. Typically, it is a timberline tree that grows above the woodland of singleleaf pinyon and Utah juniper, alone or in the company of limber pine. Rather than seeking shelter, it exposes itself on high slopes and ridges that take the full force of winter gales. In the White Mountains, bristlecone trees experience average monthly temperatures below freezing from November through April. During the hottest months of July and August, mean temperatures rarely exceed 50°F. Precipitation averages just over 12 inches per year. Thus, we hear the common observation that amid the bristlecone pines the climate ranges from cold to frigid and from droughty to arid. Despite the rigors of their environment, these trees seem always to grow upright, rather than beaten down into the shrubby timberline

The Schulman Memorial Grove has been the site of significant bristlecone pine research since the late 1950s. [White Mts.] LARRY ULRICH

krummholz one might expect in such a place. (Some bristlecone *krummholz* are found on Nevada's Mount Washington.) There are White Mountain bristlecones as tall as 60 feet, with five-foot-diameter trunks; 90-footers have been reported from other areas, but not verified.

Young Great Basin bristlecones are as symmetrical and as fine-limbed as firs. As they age their crowns spread, their branches become massive, and most top out at 30 feet or so from the ground. The foliage consists of short needles, deep green and lustrous, in fascicles of five. Unlike needles of other conifers, which live only a few years and are then shed, those of bristlecone pine may live 20, 30, even 40 years. This burdens a limb with a very heavy load of needles, but it also gives the tree the benefits of a stable needle mass, which is a possible advantage in a harsh environment. The needles pro-

duce new phloem cells each year, and their chlorophyll content remains quite stable from year to year. Thus the needles appear to function well throughout their long lives.

Great Basin bristlecones tend to grow on steep slopes with thin soils. They experience especially severe drought conditions in dry years and faithfully record them by forming narrower-than-normal growth rings. It is this sensitivity of ring width to precipitation, coupled with bristlecone's ability to live many years, that has made the tree a valuable dating tool for dendrochronologists. Schulman located 17 bristlecones in the White Mountains that were over 4,000 years old. The oldest, named Methusaleh, was estimated to be about 4,600 years of age. The oldest bristlecone known—indeed, the oldest tree known—was felled on Wheeler Peak, Nevada in 1964. Its published age, by actual ring count, was 4,844 years. A little-known second count was made, however, on another reconstructed section of this tree by the late dendrochronologist Don Graybill, and he found 4,862 rings. The tree was almost certainly over 4,900 years old when it was cut down.

Great Basin bristlecone's age record has been challenged by botanists who advocate quaking aspen or creosote bush as the longest-lived plants. Those competing plants, however, are clonal; their tissues are short-lived, and they perpetuate themselves by putting up new sprouts into nearby open ground. They never form very many annual growth rings on a stem because stems die young. To argue that they are ancient requires one to have faith that the clone itself has been around in its present genotype for thousands of years. However logical that may seem, it does require belief in the absence of data. But no faith is needed to acknowledge that a pine with 4,000 rings in its trunk has stood on the very spot where it stands today for 4,000 years.

Long sequences of tree rings allow scientists to make inferences about past climates. The rings of deadwood found lying on the ground after many centuries can be "cross-dated" with those of living trees, thus extending the record backwards in time. Some bristlecone chronologies exceed 9,000 years. Wood from rings of known ages has been used to calibrate the radiocarbon dating curve, increasing the precision of carbon dating and forcing a re-evaluation of earlier interpretations of European prehistory.

Despite its great potential for longevity, a bristlecone must still contend with a variety of survival challenges. For example, its roots are always at risk of decay by root-rot fungi. The high and dry sites of the White Mountains are not optimal environments for these fungi, so they do not decay wood rapidly, but over the long term they do kill roots. Bristlecone pine roots are also killed when erosion of the soil that surrounds them exposes them to the drying air. Here then is a disadvantage of great old age: persist too long and eventually the very ground you grow in will wash away! When a major root is thus uncovered and dies, the sector of trunk above it and the branches emerging from that sector also die. The bark eventually sloughs off the dead zone, exposing bare trunkwood. If this happens to several trunk sectors due to multiple root deaths, the trunk becomes a cylinder of mostly dead wood traversed by vertical or spiraling strips of living bark that connect the surviving live roots to the limbs they still supply with water.

Why does it take so long for some Great Basin bristlecone pines to die? The answer lies, at least in part, in the rigors of the tree's environment. As Schulman first pointed out, the oldest bristlecones are found on the most rigorous sites. Elsewhere, they grow faster and die younger. A comparison of bristlecones living on a good, low-elevation site in southern Utah with a stand high on Wheeler Peak, Nevada showed distinct differences in how and when trees of the two stands die. Trees form a denser stand on the much milder, low-elevation site. Its soils retain moisture longer, have more organic material,

and support a richer growth of shrubs, herbs, and grasses. Since there is more dead wood on the ground and the bristlecones share the site with ponderosa pine and Rocky Mountain white fir, fires can carry. Thus, many of the bristlecones had charred bases. Fungi do better on the milder site, so fire-scarred trees had decaying bases. Bark beetles can successfully breed in the warmer, low-elevation sites, and evidence of beetle infestation is common. In comparison, Wheeler Peak bristlecones showed no signs of fire injury or bark-beetle activity. On the milder site, several bristlecones had dead tops due to porcupines feeding on the trunk bark, but porcupine damage was not reported from the Wheeler Peak stand. At the lower elevation, even sapsuckers had riddled some of the bristlecone pine trunks, opening wounds for the entry of fungi and creating

Dead bristlecones stand with main limbs intact for many centuries in their cold, dry habitats. [White Mts.] JEFF GNASS

The death of a bristlecone's main root exposed by soil erosion leads to a dead sector of trunk dependent on that root along with the death of branches emerging from that sector. [White Mts.] JEFF GNASS

points of mechanical weakness. Neither sap-suckers nor their sap-holes were found among the trees of the old stand. Thus the more favorable site for tree growth is also a better site for fungi, bark beetles, and whatever other creatures live at the expense of bristlecones.

Some observers suggest that bristlecone pine has inherent characteristics, such as decay-resistant wood, that enable it to live longer than other trees—but no evidence of this has yet been offered. Others propose that the very slow growth of the ancient trees signifies reduced metabolism, which somehow allows them to stay alive for very long periods. Again, there is no evidence. Great Basin bristlecone pine's neighboring competitor in the long-life game is limber pine, which in the Great Basin reaches a maximum of 2,000 years. In Colorado, where Rocky Mountain bristlecone pine *(Pinus aristata)* has attained 2,435 years, limber pine's best is about

1,544 years. Maybe something we do not understand about the nature of bristlecones helps them to outlive other species, even on the sites where those other species reach their maximum ages.

Bristlecones are able to produce mature seed crops in most years despite the short growing season in places like the Schulman and Patriarch groves in the White Mountains. Perhaps the deep purple of their developing seed cones allows them to absorb heat from the sun, speeding the developmental process (though up to 20% of cones may be green due to a lack of the pigment anthocyanin). Pollen-shed and pollination are in mid-July to early August, remarkably late for a pine; seeds are matured and shed in late September and early October of the next year. The seed is very small and bears a long winglike membrane, making it wind-dispersible. It is capable of germinating right off the tree, with no need to winter.

50

A white-breasted nuthatch parent feeds its nestling in a bristlecone pine trunk crevice. [White Mts.]
GEORGE LEPP

Although quite small, bristlecone seeds are harvested from their cones and eaten or cached in the soil by Clark's nutcrackers. In the White Mountains a very large proportion of the bristlecone pines are members of stem clumps that arise—like those of limber and whitebark pines—from nutcracker seed caches. An inventory in the Schulman Grove found only 54% of the trees were growing as singles, and the other 46% were in clumps of two to four. In the Patriarch Grove, the proportions were 31% and 69% respectively. Perhaps the nutcrackers settle for small bristlecone pine seed in years when the preferred limber pine and singleleaf pinyon nuts are not available. At least it would save them the risk of migrating in search of greener pastures.

IDENTIFYING GREAT BASIN BRISTLECONE PINE
At a distance: Young trees are narrowly conical with a dense cover of short, dark green needles extending over much of the length of the branches. In older trees the heavily needle-clad branch tips droop. Very old trees, often massive,

have much exposed wood that oxidizes and weathers to tones of golden yellow through russet brown. Branches eroded by wind-blast are often reduced to spikes of glistening deadwood.
Standing beneath it: Bark is reddish to deep brown on trunks, pinkish gray on young shoots. Maturing cones are dark purple in summer, with conspicuous bristles. Long, needled limbs often lack branches over much of their length, appearing snakelike.
In the hand: Needles are slender, in sheathless fascicles of five, to 1 1/2 inches long, very densely set on the branchlet, and aromatic when crushed. Cones are about three inches long, with sharp-tipped bristles.

HABITAT
It grows on high, dry, windy, rocky sites usually between 10,000 and 11,500 feet. In the White Mountains most bristlecones are on dolomite, a limestone, but elsewhere quartzite, or even sandstone, is a common substrate.

DISTRIBUTION
In California bristlecone grows only in Inyo and Mono counties. It is found near the summits of the White and Inyo mountains, on Sentinel and Telescope peaks in the Panamints, and as a single tree in the Last Chance Range. Elsewhere it occurs on high mountains in the Great Basin and just beyond, in Nevada and Utah.

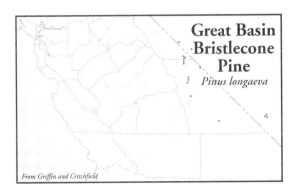

Great Basin Bristlecone Pine
Pinus longaeva

From Griffin and Critchfield

51

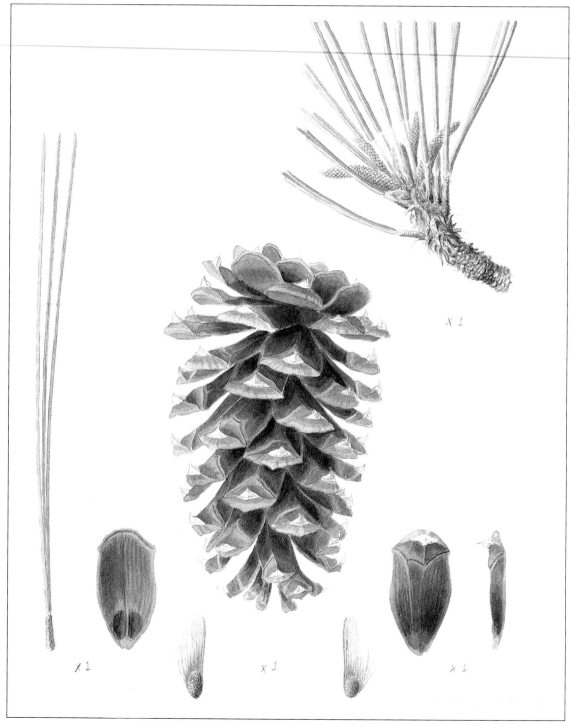

Ponderosa Pine • *Pinus ponderosa*

PONDEROSA PINE

(ALSO CALLED WESTERN YELLOW PINE)

If any tree can be said to define the region known as the American West, that tree must be ponderosa pine. Crossing the Great Plains from the east, one must pass the gauntlet of this long-needled cone-bearer somewhere: in South Dakota's Black Hills, Nebraska's pine ridges, Wyoming's Bighorns, Colorado's Rocky Mountain front, or New Mexico's cordillera. Ponderosa spreads far beyond the Rocky Mountain region, growing across much of California and the interior Pacific Northwest, and north into British Columbia's Fraser River Valley.

In California ponderosa pine has many faces. Nowhere does it grow more vigorously than on the deep, red soils of the Sierra Nevada westside; and nowhere is it as lance-pointed as on the McCloud River near Mount Shasta, where on sultry summer nights the aroma of cottonwood resin is wafted on the breeze, while bats hawk insects overhead. It is universally revered as a beautiful tree as well as a useful one whose lumber has largely supported a century-old wood products industry. Its many admirers will concur with Willis Linn Jepson, who wrote:

The traveler may journey day after day, over needle-carpeted or grassy ground, mostly free of underbrush, amidst great clean shafts forty to one hundred and fifty feet high, of really massive proportions but giving a sense of lightness by reason of their color, symmetry, and great height. No two trunks in detail of bark are modeled exactly alike, for each has its own particular finish; so it is that the eye never wearies of the fascination of the Yellow Pine but travels contentedly from trunk to trunk and wanders satisfyingly up and down their splendid columns—the finest of any pine.

Ponderosa pine regenerates most successfully after disturbances

Ponderosa pine—the conifer that defines the American West. [Yosemite Valley] CARR CLIFTON

Ponderosa pine is probably California's most common conifer. [Yosemite N.P.] FRED HIRSCHMANN

that expose bare soil and remove plants that shade its seedlings and compete with them for soil water. It often depends on flames to clear away the deep litter of fallen needles so that seedling roots can find their way to moist mineral soil. Fire also kills the young firs in whose shade ponderosa seedlings cannot get the sunlight they need. Go into a ponderosa forest and the clues to past fires will be obvious: charred snags still standing decades later, burned logs decaying on the ground, fragments of charcoal mixed into the soil, and live trees bearing basal "cat-faces"—fire scars extending up the trunk from ground level. Cat-faces form when a relatively cool-burning surface fire sends flames eddying up the upslope side of a tree, killing the cambium there despite the insulating effects of the bark. After repeated fires, the scar consists of exposed bare wood in the shape of a Gothic arch.

Researchers can reconstruct fire histories by analyzing fire scars and examining their relationship to growth rings in sections extracted from the tree. Fire histories obtained in this way show that fires have been an omnipresent influence in the ponderosa forest; they consume the forests'

accumulated fuels several times per century. The suppression of wildfires in the twentieth century has allowed massive fuel build-ups, resulting in catastrophic fires, such as those that plagued California in the 1990s. During the long intervals between these fires, shade-tolerant species, such as white fir and incense-cedar, increase their numbers exponentially and shade out the pines that would have grown up under a natural fire regime. Ponderosa pine is exquisitely adapted to that fire regime of years past. Even the younger trees have bark thick enough to help them survive many light fires, and in mature trees the scaly, plated bark may exceed three inches in thickness. Bumper seed crops come every few years in the fall, and when the masses of winged seed are released into the wind, the process of repopulating the burn with pines begins. The seeds germinate the next spring, and they quickly produce taproots that enable them to reach moist soil beneath the ashes lying in the sun.

As a ponderosa pine becomes old, its growth slows. The pointed, pyramidal crown of its youth becomes broad and round-headed, studded with twisted deadwood. The needles become fewer in number with the passing years, forming smaller tufts at the ends of branches that add less and less growth each spring from progressively shorter buds. Eventually, death will come to such a tree: bark beetles may successfully attack, lightning may strike a fatal blow, or fire may destroy the cambium, burning through bark that once had resisted flames before it began to thin in old age. The dead ponderosa may last another century or more, standing as a column of decaying wood, sheltering beetle grubs, ants, a nest of woodpeckers, perhaps a litter of fox pups, until on some windless day its last connected root silently parts and allows the now-diminished giant to fall from its place in the canopy and, in a final glorious moment, crash upon the forest floor from which it sprung.

Above, top: Reproduction tied to a regime of repeated fires creates ponderosa pine forests of various age groups. [Modoc N.F.] LARRY ULRICH
Above, bottom: Ponderosa seeds are an important wildlife food. [Yosemite N.P.] MICHAEL FRYE

IDENTIFYING PONDEROSA PINE

At a distance: It is a straight-trunked tree with yellow to reddish brown bark. It often exceeds 100 feet, with tufts of long, stiff, shiny needles clustered at the branch tips.

Standing beneath it: The bark, which is nearly odorless, sheds thin flakes with the random shapes of jigsaw-puzzle pieces. The ground is littered with old needles and the open cones of past years.

In the hand: Needles measure up to 10 inches long and are raspy to the touch when drawn through the fingers tip to base; they are three to the bundle and sweetly aromatic when crushed. Cones are three to five inches long and prickly.

HABITAT

In the Sierra Nevada it associates with gray pine at the lower edge of its elevational zone—

Prescribed burns like this one on Mt. Pinos reduce heavy fuel loads that can feed catastrophic wildfires in ponderosa pine forests. [Los Padres N.F.] MARC SOLOMON

canyon bottoms as low as 500 feet; higher up, it is found with sugar pine, incense-cedar, white fir, Douglas-fir, and black and canyon live oak. In the Transverse and Peninsular ranges it is found with bigcone-spruce and Coulter pine. It overlaps with Jeffrey pine at its upper limit, which is about 7,000 to 8,000 feet in southern California and about 5,000 to 6,500 feet in northern California. As California's arguably most common and widespread conifer, it sinks roots indiscriminately in soils derived from igneous, metamorphic, and sedimentary rocks.

DISTRIBUTION

The ponderosa pine of the Pacific coast states and British Columbia is of the typical variety, *Pinus ponderosa* var. *ponderosa.* (The other varieties are *scopulorum* in the Rocky Mountains, and *arizonica* in the Southwest and Mexico.) In California it forms near-continuous stands with its conifer associates from the Kern River north up through the Sierra Nevada, across the Cascades and Modoc Plateau, and south down the North Coast Ranges to Napa County. Other concentrations occur in the Santa Cruz Mountains, Santa Lucia Range, and the

Tehachapi, San Rafael, San Gabriel, San Bernardino, and San Jacinto mountains, as well as on Mount Cuyamaca in San Diego County. It reaches as far south in California as the slopes west of Lake Cuyamaca.

Ponderosa Pine

Pinus ponderosa

From Griffin and Critchfield

Jeffrey Pine • *Pinus jeffreyi*

JEFFREY PINE

Rampaging meltwaters descend the slopes of the eastern Sierra Nevada and Sweetwater Mountains every spring, flowing into the gorge of the West Walker River, hell-bent to fill the evaporative demands of a Great Basin summer. But when the flood-flow subsides, one can observe ragged old Jeffrey pine stumps protruding from the water. A riverbed is an unexpected place for a pine to be rooted, yet there they are. Until recently, Jeffrey pine stumps also jutted out of the shallows of Mono Lake, about 30 miles south. They were exposed when the lake was drawn down by the diversion of its feeder streams into the Los Angeles Aqueduct system, but are now slowly disappearing as Mono Lake undergoes a court-ordered increase in the lake level.

These stumps are clear evidence that sections of present-day rivers and lakebeds were once dry land. Radiocarbon and tree-ring studies show that beginning about 1,100 years ago California experienced two mega-droughts lasting 220 and 140 years, with a very wet century between them. Such droughts are more than ample to dry up streams and shrink lakes until "normalcy" returns. Jeffrey pine survived those long dry spells, perhaps by retreating to sites where moisture collects, and went on to form the extensive pure stands we see today in such places as the Mono Basin.

With its clean trunk and thick bark, Jeffrey pine is a beneficiary of frequent fires. Frequent fires are usually light ones, consuming only the forest-floor litter deposited since the last fire burned through. Where Jeffrey pine is most common, fuels are light, consisting mainly of "pinestraw," bark flakes, and fallen limbs, trunks, or cones, as well as

The fall colors of quaking aspen clones illuminate California's largest nearly-pure forest of Jeffrey pine, in the Glass Mountains. [Inyo N.F.] JOHN DITTLI

whatever thin-barked firs have gotten established since the last fire. The Sierran conflagrations of the 1980s and 1990s devastated Jeffrey pine stands in areas where decades of fire prevention had allowed fuels to build up; flames fed by high fuel levels were carried into the tree crowns. Pines that survive these hot wildfires are frequently damaged, and later become stressed by bark beetles, drought, and root rot. Ozone and other photochemical smog agents take an added toll wherever Jeffrey pine grows near or downwind from urban centers. "Chlorotic mottling," or spotwise death of needle chlorophyll, kills needles and thins the crowns of Jeffrey and ponderosa pines in the San Bernardino, San

Jacinto, and San Gabriel mountains and in the southern Sierra Nevada.

Jeffrey pine's big, beehive-shaped cones open in the fall, allowing winged seeds to spread on the breeze. Although they have inch-long wings, most of the Jeffrey's seeds do not fly very far because they are among the heaviest of winged North American conifer seeds. Unless the air is turbulent when the seeds exit the cone and start to auto-rotate their way earthwards, most will land within 30 yards or so of the parent tree. The nutritious seeds, concentrated first within opening cones and then spread out on the ground, are a powerful attractant to animals. Clark's nutcrackers harvest and make away with

Regeneration of Jeffrey pine appears to be heavily dependent on yellow pine and lodgepole chipmunks that bury its large, nutritious seeds in the soil. [Tahoe N.F.] LARRY ULRICH

some of the seeds, as do Steller's jays. Black bears search the forest floor, picking up seeds on their tongues. Golden-mantled and California ground squirrels and deer mice harvest some and "scatter-hoard" them in soil caches. But the most assiduous hoarders, and those most useful to the Jeffrey pine, are the yellow pine chipmunk, and its close relative, the lodgepole chipmunk. Research near Mount Rose, on the California-Nevada border, has shown that these two rodents concentrate nearly all the fallen Jeffrey pine seeds—within a day—into shallow soil caches, of which 70% contain one to five seeds. The caches are made not only under the forest canopy, but also among bitterbrush

shrubs growing in forest openings. As so often happens with cached seeds, some are left in the ground uneaten, and they germinate. Most of the seedlings that emerge the next spring are single individuals or clumps of two to five; occasional clumps of 50 or more can be found. Over the years, most clumps are reduced by mortality to single stems. The chipmunks are therefore important—perhaps even critical—players in the life-histories of Jeffrey pines. They disperse seeds into safekeeping, allow them to germinate, accelerate forest succession, and let natural selection operate by caching seeds in competitive situations. It appears likely that the suite of rodents and corvids that scatter-hoard Jeffrey

and in the San Bernardino, San Jacinto, and Laguna mountains. The hybrid's seed cone is intermediate in size, heft, and the ferocity of the claws on its scales.

Jeffrey pine also hybridizes with ponderosa pine. These hybrids are difficult to identify, given the general similarity of the two species in their pure form. (For many years Jeffrey was considered a variety of ponderosa pine.) They can be found at many places where the two pines overlap, especially in the Sierra Nevada.

An important difference between Jeffrey and ponderosa pines is the chemical composition of their oleoresin, the pitch that oozes out when their tissues are lacerated. Oleoresin of ponderosa—and nearly all other pines—is made up of a class of chemicals called terpenes, the ingredient of turpentine. But Jeffrey pine oleoresin contains the hydrocarbon known as normal heptane. This is a highly explosive compound. During the

Old trees in the hard pine subgenus, like this Jeffrey pine, cease adding height after their crowns "flatten." [Mono Co.] DAVID LANNER

pine seeds are of major importance in the species' natural regeneration. The pine's relationship to this community of vertebrates can be regarded as a diffuse mutualism in which one form of survival is exchanged for another.

Jeffrey pine hybridizes with Coulter pine at several places where the species occur together: in the Clear Creek-New Idria area of San Benito County, on Chews Ridge in Monterey County,

Civil War, Union manufacturers of turpentine used ponderosa pitch to replace an unavailable product from the Confederate States; Jeffrey pine pitch would sometimes get into the vats and cause an explosion. Gray pine is the only other pine known to harbor normal heptane, making California's forests unique in one more way: the only place where both of the world's "gasoline trees" reside.

IDENTIFYING JEFFREY PINE

At a distance: Mature trees have dark reddish brown bark with narrow plates between deep fissures. The foliage is grayish to blue-green in color.

Standing beneath it: Bark fissures and newly exposed bark smell like vanilla, or, to some noses, pineapple.

In the hand: The needles are fairly stiff, three to the bundle, and measure up to nine inches long. Bark scales have creamy or pinkish inner surfaces. The cones, which grow to 10 inches long, are smooth to the touch because the prickles of open cones bend inwards.

HABITAT

Jeffrey pine is found at 5,500 to 9,000 feet on the Sierra Nevada eastside. On the westside, it occurs from 5,000 to 8,000 feet in the north and from 6,000 to 9,000 feet or higher in the south. In the Transverse and Peninsular ranges it generally grows above the chaparral belt and the pinyon pine-juniper woodland at 6,000 to 9,800 feet, but it is also found on basin floors and arroyos down to 4,500 feet and lower in the Peninsular Ranges. On serpentine outcroppings in the North Coast and Klamath ranges, it dominates at elevations as low as 1,600 to 200 feet. It is often among sagebrush and bitterbrush in open, sunny stands. Its many coniferous associates include ponderosa pine, sugar pine, western white pine, lodgepole pine, singleleaf pinyon, limber pine, and red and white firs.

DISTRIBUTION

It grows throughout the Klamath Ranges, in the North Coast Ranges, in the Warner Mountains and Cascades, along the entire Sierra Nevada, in the Diablo Range, and in the San Rafael, Tehachapi, San Gabriel, San Bernardino, San Jacinto, Agua Tibia, and Laguna mountains. It also occurs along the length of the Sierra Juárez and Sierra San Pedro Mártir in Baja California.

Jeffrey pine can be identified by the aroma of its bark. [Inyo N.F.] GEORGE WUERTHNER

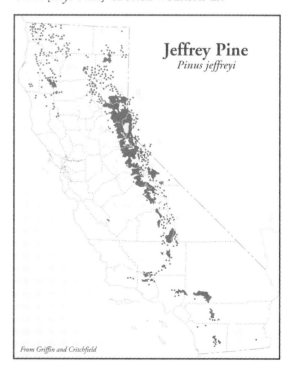

Jeffrey Pine
Pinus jeffreyi

From Griffin and Critchfield

Washoe Pine • *Pinus washoensis*   ARTWORK: SUSAN BAZELL

WASHOE PINE

Some of the yellow pine logs flumed off the Sierra Nevada eastside to supply lumber for Virginia City and mine props for the Comstock Lode were of a species that had no name until the mid-twentieth century. They were the product of Washoe pine, perhaps the rarest member of its genus in the United States after Torrey pine.

Washoe pine went unrecognized until September 1938, when University of California botanist Herbert L. Mason, acting on a tip from vegetation survey workers, botanized the east slope of Mount Rose, Nevada. Mason spotted what he at first took to be a small-coned Jeffrey pine in the upper reaches of Galena Creek. He returned the next year, and the next, collecting specimens and determining the extent of the second-growth pine stand that had come in amid the old stumps of an 1860s logging operation. One old tree found in the seven-mile-long stand rose to 200 feet, suggesting the potential of this new pine which Mason and forest geneticist Palmer Stockwell named to commemorate the Washoe Indians who had hunted on these wooded slopes.

Within three decades or so of Mason and Stockwell's 1945 publication of Washoe pine, several other locations were found, including its major concentration in the Warner Mountains of northeastern California. Great old "pumpkin pines," grow here in open stands consisting of trees of all ages and sizes. They are interspersed among openings lush with lupine, wild rose, mule ears, and big sagebrush. In the surrounding forests, California white fir is the most common species, especially on the shadier slopes; there is also a scattering of whitebark pine and stands of lodgepole pine that face quaking aspen across high, windswept meadows.

In the Warner Mountains Washoe pine is found at the upper edge of the ponderosa pine belt, often mixed with white fir. [South Warner Wilderness] ROBERT TURNER

Washoe pines tend to go unnoticed because of their resemblance to the closely related ponderosa pine and more superficial similarity to Jeffrey pine. To confuse matters, the Washoe pines at Mount Rose's Galena Creek co-occur with Jeffreys, while those in the Warners merge into ponderosas at their lower edge. Chemically, the resin of Washoe pine is similar to that of ponderosa but totally dissimilar to that of the heptane-producing Jeffrey. Nevertheless, some

At a distance, Washoe pines like these look similar to ponderosa pine. [Warner Mts.] RON LANNER

observers find that the bark of Washoe pine gives forth the vanillalike aroma of Jeffrey pine.

Washoe pine's origins remain enigmatic. One hypothesis holds that it is the product of an ancient hybridization between Jeffrey pine and the Rocky Mountain variety of ponderosa pine, but chemical data lend this idea no support. Another view is that "Washoe pine" is merely a high-elevation variant of ponderosa pine. Further study of this pine is justified.

IDENTIFYING WASHOE PINE

At a distance: This tree is much like ponderosa pine. Young trees are broadly pyramidal when growing in the open and old trees have an open crown of widely spaced horizontal branches.

Standing beneath it: The bark of old trees is in broad, yellowish plates separated by black fissures. **In the hand:** Seed cone characters are critical in identifying Washoe pine and can be used year-round. Mature Washoe pine cones that have already opened and shed their seeds feel like miniature Jeffrey cones: smooth to the touch because the scale prickles do not point outwards. However, they are much smaller than Jeffrey cones, usually only 2 to 4 inches long instead of 5 to 10 inches. Before they mature, Washoe pine cones are deep purple in color, while those of the similar-sized ponderosa pine are usually green. But this character must be used cautiously since high-elevation ponderosa pine can have purplish cones.

HABITAT

Washoe pine is found on sites ranging from glacial moraines to volcanic ridges, from about 5,500 to 8,500 feet. It grows in forests of other yellow pines, firs, and aspen.

DISTRIBUTION

In California, the most extensive stand is found in the southern Warner Mountains of Modoc County. It also grows near Babbit Peak in the Bald Mountain Range of Sierra County and has been recorded in the Butte Lake area of Lassen Volcanic National Park. Elsewhere it occurs near Mount Rose in Washoe County, Nevada, and has been reported from sites in Oregon and British Columbia.

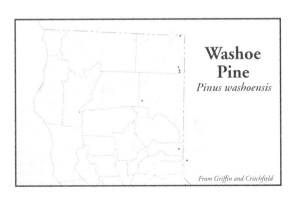

Washoe Pine
Pinus washoensis

From Griffin and Critchfield

Gray Pine • *Pinus sabiniana*

GRAY PINE

(ALSO CALLED DIGGER PINE, FOOTHILL PINE)

In November 1831 botanist David Douglas notified his patron in London, Dr. William Jackson Hooker, of his exciting rediscovery of a new species. For some months Douglas had been traveling the California coast between Fort Ross and Santa Barbara. He was probably in the Gabilan Mountains, near Mission San Juan Bautista, when he collected the specimen, about which he wrote to Hooker:

I have added a most interesting species to the genus Pinus, P. sabinii, *one which I had first discovered in 1826, and lost, together with the rough notes, in crossing a rapid stream. When compared with many individuals of the genus inhabiting the western parts of this continent, its size is inconsiderable, from 110 to 140 feet high, and 3 to 12 feet in diameter.*

Today we do not see many gray pines as large as the ones Douglas encountered, though the reigning champion near Redding stands just over 160 feet with a diameter of 59 inches. In 1910 Willis Linn Jepson wrote that gray pines were occasionally 90 feet high and to four feet in diameter, and the *Flora of North America* (1993) pares them down to a scant 25 meters; so our expectations of gray pine seem to be progressively declining as time marches on. Even in its present diminished state this is a pine to be remembered. One's first impression is of a wispy crown supported on a slender, often branched trunk. Most of the trees stand upright in their semi-arid surroundings and are sometimes garnished with poison oak vines. Many lean and tilt this way and that, creating the suspicion of a drunken forest staggering as it ascends the oak-studded foothills.

Gray pine has never been prized for its wood, which is reputed to be coarse-grained, pitchy, and highly subject to warping. Today that wood finds its way into railway ties and shipping pallets, but in the nineteenth century it was burned in great quantities to get up steam for the hoists at Sierra Nevada mines. Perhaps the big old trees of bygone days went up in smoke. Unlike all our other pines but Jeffrey, the oleoresin of this species—yielded by tapping the trunk—contains normal heptane instead of terpenes. Distillation of the resin cannot, therefore, result in production of turpentine, but can threaten life and property. Because of their non-conforming chemistry these pines have been referred to as "gasoline trees."

Gray pine usually grows in open woodlands rather than forests. [Kern Co.] DAVID LANNER

What gray pine lacked in wood value, chemical utility, and the ability to offer the "comfort of shade to the inexperienced wayfarer who, dusty and sun-bitten, seeks its protection" (Jepson), it made up for with its large thick-hulled nuts. John Muir wrote of Indian men climbing the trees to beat down the cones with sticks and the women opening them with fire-heat. These early Californians were wise to harvest the large nuts of this pine. The kernels are 25% protein and 49% fat, and over 95% of the fats are the polyunsaturated oleic and linoleic acids. The large seed, which has only a short, thick, removable wing, is almost certainly

dispersed less by the wind than by animals, perhaps gray squirrels and scrub jays. Surprisingly, this aspect of gray pine's biology has yet to be explored in the detail it deserves.

Many Californians known that gray pine long went by the name Digger pine. Why the change? John G. Lemmon challenged posterity in 1895 when he wrote, "Vernacular names, with their frequent unfitness, are apt to be long-lived. Shall we see to it that only appropriate ones are used?" In this case Digger refers to California Indians in a way that is inaccurate, as well as offensive to them, so it is clearly not appropriate. Nor has it ever been the only common name in use. Even crusty old Jepson, to whom the objections to Digger pine weighed "not in the slightest," acknowledged that as far back as 1874 it was also called nut pine, blue, grayleaf, bull, and ghost pine. Lemmon liked the descriptive accuracy of grayleaf, which gray pine makes more succinct. In 1855 John Newberry referred to it as Sabine's pine or nut pine, and even by 1908, George B. Sudworth was using gray more often than Digger. Today one often hears this tree called foothill pine. Dendrology is under no obligation to prolong historic insults, thus the use of gray pine here.

IDENTIFYING GRAY PINE
At a distance: Note the spindly dark trunks, often forked and tilted, supporting crowns of wispy gray needles.
Standing beneath it: The slender needles are up to a foot long and hang loosely. The gray-barked limbs are studded with brown cones varying in size from apple- to pineapplelike.
In the hand: Needles are three to the bundle, 8 to 12 inches long, and droopy. Cone scales have sharply pointed tips, and those at the cone base are usually prolonged into nasty hooklike spurs.

HABITAT
Gray pine grows scattered or in small groves on dry, rocky foothill slopes or on valley floors.

Forked and tilted black trunks and wispy, ghost-like foliage immediately signify gray pine. [Mariposa Co.] DAVID LANNER

It can survive a mere 10 inches of rainfall annually, and tolerates "ultramafic" soils—soils very high in magnesium—such as those that develop on serpentine. It is most common between 1,000 and 3,000 feet but drops to 100 feet in some northern Sacramento Valley locations and nears 7,000 feet on Sawtooth Peak in southwest Inyo County. Some common associates in its usual hot, dry foothill stands are blue oak, valley oak, and interior live oak. The lower edge of the ponderosa pine forest often merges with the uppermost gray pines. California buckeye may grow on shaded north slopes in these foothill woodlands along with numerous shrubs and annual grasses. In the Tehachapi and Piute mountains blue oak and gray pine merge into open stands of singleleaf pinyon and California juniper, forming a unique combination of drought-resistant trees.

DISTRIBUTION

Gray pine's distribution is noteworthy for two reasons. First, it is a true Golden State endemic—

in other words a native to California alone—without any Nevada or Oregon outliers. Second, more than any other conifer, more than any other tree except for blue oak, gray pine encircles the Central Valley. There is an intriguing gap 55 miles wide in the southern Sierra Nevada, between the Kings River and the South Fork of the Tule River. Otherwise, the Sacramento and San Joaquin valleys are fairly ringed with groves of this California original. There are additional significant populations in the Klamath Ranges, where it reaches its northern limit along the Salmon River drainage, and in the Pit River country of northeast Shasta County. It is found in many of the inner Coast Ranges and reaches its southern limit at foothill locations in northern Santa Barbara, Ventura, and Los Angeles counties. In Monterey County, gray pine breaks out of the Nacimiento Valley, and leaving even blue oak behind, crosses the Santa Lucias to raise cone-studded limbs almost down to the Pacific on the Big Sur coast.

Gray Pine
Pinus sabiniana

From Griffin and Critchfield

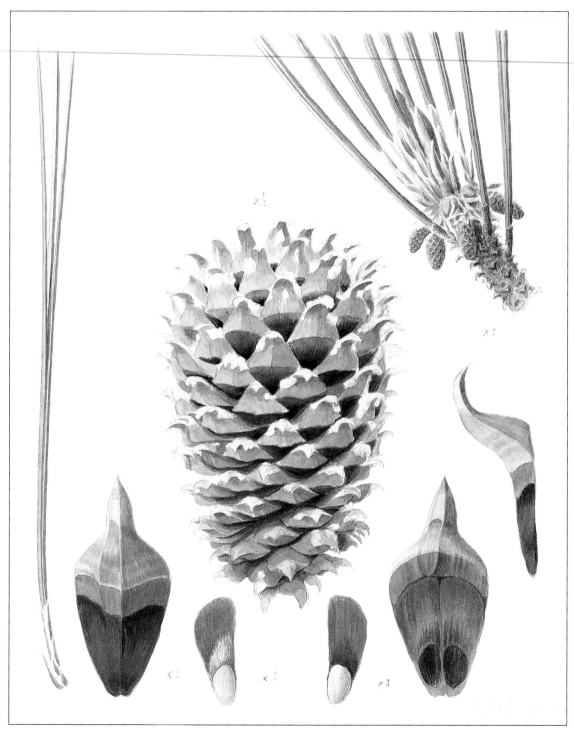

Coulter Pine • *Pinus coulteri*

COULTER PINE

Imagine Thomas Coulter's self-satisfaction, perhaps bordering on gloating, as he stood on a steep, grassy slope in the Santa Lucia Range one fine day late in 1831. His much better-known contemporary, David Douglas, had immortalized himself several years earlier by discovering the world's longest-coned pine, sugar pine. As Dr. Coulter gazed down upon the Pacific shore from his 4,000-foot perch, there were indeed some sugar pines in his field of view. But more importantly, there was also a thick-limbed, glossy-needled pine whose cones resembled great tawny porcupines and were of a massiveness unknown in the pines. Douglas himself had been collecting plants in this very area before and during Coulter's brief stay in California, but the great plant explorer had somehow, inexplicably, confused two pines. One Douglas had rediscovered after having lost specimens of it collected some years previously, and had named it *Pinus sabinii.* But the other—before which Coulter now stood—Douglas had overlooked, not realizing it was of a hitherto undescribed species. Seizing the opportunity, Coulter sent specimens of this remarkable pine to botanist David Don in England. Don memorialized Coulter by naming the new conifer *Pinus coulteri.* Surely no Irish botanist had ever been introduced so felicitously to the California dendroflora.

The cones that Don found to be "very large—twelve inches in length by six in diameter—comparable to sugar loaves" have scales variously described since as horribly armed, curved like a nail-grab, with talonlike appendages, tusklike spurs, and incurved spines. In 1895, California's first conifer expert, John G. Lemmon, recorded a maximum

Coulter cone length of 20 inches and a weight of eight pounds. The latter figure must refer to a cone still green and moist as it approached maturity in its final summer. Within these ponderous cones there are about 150 seeds, measuring $1/2$ inch long. Each seed is grasped by the thickened claws of an inch-long reddish brown wing that appears incompetent in dispersing the heavy, thick-hulled propagule much beyond the shadow of its parent tree. Western gray squirrels and scrub jays feed on Coulter pine nuts, but their role in further dispersal or in establishment of seedlings remains to be learned. The squirrel harvests nuts by cutting the cones from the tree, thus endangering the life and limb of any passerby; it then gnaws off the scales from the base upwards. Coulter nuts are a reliable food source for the squirrel because they are often retained for years in closed cones.

The "closed-coneness," or serotiny, is a variable character in Coulter pine. In some stands it is relatively uncommon, and only a few cones remain closed for as much as four years. But in other stands a majority of cones may stay closed for more than six years; some even remain tightly sealed with viable seeds inside for as many as 25 years while weathering and even disintegrating on the tree. Serotiny is a helpful trait for

Coulter pine adds a measure of diversity to California forests. [Los Padres N.F.] JOHN EVARTS

Coulter pines growing amid chaparral or with canyon live oak where stand-destroying crown fires commonly burn. The heat of the fire can open the long-sealed cones, allowing the seeds to exit and, typically, produce a flush of new seedling growth the next spring. Unfortunately, fire control exerted by forestry authorities can work against the long-term regeneration prospects of Coulter pine.

The relatively high content of protein, fat, and carbohydrate found in Coulter pine nuts is quite similar to gray and sugar pines, both of which were extensively harvested by Native Americans. Surprisingly, there is little information about the use of Coulter pine's nutritious nuts among California Indians. The wood of Coulter pine is brittle and prone to warping, and it has never been in demand for lumber.

Coulter pine can be quickly identified by its long needles and massive cones. [Los Padres N.F.]
JOHN EVARTS

Lower limbs of open-grown Coulter pines are not shaded and can live for many years. [San Bernardino N.F.] DAVID LANNER

IDENTIFYING COULTER PINE

At a distance: Coulter pine is a medium-sized, single-trunked tree three feet in diameter, up to 70 or 80 feet tall, and often with a spreading crown of stout branches bearing long, stiff, shiny needles and very large cones.

Standing beneath it: The bark of mature trunks is dark brown, even blackish, with furrows separating wide, scaly ridges. Generations of cones in various stages of decay repose on the long-needled litter.

In the hand: Needles are three to the bundle, stiff, sharply-tipped, to 12 or 14 inches long. Cones are about the same length, with sharply hooked scale tips often exceeding an inch in length. Inner portions of the scales are chocolate brown, while the tips are yellow and encrusted with dried yellow pitch.

HABITAT

It grows on dry foothills and mountainsides between 2,500 and 7,200 feet in chaparral, oak woodlands, or forests with ponderosa, gray, or

knobcone pines, Santa Lucia fir, or incense-cedar. In the Transverse and Peninsular ranges it can also overlap with Jeffrey pine, with which it sometimes hybridizes. It is usually found on coarse-textured or gravelly sandstones or granites.

DISTRIBUTION

This pine ranges from northern Contra Costa County through the South Coast Ranges, including the Diablo, Gabilan, and Santa Lucia ranges and the San Rafael Mountains. It also grows in the Transverse Ranges, including the Santa Ynez, San Gabriel, and San Bernardino mountains, as well as the Peninsular Ranges, including the San Jacinto, Santa Ana, Agua Tibia, Cuyamaca, and Laguna mountains; it continues south into Baja California, ranging through the Sierra Juárez and into the Sierra San Pedro Mártir. A curious gap in Coulter pine's distribution occurs in the Transverse ranges of western Los Angeles County and Ventura County, where it is entirely absent.

Coulter Pine
Pinus coulteri

From Griffin and Critchfield

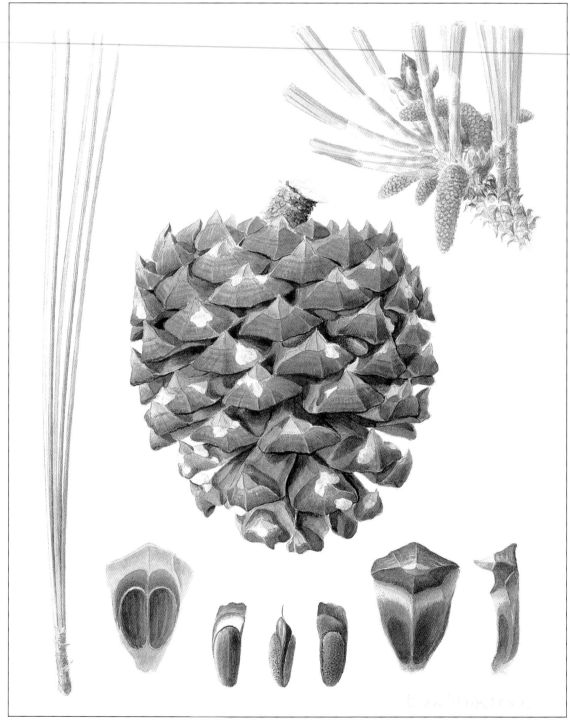

Torrey Pine • *Pinus torreyana*

TORREY PINE

Torrey pine is one of those unusual plants that qualifies as a "narrow" endemic. Not only is it restricted, or endemic, to California, but it occupies only a tiny fraction of the state's territory. In fact, Torrey pine is the rarest member of its genus in the United States. The native Torrey pine groves comprise perhaps 9,000 to 10,000 trees, all of which are concentrated in two places: a five-mile stretch of sea bluffs along the north edge of San Diego and the adjacent community of Del Mar, and the northeast side of Santa Rosa Island, about 25 miles from Santa Barbara.

Among the California conifers, Torrey pine is something of an enigma. Since no fossils of Torrey pine have been found, there exist no records of its earlier distribution. Moreover, the genetic uniformity exhibited by this species suggests that its numbers were greatly reduced—perhaps to the brink of extinction—in the not-too-distant past. The two Torrey pine populations, separated by 175 miles, may be holding on to their little pieces of Earth's surface, but they do not appear to be enlarging their range. The mainland Torrey pine popula-tions are now confined by urbanization, yet their total acreage was tiny even at the time of their discovery by Charles Parry in 1850. The Santa Rosa Island trees may simply have filled the available habitat suitable to their needs.

There may be another reason that this species has so confined its range: an inherently inefficient system for dispersing its seeds into new territory. Like its closest relatives, gray and Coulter pines, Torrey pine's large, heavy seeds are enclosed in massive, woody cones that open very slowly. The cones sometimes remain on the trees for 15 years, gradually

Mainland Torrey pine, growing here among sandstone outcrops, forms southern California's only coastal coniferous woodland. [Torrey Pine S.R.] BILL EVARTS

releasing their seeds over a number of seasons. When a seed falls out of a cone, the short wedge of a seedwing will do little to help it disperse, even if a brisk wind is blowing. The situation seems made to order for an animal disperser, but none has been convincingly shown to move Torrey pine seeds. Some biologists think the delayed opening of Torrey pine's cones helps the tree regenerate in burn areas.

In their widely separated enclaves, Torrey pines differ in subtle ways. Island trees tend to sprawl more, and they grow less tall. They have broader cones and shorter needles. Mainland trees have hardly any presence of the compound beta-phellandrene in their oleoresin, but on Santa Rosa Island that substance reaches levels of over 12%. Genetic analysis of enzyme systems has shown the two populations to be distinctly different from each other in two of 59 genes studied. That clear difference has supported the proposal that the population on Santa Rosa Island be considered a separate subspecies, *Pinus torreyana* ssp. *insularis.*

IDENTIFYING TORREY PINE
At a distance: Torrey pine is a short to medium-sized tree with crooked or forked stems bearing tufts of long needles and conspicuous cones.

Mainland Torrey pine grows among coastal chaparral. [Torrey Pines S.R.] BILL EVARTS

Contorted or semi-prostrate specimens are common on exposed bluffs, while straight, upright trees to 70 feet or more occupy more wind-protected arroyos and alcoves.

Standing beneath it: Mature cones are nut brown in color, fading to gray with age; they are mostly closed and set apart from the branch by a thick stalk as much as an inch in length.

In the hand: The needles average about 9 inches in length and may reach 13 inches; they are mainly in bundles of five, but three- and four-needled bundles are also found. The cone scales are sharply prickle-tipped and make the cones uncomfortable to handle.

HABITAT

It grows on sandy or sandy loam soils, between 100 and 500 feet above sea level, on seaside cliffs, ridges, and mesa tops. Annual precipitation averages about 10 inches at the mainland groves and 12.5 inches at the island stand.

Santa Rosa Island Torrey pine is 175 miles from its coastal relative. [Channel Is. N.P.] JOHN EVARTS

It associates with coastal chaparral on the mainland, including an unusual assemblage of drought-tolerant species, such as yucca, agave, and cacti. The Santa Rosa stand is home to several other endemics, including island monkey flower, island scrub oak, and Santa Rosa Island manzanita.

DISTRIBUTION

The mainland population (subspecies *torreyana*) is largely within Torrey Pines State Reserve on both sides of the mouth of Los Peñasquitos Lagoon near Del Mar in San Diego County. The insular population (subspecies *insularis*) is on the eastern coast of Santa Rosa Island (part of Channel Islands National Park), primarily on steep slopes that overlook the Santa Barbara Channel.

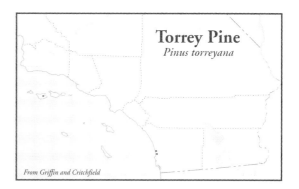

Torrey Pine
Pinus torreyana

From Griffin and Critchfield

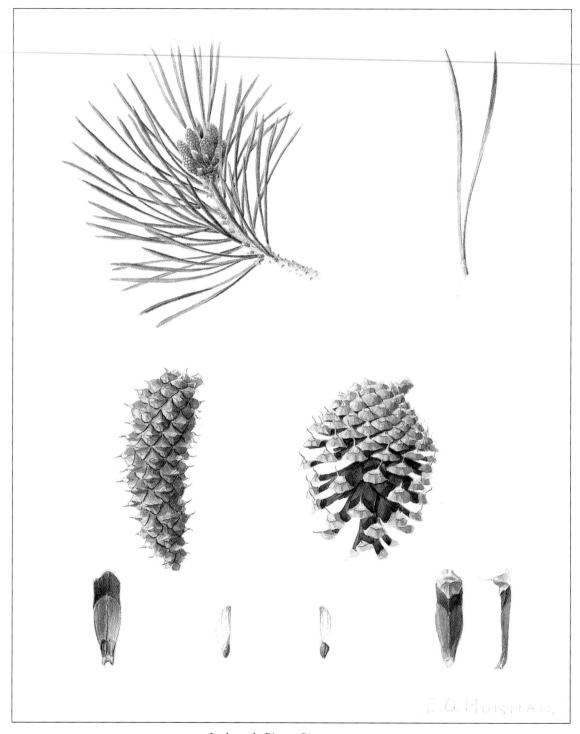

Lodgepole Pine • *Pinus contorta*

LODGEPOLE PINE

(SEE TEXT FOR ADDITIONAL COMMON NAMES)

The pine described under this name is one of the most interesting of Pacific species on account of its variable characters and... its enormously wide range. For many years a fruitless effort has been made to keep the tree which inhabits the northern Pacific coast region distinct from the tree of the high Sierras and Rocky Mountain plateaus. . . . Differences are not too great to be consistently merged in one polymorphous species, as it is proposed to do here.

—George B. Sudworth
Forest Trees of the Pacific Slope

Sudworth's judgment, as expressed in his classic, has since been borne out by decades of research. No longer do botanists recognize as a species *Pinus murrayana* of the Sierra Nevada, or *Pinus latifolia* of the Rockies. Since W. B. Critchfield's 1957 study of lodgepole pine in all its variations, this most widely ranging of all western conifers has been viewed as a complex species made up of four quite well-differentiated subspecies. Three of these subspecies can be found in California, one of which is endemic to the state.

Lodgepole pine has not left behind very much fossil evidence. We can place it in the Pacific Northwest during the late Miocene to early Pliocene (five to six million years ago) and in the Yukon by perhaps early Pleistocene (two million years ago). By then it had already become subdivided into several populations that occupied varying environments. They had therefore been exposed to different spectra of natural selective forces and responded by evolving into distinctive races, each

Sierra-Cascade lodgepole pine typifies moist sites in the upper montane forest. This old tree continues to close an old axe blaze. [Ansel Adams Wilderness] CARR CLIFTON

with its own environmental tolerances and physical characteristics.

Due to western geomorphology and the north-south axes of most of our mountain ranges, the three major lodgepole pine races found refuges from Pleistocene glaciation: south down the Pacific coast, south down the Sierra Nevada range, and south down the chains of the Rockies. Thus all three of these races survived the Pleistocene and were able to expand northwards when the ice retreated. The three main subspecies of lodgepole pine that we recognize today represent formal acknowledgment of those earlier races. They are Rocky Mountain lodgepole pine (*Pinus contorta* ssp. *latifolia*), Sierra-Cascade lodgepole pine (*Pinus contorta* ssp. *murrayana*), and Coastal lodgepole pine (*Pinus contorta* ssp. *contorta*). The fourth subspecies, Mendocino White Plains lodgepole pine (*Pinus contorta* ssp. *bolanderi*), is believed to have evolved in place from a soil race or ecotype of coastal lodgepole.

Sierra-Cascade lodgepole, often called "tamarack" or "tamrac pine," grows rather slowly in height, but reaches greater trunk girth than lodgepoles elsewhere. Near the start of the twentieth century forester John Leiberg observed trees up to four feet in diameter, and some were reputed to have attained diameters exceeding six feet. Cones of this subspecies open when they mature and shed their winged seeds on the wind. They do not require heat to open them, so this subspecies is not dependent on fire for its regeneration. Seedlings come up in the small openings created when dead trees fall, or the ground slumps, or small fires burn out competing growth. Thus Sierra-Cascade lodgepole pine stands can be self-perpetuating, at least for several centuries.

In upper montane forests of the Sierra Nevada and Cascades lodgepole pine is a tree of moist places—creek banks and meadow margins—where it consorts with red and white firs, Jeffrey pine, and quaking aspen between

Coastal lodgepole is short, crooked, and broad-crowned. It grows on dunes, cliffs, grasslands, and bogs north to Alaska. [Mendocino Headlands] LARRY ULRICH

6,000 and 9,000 feet. Farther upslope, to 11,000 feet, it grows on dry sites as well, with whitebark, limber, foxtail, and western white pines, and with mountain hemlock. Throughout the Sierra Nevada, lodgepole pine is periodically attacked by its very own little moth, the lodgepole pine needle miner. This creature is known only from the Sierra Nevada, and it has a perverse interest in lodgepole needles. It lays its eggs in lodgepole needles, and the first-instar (earliest stage) larva spends 10 to 12 months mining out and digesting the contents of that needle! The larva becomes more active as it matures, and by the time it pupates it has destroyed about half a dozen needles. This insect infestation does occasionally become epidemic, and it has killed large numbers of trees in Yosemite National Park and elsewhere.

The coastal lodgepole, known to many as "shore pine" or "beach pine," offers a marked contrast to its upper-elevation kin. Where the Sierra-Cascade subspecies has straight, cylindrical trunks clothed in thin, flaky, light bark, coastal trees are crooked and limby, with thick,

Sierra-Cascade lodgepole is common on moist sites such as this lakeshore, but it also grows on dry, upland slopes. [Yosemite N.P.] ROBERT TURNER

in "the low mountains of central Del Norte County." Its affiliation with the coastal subspecies needs further study.

The most remarkable lodgepoles are those of the Mendocino White Plains. Here on the uppermost—and oldest—of the Pleistocene marine terraces, a pygmy forest grows on soils of astonishing acidity (pH as low as 2.8). It is these ash-colored, podzolized soils that give the White Plains their name. The lodgepoles, bishop pines, and cypresses that grow here are doomed to a dwarf's life because of the terraces' nutrient-poor soils. One can stride, Gulliver-like, among cone-bearing trees that are barely knee-high, while in the distance the spiked tops of old redwoods pierce the sea-fog.

Experiments have shown that when Mendocino White Plains lodgepoles are grown in normal soils, they grow as normal trees. Thus their pygmy habit is not genetically determined, but is soil-induced. However, the same cannot be said for their needles, which lack resin canals, making them unique among the world's pines. Crush any other pine needle between your fingers and they become sticky; crush the needles of this pygmy lodgepole and no sticky resin is released.

Pygmy lodgepoles also differ from other California lodgepoles in having heavy cones that are often serotinous. The bishop pine and Mendocino cypress that grow on Mendocino's White Plains are also closed-coned. Perhaps this environment is more fire-prone than that of the

furrowed, dark bark. In California, coastal lodgepole is usually found on the youngest Pleistocene marine terraces, which were cut by wave action of the rising sea during interglacial periods and then uplifted by tectonic forces. Genetically, this subspecies is relatively homogeneous, despite being spread over 20 degrees of latitude. In Washington, British Columbia, and Alaska it leaves the coastal dunes, cliffs, and grasslands of its California range, and sinks its roots in bogs and muskeg. Though coastal lodgepole is typically open-coned, James R. Griffin and William Critchfield reported a closed-coned race

downslope terraces that are closer to the shore; this might explain why the pygmy lodgepole and its conifer associates have a more serotinous character.

IDENTIFYING LODGEPOLE PINE

At a distance: Sierra-Cascade lodgepole is a medium to tall forest tree with a straight trunk, light brownish gray bark, and a narrow crown. Coastal lodgepole is short, crooked, and forked, with a domelike crown.

Standing beneath it: Sierra-Cascade lodgepole is finely branched unless open-grown, and the bark is flaky and thin; there are numerous cones, even on small trees unless shaded. Coastal lodgepole is heavy-limbed, with thick, deeply furrowed, dark red-brown to purplish bark.

In the hand: Needles are in bundles of two and usually about two inches long. Cones are prickly and measure about two inches long in Sierra-Cascade and down to one inch in coastal lodgepole. Sierra-Cascade needles are broad, coastal are thin, and Mendocino White Plains are very thin.

HABITAT

Sierra-Cascade lodgepole grows on moist sites between 6,000 and 9,000 feet and on drier sites to 11,000 feet; in some locales it is found even higher, forming *krummholz*. Coastal lodgepole is found on coastal dunes, cliffs, and inland bogs and in the Klamath Ranges on ultramafic soils, granite, and sediments.

DISTRIBUTION

Sierra-Cascade lodgepole is scattered from the Klamath Ranges east to the Cascades and Warner Mountains and is widespread throughout the length of the Sierra Nevada to northern Kern County. It also has outposts in the San Gabriel, San Bernardino, and San Jacinto mountains, and reappears again about 300 miles south in Baja California's Sierra San Pedro Mártir. Coastal lodgepole grows in coastal Del Norte, Humboldt, and Mendocino counties, ranging no farther south than Manchester. Mendocino White Plains lodgepole is located near Fort Bragg in Mendocino County.

Mendocino White Plains lodgepole grows as a dwarf on podzol soils. [Mendocino Pygmy Forest] J. R. HALLER

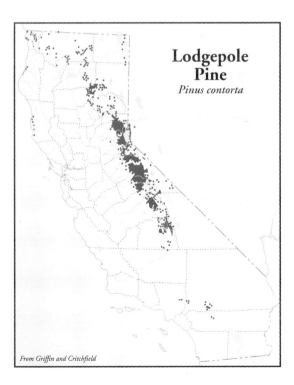

Lodgepole Pine
Pinus contorta

From Griffin and Critchfield

THE "CALIFORNIA CLOSED-CONE PINES"

Most of the world's pines have cones that dry out and open up when the seeds mature, and then they shed their winged seeds on the autumn wind. There are numerous variations on this theme, however, and California's pines show the whole spectrum of variability. For example, whitebark pine cones never open quite enough to let the seeds passively fall out, while Torrey and Coulter pines flirt with serotiny—the delay in cone opening that adapts some pines to fire-prone environments. California also harbors one subspecies of lodgepole pine that has closed cones, and three other pines that are so closely related and genetically intertwined, they are often put into an informal taxonomic category of their own: the "California closed-cone pines." They are bishop, Monterey, and knobcone pines.

It is generally accepted that serotiny

After fire, bishop pine cones open and deposit their seeds on the ashes. Seedling thickets result. [Santa Barbara Co.] JOHN EVARTS

Until a fire occurs, closed cones of knobcone pine protect their seeds from loss or deterioration. [San Bernardino N.F.] ROBERT TURNER

has evolved through natural selection in droughty environments where fire is a frequent visitor. Studies of lodgepole pine (*Pinus contorta* ssp. *latifolia*) in the northern Rockies have shown that its serotinous cones are sealed with resin that has a melting point around 145°F. When the resin is melted, the scales are allowed to spread and the seeds are released. The usual source of sufficient heat to do that job is fire, though heat reflected from the ground can open the cones of limbs lying on the forest floor due to logging, breakage, or windfall. Serotinous cones are always persistent on the tree, so a fire burning through a stand of such trees can simultaneously open the cones of many prior crops that have been stored for years in the forest canopy. Following a burn, a myriad of seeds alights on the mineral-rich ash below, and if sufficient fall or winter rains follow, a massive crop of seedlings rises weedlike from the scorched earth.

Although bishop, Monterey, and knobcone pines all share the serotinous cone habit, they do so to an unequal degree. Bishop pine are themselves notably variable: mature cones from some of the species' northern popula-tions hardly stay closed at all, while some of those from the southern range remain tightly closed for decades. Monterey pine

Dense growth of Monterey pine rapidly accu-mulates fuel that will burn in future fires. [Monterey Peninsula] GARY GEIGER

cones may start opening on the tree after a few years, even without benefit of fire. Donald Culross Peattie commented on the "crackling and snapping" of these cones on hot autumn days. Of all the California closed-cone pines however, none have cones that remain more tight-ly closed than those of knobcone pine, perhaps the least appreciated species of the group.

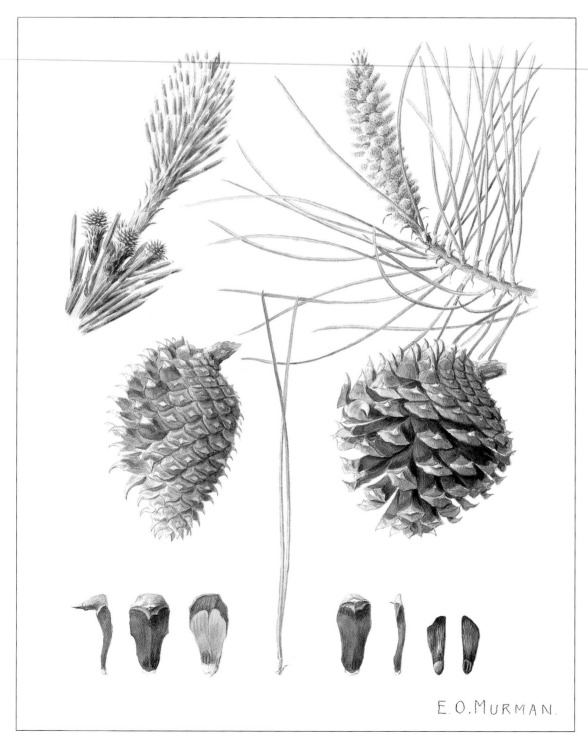

Bishop Pine • *Pinus muricata*

BISHOP PINE

Bishop pine always grows within 12 miles or so of the Pacific shore, and most are within sight or earshot of pounding surf. Therefore bishop pine is often thought of as a picturesque tree distorted by the seawind. It is that, but it is also a straight-boled "timber pine" reported to reach well over 100 feet in height, and it forms pure, dense forests of limited extent. In addition, it is a dwarfish little tree that can bear cones while only knee-high, when it is deprived of nutrients, as on Mendocino County's White Plains. In truth, bishop pine is a hard tree to stereotype.

This tree is exceedingly variable in growth habit, cone shape and prickliness, and even the chemistry of its resin. During the last several decades it has engendered more than one heated argument as to its ancestry and its very identity. These questions have been complicated by the ambiguities of interpreting a rich macrofossil resource of needles and cones, the possibility of hybridization with Monterey pine, divergent characteristics of trees on offshore islands, and the inability of certain northern and southern bishop pine populations to breed with each other. This last point is especially vexing, because no such crossing barrier has ever been found elsewhere in a pine species, and pines are relatively well-known genetically. It suggests that bishop pine's northern and southern populations have been isolated from each other for a long time.

Perhaps the strongest position that can now be defended in regard to bishop pine's complex nature maintains that the species has two varieties, separated by about 200 miles, with trees in between that are more intermediate in character. The distinctive northern variety, *Pinus muricata* var. *borealis,* ranges from the Sonoma County coast northwards to

A member of bishop pine's southern variety grows amid dense manzanita and coast live oak in the Solomon Hills. [Santa Barbara Co.] JOHN EVARTS

Trinidad in Humboldt County. To add to the confusion, this variety has both a more southerly "green" race and a more northerly "blue" race, based on foliage color; the two meet at Sea

Bishop pine on the Channel Islands is also of the southern variety. [Santa Rosa Island] JOHN EVARTS

Ranch in Sonoma County. (As is generally the case with conifers, a blue coloration is due to deposits of wax in the pits of the numerous stomates that are deployed in lines extending the length of the needles.) The southern variety, *Pinus muricata* var. *muricata,* comprises populations in San Luis Obispo County (mainly in and around Montaña del Oro State Park), Santa Barbara County, the Northern Channel Islands, and the vicinity of San Vicente, Baja California. Bishop pines from the Monterey area and Marin County are intermediate to the two varieties.

The trees on Baja California's Cedros and Guadalupe islands are no longer considered bishop pine, nor is there any such species as *Pinus remorata.* These conclusions are based on a wide range of genetic and other evidence and may help to sort out the confusion that has sur-rounded bishop pine taxonomy.

IDENTIFYING BISHOP PINE

At a distance: It ranges from a bushy or stocky wind-swept tree to a slender, straight-trunked one. Foliage is green in the south, blue-green from Sea Ranch to Trinidad.

Standing beneath it: Mature trees have gray-brown to almost black bark with scaly ridges separated by fissures, which in young trees may show some orange coloration. The crown retains large numbers of cones arranged in circles on the branches.

In the hand: Although extremely variable, the cones are often egg-shaped and measure up to four inches long with strongly prickled scales. Depending on their age, the cones are reddish brown to weathered gray and usually tightly closed. The needles are up to six inches long and in bundles of two.

HABITAT

It grows in mild, foggy coastal areas on terrain that includes seaside bluffs and headlands, infer-tile granitic ridges, and old marine terraces with highly acidic soils.

DISTRIBUTION

This pine forms scattered groves and forests of limited extent from Luffenholz Creek near Trinidad Head in Humboldt County south to the Purisima Hills and westernmost Santa Ynez Mountains in Santa Barbara County. It is also found on Santa Cruz and Santa Rosa islands. A southern outlier exists near San Vicente, Baja California, more than 250 miles from the closest population.

Bishop pines at Inverness are intermediate to the species' two varieties. [Marin Co.] RICHARD BLAIR

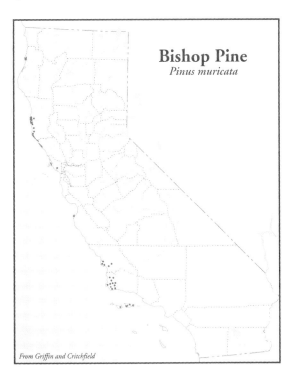

Bishop Pine
Pinus muricata

From Griffin and Critchfield

91

Monterey Pine • *Pinus radiata*

MONTEREY PINE

(ALSO CALLED RADIATA PINE)

One day in 1955, Ib Thulin, a transplanted Danish forester employed by the New Zealand Forest Research Institute, came out of a 24-year-old test plantation of Monterey pines in a state of high excitement. Moments earlier he had found a Gulliver among dwarfs, a tree later known as "Super 80055" that far exceeded in size all of its relatively spindly neighbors. Where most of them were slender poles less than six inches in diameter and 60 feet tall, 80055 had a massive trunk more than two feet thick and a terminal shoot that projected 135 feet into the filtered New Zealand sunlight. Because of its youth, it eclipsed even a locally famous Monterey pine growing near Nelson on the South Island, a tree which measured three feet thick and 190 feet tall at 65 years. Clearly, these were trees that could make New Zealand a powerhouse of timber production. Within a few years New Zealand's ongoing pine breeding program had focused on 80055, and by the 1990s its genes had been incorporated into nearly every Monterey pine seed orchard in New Zealand and Australia.

By now, the story of Monterey pine's domestication is well known. A coastal tree usually contorted where exposed to steady onshore winds, or lanky, limby, and crooked when sheltered behind higher ground, Monterey pine has become the world's most planted conifer species. Native groves of Monterey pine are restricted to three small locales on the California coast and two offshore islands, totaling no more than 11,000 acres of forest. But worldwide, Monterey pine plantations now surpass 10 million acres, and they continue to expand every year. Chile's paper industry depends on this California import. Over two million Australian

The southernmost mainland Monterey pines are near Cambria. [San Luis Obispo Co.] GALEN RATHBUN

acres are devoted to it. New Zealand boasts three million acres of Monterey pine, which contributed one billion dollars to that country's economy in 1992. South Africa, Kenya, Spain, Argentina, and Uruguay all manage significant acreages of Monterey pine, which is usually known in the timber industry as "radiata pine."

Monterey pine's rapid growth and excellent pulping and lumber qualities assure its future throughout the world's subtropics, where soft-wood requirements cannot be filled by native species. In many wet, tropical areas Monterey pine is notable for its ability to grow year-round. If temperatures remain mild, and there are no seasonal droughts, this pine can depart from the strict seasonality of growth in a Mediterranean climate and form wood that lacks annual rings while putting up totally branchless leaders 20 feet tall.

Despite its restricted natural range, Monterey pine has a wealth of genetic variability in traits related to growth rate and other economically important characters; such genetic diversity is the first requirement for a selective breeding program. It is easily control-pollinated and readily cloned by growing plantlets from tissue cultures, making it possible to propagate, almost infinitely, highly desirable genotypes. These attributes of Monterey pine have allowed its domestication—breeding and propagation of genotypes that provide for human needs—to proceed briskly. Molecular methods of genetic engineering promise further long strides in the near future.

Monterey pine was widely distributed along the California coast during Pleistocene times, but since then its native range has shrunk into just a few fragments. These are in the Año Nuevo-Swanton area, the larger Monterey-Carmel area 30 miles to the south, and the Pico Creek-Cambria groves 65 miles farther south. All of these localities have cool, foggy climates. Near Swanton, Monterey pine hybridizes sparingly with scattered knobcone pines, producing trees that grow almost as rapidly as the Monterey parent and that are nearly as frost-hardy as the knobcone parent.

Monterey pine's insular populations are both in Mexico. One is found on rugged Cedros Island, a few miles north of Punta Eugenia, Baja California Sur; the other is located on Guadalupe Island, a volcanic island some 200 miles northwest of Cedros. The Guadalupe Island population, heavily browsed by feral goats, declined from 383 trees in 1964 to just 150 in 1992 and is clearly on the way to extinction. Fortunately, plantings have been made in Australia to preserve some of the island's germ plasm. Controversy exists over the identity of the island pines. The totality of the evidence, however, best supports the conclusion that the two-needled Guadalupe trees consti-tute variety *binata,* and those on Cedros Island variety *cedrosensis.*

The history of some of our domesticated agricultural plants has highlighted how important

Monterey pine forests are never far from the coast. *[Point Lobos S.R.]* MARK J. DOLYAK

humidity. Needles are bright, grassy green, slender, to six inches long, and in fascicles of three (except for var. *binata* on Guadalupe Island, which is two needled).

HABITAT
Monterey pine is native to cool, humid, foggy coastal and insular areas. Rain falls mostly in the winter, and is often 15 to 35 inches annually; this may be augmented by summer fogs, which condense on the needles and can drip $1/2$ inch per week. Soils are usually sandy loams with ample organic litter. Elevation ranges from sea level to 1,000 feet in the Santa Lucia Range, and to 2,100 and 3,600 feet on Cedros and Guadalupe islands respectively. Monterey pine grows among Douglas-fir, redwood, Monterey and Gowen cypresses, and knobcone and bishop pines; the most common tree in the Monterey pine forest understory is coast live oak.

it is to preserve their wild, ancestral forms in the species' natural distribution area because this is where the genetic variability of the species has been generated. These areas are also where researchers look when adapted genotypes suddenly are needed to counter new threats, such as pine pitch canker. In recent years the canker has become established in all three of California's native mainland stands, and it appears likely to become a major killer of wild and planted trees in the twenty-first century.

DISTRIBUTION
It occurs in the Año Nuevo-Swanton area (San Mateo and Santa Cruz counties), on the Monterey peninsula and south around Carmel (Monterey County), and around Pico Creek, Cambria, and Santa Rosa Creek (San Luis Obispo County). It also grows on Baja California's Guadalupe and Cedros islands.

IDENTIFYING MONTEREY PINE
At a distance: When grown in the open, it forms a densely-needled, domelike crown set on a thick, branchy trunk clothed in fissured gray-brown bark. In dense stands its crown is short and sits atop a slender, cylindrical bole.
Standing beneath it: The branches are laden with masses of cones, open and closed, young and old, and retained in many whorls or circles. Cone stalks are "swallowed" by growth of the branches.
In the hand: The cones are massive, to six inches long and five inches wide, with basal scales opposite the branch swollen into rounded beaks. The glossy scales open and close frequently and erratically with changes in

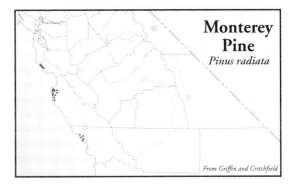

Monterey Pine
Pinus radiata

From Griffin and Critchfield

Knobcone Pine • *Pinus attenuata*

KNOBCONE PINE

This pine is named after its knobby cones, which grow in clusters of three to five on almost every year's growth of the trunks and major branches. These heavily woody cones remain tightly sealed, their varnishlike glaze of dried resin slowly breaking down over the years as they weather from nut brown to a dull gray. The steadfastness with which these cones are retained on the trees is legendary. Trunk cones are frequently engulfed in the expanding mass of wood of a fast-growing tree. Stories are told of knobcone pine lumber containing sections of perfectly intact cones full of viable seeds—cones that were swallowed up as they defiantly withstood the silent onslaught of new annual rings. The significance of this tenacity is that when a tree finally burns, it still holds in its crown nearly all of the cones and seeds it has ever produced. The heat of fire, or at least the first 200°F of it, melts the resin that bonds the cone scales to each other, letting them begin their gradual opening with audible crackling and popping sounds. There are some places where cones can open without fire-heat, but on the whole, knob-cone pine is one of our most fire-dependent conifers.

Knobcone pine was never held in high esteem by admirers of the California conifers. Willis Linn Jepson referred to it as a scrub pine and observed that it grows "as thickly as corn stalks" on sites that are the "most hopelessly inhospitable in the California mountains." According to John Muir, mountaineers called it "that queer little pine tree covered all over with burs." Even Donald Culross Peattie, who rarely saw a tree he didn't admire, was compelled to mention knobcone pine's thin, faded-looking foliage, though he did left-handedly compliment it as "the best of all possible trees where one finds it."

When considering the ecology of knobcone pine, one gets the eerie feeling that this slender, thin-crowned, thicket-former is a strangely take-charge kind of tree, a near-autonomous participant in its own fate. Take, for example, the stands of "knobbies," as they are sometimes called, on the upper slopes of Pleasants Peak in the Santa Ana Mountains. Speaking anthropomorphically, these trees appear to choose what is for them the right neighborhood. In the Santa Anas, knobcone pine is the dominant plant on serpentine outcrops. Few shrubs grow on these outcrops, and those that try become dwarfish and chlorotic. On adjacent non-serpentine soils, there is a dense chaparral mantle with virtually no pines at all. The major plants here are scrub oak and chamise. The pines are apparently

Knobcone pine grows rapidly on good sites, reaching 60 to 80 feet. [Shasta-Trinity N.F.] DAVID LANNER

unable to compete with the dense shrub cover on the nonserpentine soils, so they are not found there. But since they, and not the chaparral shrubs, can tolerate the more acid, nitrogen-poor, phosphate-deficient serpentine soils, knobcone has these "hopelessly inhospitable" sites to itself. Growth conditions there are not ideal for knobcone pines, but they are tolerable, and in nature tolerable is often good enough.

When knobcone stands burn up, many unconsumed trunks remain as standing snags. After five or six years, strong winds topple these snags. When a snag falls, the undecayed bases of its major roots are pulled out of the ground, scattering on the surface the thin serpentinite soil they were rooted in and exposing bedrock. This process retards normal soil genesis, which helps keep out plants that might compete with knobcone pine. Soil erosion, which is accelerated on burned-over knobcone pine sites, has a similar effect.

Once established, knobcone pines must survive California's long dry season. Where it grows in coastal mountains, knobcone benefits from the deep marine layer that is common in spring and early summer. Riding the onshore winds, fog stacks up against the slopes and enshrouds the pines. Condensate drips from the pine needles into the water-retentive soils beneath each tree. In the Santa Ana Mountains, for example, fog-drip adds up to four inches of precipitation per month in May and June, when there would normally be almost no rain at all.

As a knobcone stand develops, open-grown trees retain long branches low on the trunk, sometimes resting them on the ground. Trees in dense thickets crowd each other, interlocking their limbs. When fire spreads into knobcone stands, the resinous foliage and stems explode in flames. In its aftermath, little is left except charred, cone-studded, woody skeletons. After such a burn, the cones open. Most of the seeds are probably shed onto the burnt ground within days or weeks. Others may be retained longer,

*Knobcone pine amid chaparral is highly suscepti-
ble to wildfire. [Los Padres N.F.]* JOHN EVARTS

as the cone responds to changes in relative
humidity by alternately closing and opening its
scales. The dispersal of the seeds sets the stage
for the establishment of a new stand.

IDENTIFYING KNOBCONE PINE

At a distance: It often forms dense thickets.
Individual trees are slender, with pale green
foliage, and the major limbs and trunks bristle
with clusters of cones at regular intervals.
Standing beneath it: The numerous cones are
tightly closed and grow in clusters of three to
five. Those nearer the ends of the shoots are
green, yellow, or brown. Those further down
the shoot—the older ones—are brownish gray
to weathered gray.
In the hand: Needles are usually four to five
inches long, stiff, slender, and in fascicles of
three. Cones are three to six inches long and
half as wide, hard, heavy, tightly closed, and difficult to remove from the tree; they point down
the shoot, with protuberant scale tips ("knobs")
on the side away from the shoot.

HABITAT

Knobcone pine is usually found on dry, rocky
slopes in thin serpentine or granitic soil, from

near sea level in Santa Cruz County
to almost 6,000 feet on Mount
Shasta. Its long list of associates
includes Sargent, McNab, and Santa
Cruz cypresses; Monterey, sugar,
Jeffrey, ponderosa, lodgepole, and
western white pines; and white fir,
incense-cedar, and Douglas-fir.

DISTRIBUTION

This is the most widespread of the
three California closed-cone pines.
It grows mostly in the Coast Ranges
from the Santa Lucias north
through the Klamath Ranges and
into southwest Oregon. It also spreads across
the Cascades and on to the Modoc Plateau, and
it sporadically occurs on the Sierra Nevada
westside from Tehama County south to
Yosemite. Outliers are in the San Bernardino
and Santa Ana mountains and near Ensenada,
Baja California.

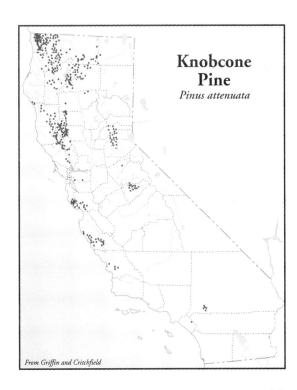

Knobcone
Pine
Pinus attenuata

From Griffin and Critchfield

FIRS

Most of the world's 40 species of firs live in forests that are cool and humid due to these forests' high elevation, ample precipitation, or close proximity to the sea. But a few firs break that stereotype by surviving in droughty habitats. Both situations occur in California, which is exceptionally rich in firs. It contains within its borders all of the seven western species, including the endemic Santa Lucia fir, perhaps the most unusual member of its genus.

Firs usually have short, flat, blunt, spreading needles on their lower limbs, and thicker, sharply-pointed, upright ones higher in the crown. The sharp-pointed needles have been associated by many botanists and dendrologists with cone-bearing, but they occur also on trees that have not yet borne cones. When they fall off, the needles leave flat, circular scars on the twig. The cylindrical trunks of firs are smooth, gray, and dotted with resin blisters until age roughens the bark. The elliptical blisters can be made to squirt a stream of sticky, aromatic resin when squeezed.

Fir cones are barrel-shaped, stand upright high in the treetops, and glisten with exuded resin droplets as they mature. After drying in the warm sun of early autumn they begin to disintegrate scale by scale, until the seeds have all flown off into the wind and only the spiky central axes remain. Among North American conifers, only the firs—or "true firs" as they are often called to distinguish them from the Douglas-firs—exhibit this self-destructive mode of behavior. The vigor with which the scales become distorted, before breaking loose, has been described by one researcher as "violent."

Opposite: Shasta red fir on the slopes of Mt. Shasta. [Shasta-Trinity N.F.] JEFF GNASS

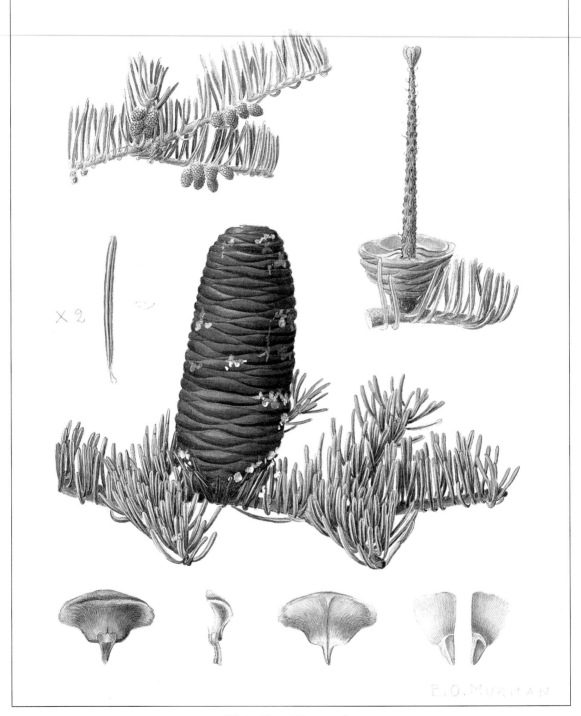

White Fir • *Abies concolor*

WHITE FIR

Abies concolor, the white fir of the mountain West, extends from the Colorado Rockies to northern Sonora in Mexico and from the Coast Ranges of Oregon to the Sierra San Pedro Mártir in Baja California. The climatic diversity within its vast distribution is enormous, especially given white fir's elevational range of 2,000 to 11,000 feet. An organism this widespread is subjected to a variety of natural selective factors across its range, and it responds differently to the components of its environment from one place to another. Thus it can become differentiated into geographic strains, or races. If these races are sufficiently pronounced, they will probably be singled out by taxonomists as varieties or subspecies and will be assigned names to distinguish them from each other. This has indeed been the case with white fir, and two geographically distinct races have been given varietal status.

The name *Abies concolor* was first applied to members of what is now regarded as the Rocky Mountain variety of white fir, and that variety is called *Abies concolor* var. *concolor,* referred to as the "typical" variety. The other variety, whose perceived distinctness triggered this splitting asunder of a species, is the California white fir, *Abies concolor* var. *lowiana.* Some plant scientists think the two are different enough to warrant being considered separate species, *Abies concolor* and *Abies lowiana.* Others think the differences are too slight even to differentiate varieties, and they lump all these firs together simply as *Abies concolor.* This book uses the two-varieties solution.

Rocky Mountain white fir, which in California appears to be restricted to several mountain ranges in the eastern Mojave Desert, has a

White fir regenerates profusely in the westside Sierran mixed-conifer forest. [Kings Canyon N.P.]
FRED HIRSCHMANN

relatively broad crown of steely blue needles. In contrast, the crown of California white fir is more narrowly cylindrical, sometimes almost spirelike, and has darker, greener foliage (though still pale and bluish compared to other conifers it grows with). Another difference is that California white fir is much larger than the Rocky Mountain variety. Apparently the tallest documented California white fir is a 240-footer measured several decades ago by this writer in Plumas National Forest. The largest recorded diameter, 74 inches, came from a tree in Oregon. The bark on such massive old trees has long passed the thin, smooth, whitish gray, resin-blistered stage of youth and has become thick, dark, and deeply furrowed with corky ridges. The trunks are often severely malformed or broken off where dwarf-mistletoe infections have created weak spots that can give way when the wind blows hard.

At lower-elevation sites on the Sierra Nevada westside, California white fir is usually found in a mixed-conifer forest with sugar and ponderosa pines, incense-cedar, and Douglas-fir.

It is also prominent in giant sequoia groves, where even very large white firs are dwarfed by their red-barked neighbors. White fir has enjoyed a recent population boom in these coniferous forests. Thin-barked young firs that seeded into the understory of the predominantly ponderosa pine forests seldom survived the relatively frequent ground fires, but the control of wildfire that is a hallmark of twentieth-century forest management has allowed the shade-tolerant firs to mature there in greater numbers than ever before. Thus as the pines grow old, and begin to succumb to root diseases and bark beetles in ever-increasing numbers, it is firs that grow up to replace them. The firs' resinous foliage becomes an incendiary device when wildfires burn, and the trees act as "fire ladders," conducting flames into the crowns of the pines. The pines are not tolerant of shade and do not become established in large numbers beneath the canopy of the white firs—so one unexpected effect of fire suppression is to exchange pines for firs.

At higher elevations in the Sierra Nevada, white and red firs coexist in extensive, shady forests. These species have not been found to hybridize. Elsewhere, white fir associates with nearly all of California's mountain conifers, including even singleleaf pinyon. (For details of its genetically significant relationship with grand fir, see page 115.)

Throughout its range, white fir is browsed by mule deer, despite the strong, citruslike, aromatic essential oils of its foliage. Chickarees, or Douglas squirrels, cut its barrel-shaped cones for storage on or in their middens. The great hollowed-out trunks of old trees, dead or alive, are favorite sites for mammals ranging from weasels to porcupines to black bears.

IDENTIFYING WHITE FIR
At a distance: Young trees are neatly pyramidal. The crowns of older California white fir become cylindrical. The foliage has a grayish frosted appearance when seen from below. Cones are in

White fir replaces pine when the fire cycle is interrupted. [Inyo N.F.] STEPHEN INGRAM

the treetops only, barrel-shaped, upright, green in summer and brown when mature.

Standing beneath it: Bark changes with age from light gray, smooth, thin, and blistered to dark gray or brown, roughly furrowed, and thick.

In the hand: Needles are one to three inches long, broad and flat, soft to the touch, and aromatic when crushed. Those of California white fir tend to be longer than those of the Rocky Mountain variety, with rounded to notched rather than pointed tips and a definite twist at the base. New branchlets are olive green but become light brown. Bark of older trees shows yellowish brown, not reddish brown, when cut (see pages 116 to 117 of "Grand Fir").

HABITAT

White fir grows on a great variety of slightly to strongly acid soils as low as 3,000 feet in the North Coast Ranges and to over 10,000 feet in the San Bernardino Mountains and the Sierra San Pedro Mártir of Baja California. Within its distribution, annual precipitation ranges from 20 to 75 inches.

DISTRIBUTION

California white fir (var. *lowiana*) is widely distributed in the Sierra Nevada, Cascades, Warner Mountains, Klamath Ranges, and in the North Coast Ranges as far south as Colusa County. In southern California it grows in the Tehachapis and at scattered locales throughout the Transverse and Peninsular ranges, reaching its southern terminus in the Sierra San Pedro Mártir, Baja California. Rocky Mountain white fir (var. *concolor*) is sparingly distributed in the Clark, Kingston, and New York mountains of the eastern Mojave Desert.

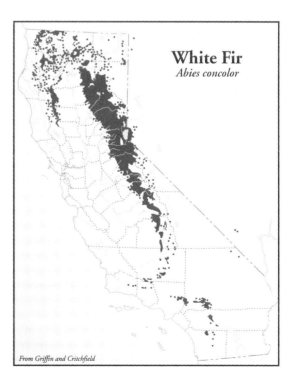

White Fir
Abies concolor

From Griffin and Critchfield

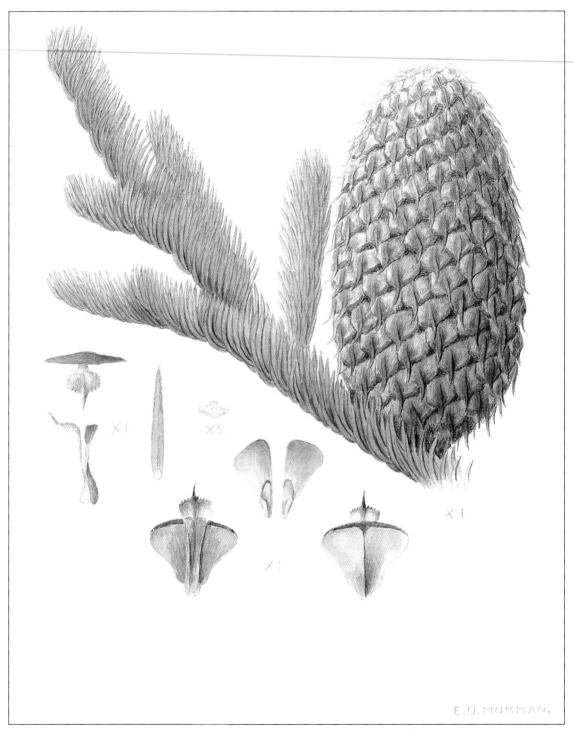

Noble Fir • *Abies procera*

NOBLE FIR

It is unclear whether typical noble fir really extends southwards into California, or if the noble firlike trees of the Siskiyou Mountains are all hybrids of noble fir and Shasta red fir. Noble fir is essentially a giant forest tree of middle elevations in the Cascade Range. There it may attain a height of 260 feet, making it the tallest of all firs. It is relatively long-lived for a fir, occasionally reaching 600 years of age before succumbing to fire, root rots, or gravity.

The northern end of red fir's range consists of trees that are intermediate in appearance between the typical red fir to the south and noble fir further north in Oregon. This population has long been known as *Abies magnifica* var. *shastensis,* the Shasta red fir. Its location in what may well have been an overlap zone of red and noble firs, and the intermediacy of the phenotypes (the observable characteristics) of the trees there, strongly suggests that Shasta red fir is the product of hybridization rather than a subspecies of red fir. Some observers believe that the pure noble fir end of the genetic spectrum is not present in California at all. Others think it is. (See pages 112 to 113 for a discussion of how to differentiate between red and noble firs, species photo, and distribution map.)

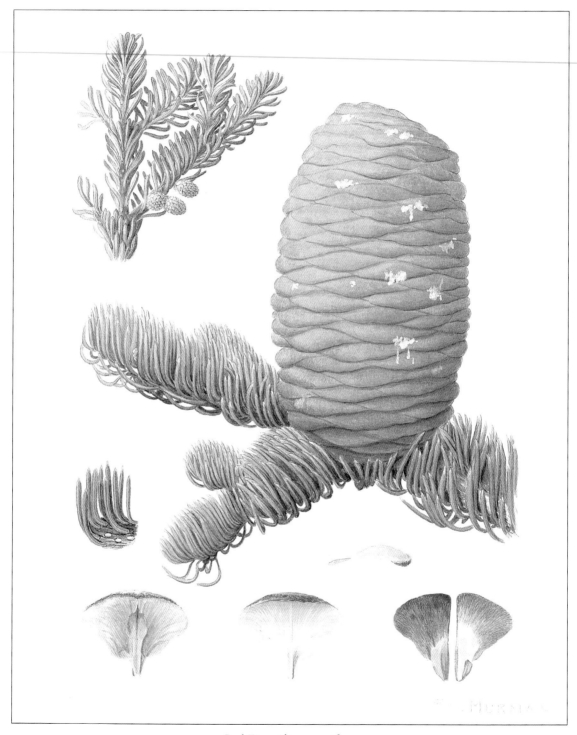

Red Fir • *Abies magnifica*

Abies magnifica

RED FIR

(ALSO CALLED SILVERTIP)

The fir woods are delightful sauntering-grounds at any time of year, but most so in autumn. Then the noble trees are hushed in the hazy light, and drip with balsam; the cones are ripe, and the seeds, with their ample purple wings, mottle the air like flocks of butterflies. . . . No wonder the enthusiastic Douglas went wild with joy when he first discovered this species.

—John Muir
The Mountains of California

The "Magnificent Silver Fir," as John Muir called it, is one of the most impressive of western conifers, both for size and beauty. It can become a giant—rising to 230 feet and growing to 10 feet in diameter—and can survive half a millennium. There are still old-growth stands with 200-foot-high red fir, but the depletion of lower-elevation pine forests has increased the pressure to liquidate these shady forests.

In the Sierra Nevada, where much of the state's red fir grows, it is often found among upper-elevation white fir or with a suite of high-elevation conifers: Jeffrey, lodgepole, western white, and whitebark pines, and mountain hemlock. But red fir also forms dense, practically pure forests of its own in which undergrowth is largely restricted to the sunny openings around dead or fallen trees. Donald Culross Peattie dubbed the snowy belt in which red fir dominate a "snow forest," analogous to the rainforests of other regions.

The tallest red firs are often hit by lightning, and old-growth forests harbor many trees with damaged crowns and snag-tops.

It was the red fir whose "plushy branches...with ferns and flowers for a pillow" formed the mountaineers' bed favored by John Muir. [Inyo N.F.] CHRISTOPHER T. FRANK

Williamson's sapsuckers and hairy and white-headed woodpeckers forage for grubs in the snags, while owls, chickarees, and flying squirrels use them as nesting sites.

Mature red fir bear periodic large crops of purplish brown cones high in their crowns. The upright cones can reach nine inches in length and are the largest of the world's fir cones. They disintegrate on the tree, releasing their very large, winged seeds throughout fall and winter. Like the seeds of some other high-elevation firs, these can germinate atop the snowpack in the

Most fires in the red fir forest are caused by lightning. The absence of ground fuels at Red Fir Flat suggests fires in the recent past. [Shasta-Trinity N.F.] JOHN EVARTS

warm spring air, but it is unlikely that such precocious seedlings ever survive long enough to become properly rooted.

In some parts of California, there are populations of red fir whose cones have pointed papery bracts that protrude from between the cone scales. These firs are often regarded as a genetically distinct variety, *shastensis,* or Shasta red fir. They are principally found in the vicinity of Kings Canyon and Sequoia national parks and from Lassen Peak north to Crater Lake, Oregon, including the area around Mount Shasta. In northwestern California, the bracted cones can be reasonably attributed to hybridization with nearby populations of noble fir, which has decidedly bracted cones. However, no such hybridization is occurring in the Sierra Nevada stands of Shasta red fir.

IDENTIFYING RED FIR

At a distance: Young trees have narrow, symmetrical crowns of blue-green foliage carried on horizontal limbs. They become more ragged with age.
Standing beneath it: Bark of young trees is thin, smooth, and gray, with elliptical resin blisters. In old trees it is thick, deeply furrowed, and reddish brown to reddish purple.
In the hand: The needles are short, thick, stiff, and blunt, and square enough in cross-section to be rolled between the fingers. In the first year they are silvery, thus the name "silvertip" fir. They leave flat, round scars on the branchlet when they fall. The cones are purplish brown and measure up to nine inches long. Shasta red fir has cones with exposed bracts, but these cover less of the cone's surface than those of noble fir.

Snow depth in the red fir belt exceeds 30 feet in a wet winter. [Inyo N.F.] CHRISTOPHER T. FRANK

Red fir is afflicted with rots and mistletoe and seldom exceeds 300 years. [Trinity Alps] ROBERT TURNER

HABITAT

Red fir grows on deep soils and glacial moraines; the soils are often recently weathered from bedrock and have little organic content. The tree ranges in elevation from about 4,600 to 9,000 feet, depending on its location, and occurs on slopes and flats where snowfall may exceed 30 feet in a wet winter. The heavy Sierran snow can persist into July, guaranteeing a brief growing season during which virtually no rain will fall.

DISTRIBUTION

Red fir occurs nearly the full length of the Sierra-Cascade system in California, from Sunday Peak in the Greenhorn Mountains of Kern County north to the Cascade peaks east of Yreka. It is widespread in the Klamath Ranges, and a peculiar scattering of relatively low-elevation stands extends down the North Coast Ranges to Lake County.

DIFFERENTIATING RED AND NOBLE FIRS

Red fir may overlap and hybridize with noble fir in northwestern California. Here are a few characteristics to help the field observer discern the differences between the two.

Needles of lower (shaded) limbs: Typical red fir needles are square in cross-section and easily rolled in the fingers. They lie flat, spreading laterally from the branchlet. Their upper surface has no groove down the center. Noble fir needles are flattened and do not roll. They are upturned as they leave the branchlet. They have a deep groove running down the upper surface.

Seed cones: Typical California red fir cones are up to nine inches long and purplish brown when mature. No papery bracts protrude from between their scales. Noble fir cones reach about seven inches in length and are light brown when they mature. They have prominent papery bracts that protrude from between the cone scales, bend back, and conceal 90% or more of the cone surface. Trees that have been called Shasta red fir usually have cones with protruding bracts, but they protrude less than do those of noble fir and do not conceal as much of the cone's surface. Reliable field studies and genetic analyses of this apparent long-standing hybrid zone are needed to clarify a confusing situation.

Noble fir is the tallest of the world's firs, reaching 260 feet in height in the Cascade Range. [Snoqualmie N.F., WA] RON LANNER

The Shasta firs of the southern Sierra Nevada are of puzzling origin. [Kings Canyon N.P.] JOHN SAWYER

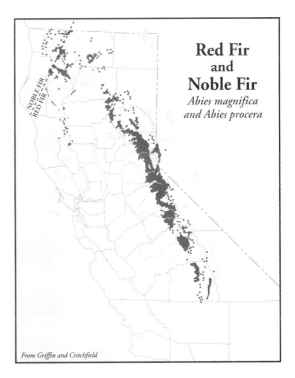

Red Fir and Noble Fir
Abies magnifica and Abies procera

NOBLE FIR
RED FIR

From Griffin and Critchfield

Grand Fir • *Abies grandis*

Abies grandis

GRAND FIR

I t is easy to overlook even a large fir in California's north coast forests, dominated as they are by gargantuan redwoods, enormous Douglas-firs, and massive Sitka spruces. But grand fir—as its name implies—deserves at least a second look. In its limited California range scattered individuals and groups of this so called "lowland fir" grow with amazing speed and quickly project their crowns 200 feet into the over-story. The tops of free-growing grand firs support clusters of upright seed cones that are bright green throughout their summer of growth, turning slightly brownish or purplish with maturity.

Grand fir that are farthest from the shore and growing at the higher elevations find themselves in close proximity to California white fir. Starting with a very similar DNA heritage, and shedding pollen to their receptive young seed cones at the same dates, these closely related species interbreed, creating between their pure populations a belt of intermediates. The intermediates are hybrids. Fir hybrids can breed between themselves and breed back into their parent species as well. This creates confusing populations known as "hybrid swarms," which are stands of trees that show past influence of hybridization. Scientists have found hybrid swarms of firs in Del Norte and western Siskiyou counties and northeastwards across Oregon into west-central Idaho.

IDENTIFYING GRAND FIR
At a distance: Young trees are narrowly pyramidal with deep green foliage. Old trees have rounded crowns.
Standing beneath it: The bark of young trees is thin, smooth, blistered,

Grand fir hybridizes with California white fir in a belt extending from northwest California, across Oregon, and into central Idaho. [Nezperce N.F., ID] JEFF GNASS

and grayish brown with chalky patches. The bark of mature trees is reddish brown, or even purple, with long, flat ridges or plates bounded by narrow furrows. Cones are like miniature casks, three to four inches long and one to two inches wide.

In the hand: Needles are glossy green and deeply grooved on the upper surface, with two silver-white stripes (of wax-filled stomates) on the lower surface. The longer needles are almost as long as those of white fir, but are more consistently notched at the tip. Those borne on the

In coastal northwestern California grand fir is usually found below 2,000 feet, scattered among redwoods, Douglas-firs, and other conifers. [Humboldt Co.] J. R. HALLER

upper side of the shoot are much shorter than the others and lie flat, pointing forward. If the bark of a mature grand fir is cut into with a knife, the tissue inside will appear reddish, never yellowish as in white fir. Trees found above approximately 2,000 feet in northwestern California with characteristics that are intermediate between California white fir and grand fir should be considered to be of hybrid origin.

HABITAT

Grand fir grows on rich, moist soils derived from such varied parent rocks as lava, gneiss, sandstone, and granite. In California it grows to about 2,000 feet, where most of the precipitation is from winter rains. Grand fir often grows in river valleys and along streams, but it is also found on exposed headlands, such as those along the coast of Mendocino County.

DISTRIBUTION

In California, grand fir occupies a coastal strip from the Oregon border south to about Humboldt Redwoods State Park in Humboldt County, then from about Westport south down the coast to Fort Ross, with an outlier across the Russian River on Willow Creek. Elsewhere, it ranges widely in Oregon, Washington, Idaho, and British Columbia.

Grand Fir
Abies grandis

From Griffin and Critchfield

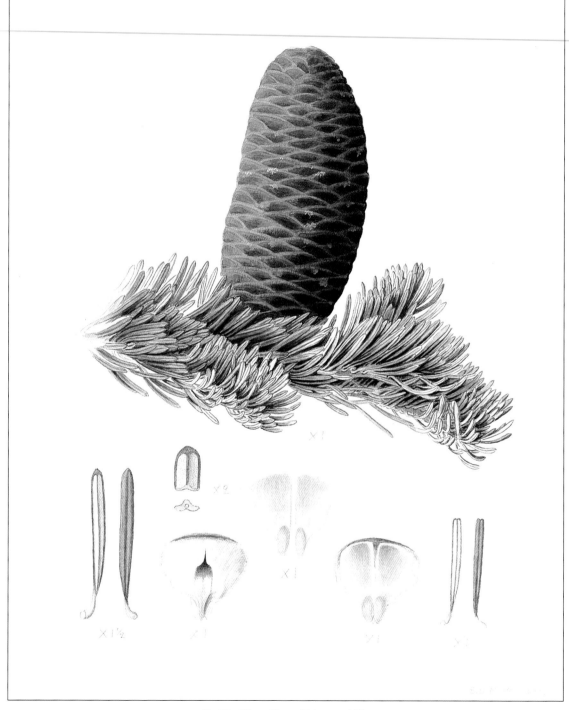

Pacific Silver Fir • *Abies amabilis*

PACIFIC SILVER FIR

Pacific silver fir is one of the state's rarest conifers, and to see this beauty most Californians will have to travel north. One of those northern stragglers trapped in that outdoor museum of the Klamath Ranges, it was not correctly identified until 1932, having been confused for several years after its initial discovery with subalpine fir. Pacific silver fir is a Pacific northwest species, distributed from sea level in southeast Alaska to continually higher elevations proceeding southward, culminating at 7,000 feet within its California range. Outside California it is a large, forest tree and a high-yielding lumber producer. It is often found with western hemlock, Douglas-fir, Alaska-cedar, Sitka spruce, and several other conifers.

Pacific silver fir is the most shade-tolerant of western firs. Conspicuously flat-topped saplings may persist in the gloomy understory for a hundred years or more, growing perhaps an inch or two a year in height as their limbs continue to spread horizontally. When finally exposed to more sun, such as when a fallen tree opens up a hole in the canopy, the sapling can markedly accelerate its growth.

Like the other firs, this one has thin bark and shallow roots, making it vulnerable to fires and strong winds. On its more humid sites, the bark may be totally obscured by heavy encrustations of mosses and club mosses.

There is little question of the appropriateness of "silver" in this tree's common name. The color comes from the twin silvery white bands of stomatal wax flanking the midrib on the needle's underside.

IDENTIFYING PACIFIC SILVER FIR
At a distance: Pacific silver fir is a tall, straight tree with a spirelike tip that becomes rounded on old trees.

Standing beneath it: Foliage layers are brilliantly whitish or silvery when viewed from below. The smooth, gray, blistered bark of young trees has whitish blotches; old trees' bark is covered with reddish scales. Mature cones are up to six inches long and deep purple.

In the hand: Among northwestern firs, only Pacific silver fir has needles that are silvery below, shiny, dark green above, with a usually-notched apex, and a deep groove on the upper surface.

HABITAT
This is a tree of cool, wet conditions—including coastal fog belts—where there is a long growing season. It tends to grow with mountain hemlock or in pure stands.

DISTRIBUTION
In California it is restricted to isolated groves near Hancock Lake in the Salmon Mountains and at several locations in the Siskiyou

A new stand of Pacific silver fir develops at the foot of a slope dominated by old Douglas-fir and noble fir. [Mt. Hood N.F., OR] STEVE TERRILL

Pacific silver fir saplings grow slowly in the shade of the understory for many decades until they can exploit an opening to grow into. [Columbia River Gorge, OR] GARY BRAASCH

Resin blisters adorn young silver fir bark.
[Columbia River Gorge, OR] GARY BRAASCH

Mountains between 5,000 and 7,000 feet (between Copper Butte and Joe Creek, and in the Slaughter House Flat-White Mountain-Black Mountain area). All these locations are in Siskiyou County and the Klamath National Forest. Elsewhere it ranges from coastal southern Oregon to southeast Alaska.

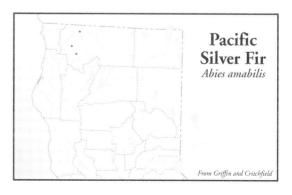

Pacific Silver Fir
Abies amabilis

From Griffin and Critchfield

121

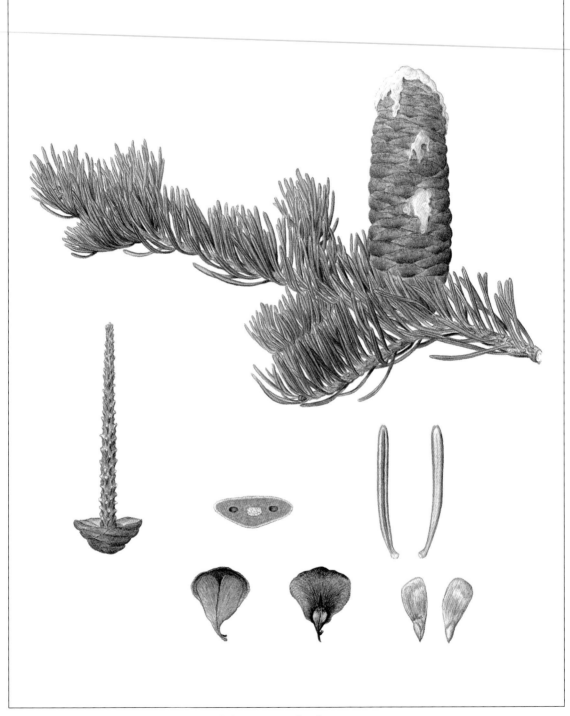

Subalpine Fir • *Abies lasiocarpa*

ARTWORK: SUSAN BAZELL

SUBALPINE FIR

(ALSO CALLED ALPINE FIR, BALSAM)

An enduring myth of forest ecology is that as a tree species approaches the edge of its natural area of distribution, it invariably grows under ever more arduous conditions until, at the furthest fringe, it can barely survive and cannot reproduce. One of the many exceptions to this overgeneralization is the status of subalpine fir in its limited California range near Russian Peak in the Salmon Mountains of Siskiyou County. Here, about 50 miles beyond its nearest congeners in Oregon, this fir forms the southern tip of a western range that begins in the subarctic. Are these coniferous outliers living at the margin? Hardly. According to their 1968 discoverers, they are growing vigorously, reproducing well, and even invading wet meadows.

Subalpine firs in the open retain their lower branches, which grow long and rest their weight upon the ground. Branches root into the moist soil beneath them, and the tips of these rooted limbs, which are called "layers," turn upwards as though presuming to be trees. A "mother hen and chicks" scenario can result, with a ring of apparent saplings surrounding the parent tree. If decay severs rooted branches from their tree, they may survive to form a clone—a group of genetically identical plants derived vegetatively from a single parent.

IDENTIFYING SUBALPINE FIR

At a distance: With the possible exception of Santa Lucia fir, this is the most narrowly spire-shaped western conifer. It appears from afar as the point of a sharpened pencil. The newest foliage has a bluish tinge.

Standing beneath it: Bark of young trees is smooth, gray, and blistered.

Subalpine fir, seen here in Utah's Bear River Range, is widespread in the Rockies, Cascades, and coastal ranges north to Alaska. It barely enters California, in the north. [Wasatch-Cache N.F.] SCOTT T. SMITH

which it has been confused in its California range, see "Identifying Pacific silver fir, In the hand" on page 120. If further reassurance is needed, cut a needle across the middle with a razor blade and inspect the cut surface with a 10 X lens. If resin issues from two prominent openings (resin canals) set deeply in the needle tissue, it is subalpine fir. If the resin canals are inconspicuous and at the edges of the needle, it is Pacific silver fir.

HABITAT

It grows around and in wet meadows and along terraces above creeks between 5,800 and 6,400 feet. Its typical associates are Engelmann spruce, mountain hemlock, western white pine, and Shasta red fir.

DISTRIBUTION

In the Salmon Mountains subalpine fir is found in the Russian Peak area (Duck Lakes, Sugar Creek), in Shelly Meadows, and in the Virginia Lake area. In the Marble Mountains it is in the Sky High Lakes and Deep Lake areas.

Subalpine fir contributes to the rich conifer flora of the Klamath Ranges. [Klamath N.F.] TODD KEELER-WOLF

On older trunks, fissures form between shedding gray plates marked with the horizontal lines of the old resin blisters. The underside of the foliage is almost as dark as the upper side and never silvery.

In the hand: The needles of lower limbs are flat, to 1 1/2 inches long, blunt or notched at the tip, and sharply aromatic when crushed. Cones are never more than four inches long. To definitively separate this species from Pacific silver fir, with

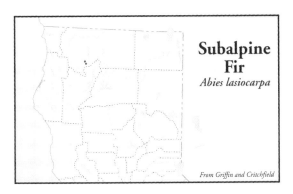

Subalpine Fir
Abies lasiocarpa

From Griffin and Critchfield

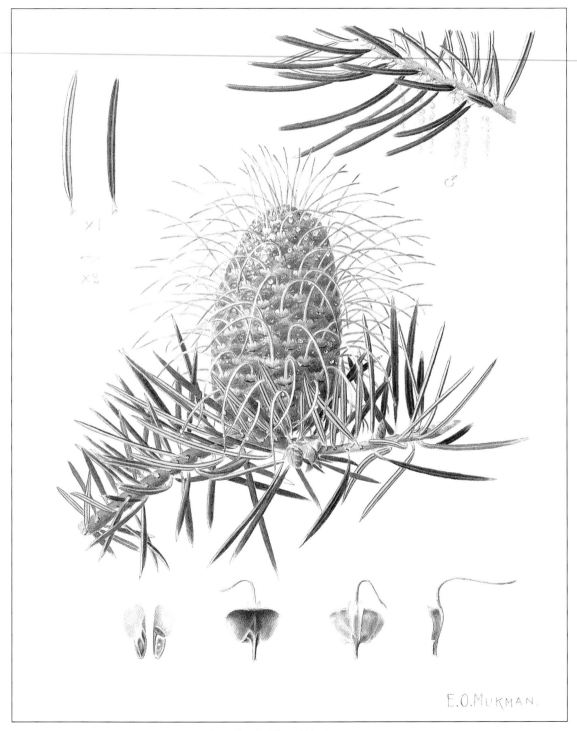

E.O.MURMAN.

Santa Lucia Fir • *Abies bracteata*

SANTA LUCIA FIR

(ALSO CALLED BRISTLECONE FIR)

Forming a mere remnant in the Santa Lucias they give to this
distinctive mountain range a singular interest and are the quest
of botanical travelers from all parts of the scientific world.
                                                    —Willis Linn Jepson
                                                    The Silva of California

Santa Lucia, or bristlecone, fir is generally considered the most non-conforming of its genus worldwide. Where other firs have short, blunt, almost spherical buds, those of Santa Lucia fir are up to an inch long, narrow, and sharply pointed. And while nearly all other firs have short, relatively thick, blunt needles soft to the touch, those of this fir can reach two inches in length; blade-thin and dagger-tipped, they easily pierce the skin of an impetuous foliage grasper. In fact, these remarkable needles seem to belong more on a California nutmeg tree than on any fir. But the most noteworthy feature of this tree is the cone, which gives it the name of bristlecone.

Like cones of other firs, those of Santa Lucia fir form only in the very top of the crown and perch upright on the bearing branch. They are almost cream colored as they approach maturity, then turn to a pale purplish brown. What sets them apart are their bristles. Many firs have papery bracts protruding from between the cone scales, but only in Santa Lucia fir are the midribs of those bracts so long and drawn out— to over two inches—that the cone looks like a vegetable hedgehog. The bristles, which are much narrower than the tree's needles, are at first glossy green on top, and have two white bands of stomates below, just

Santa Lucia fir is the rarest and most unusual of North American firs. [Ventana Wilderness] ROBERT TURNER

in moist canyon bottoms and on steep, rocky, north slopes and summits, always within 13 miles of the sea coast. It was first encountered by Thomas Coulter late in 1831, then by David Douglas a few months later. The names *Abies bracteata* (based on Coulter's specimens) and *Abies venusta* (based on Douglas's) were both published in Europe in 1836, but since Coulter's *bracteata* appeared a bit earlier, the rule of priority makes it the name we must use.

This fir grows among a rich collection of forest trees whose affinities are both southern Californian and Sierran: California black oak, coast, canyon, and interior live oaks, tanoak, Pacific madrone, incense-cedar, ponderosa, Coulter, and sugar pines. It usually grows singly or in small groups, not in continuous forest, and can reach 100 feet or more in height. The lower limbs of its narrow, spirelike crown often reach close to ground level. Some logging of this species occurred in the nineteenth century, but its rarity and the steep topography it inhabits have protected it. Few pests of Santa Lucia fir are known: a fungus on the needles, an insect that mines the seeds. Its greatest potential danger is probably a catastrophic fire that could render it near-extinct. Fossil evidence places *Abies bracteata* in western Nevada during the early Miocene, perhaps 20 to 25 million years ago. With luck, it will continue well into the future, but it must be considered vulnerable and should be constantly monitored.

like the needles; as the cone ripens they die and turn brown. Gobs of resin congeal at many of the bristle tips, presumably exuding from breaks in the epidermis. In the nineteenth century the Franciscans at nearby Mission San Antonio used Santa Lucia fir resin for ceremonial *incensios,* candles that contributed more aroma than light.

Santa Lucia fir is endemic, or "stranded," as John G. Lemmon put it a century ago. In the mountain range whose name it bears, it grows

The "bristlecone fir" forms small groves in the Santa Lucia Range and nowhere else. Associates include black and live oaks, Coulter, ponderosa, and sugar pines, and incense-cedar. [Ventana Wilderness] JIM GRIFFIN

IDENTIFYING SANTA LUCIA FIR

At a distance: A dense, deep green, conical crown with a long, tapering tip immediately signals Santa Lucia fir when seen in the Santa Lucia Range.

Standing beneath it: Bark changes with age from smooth, blistered, thin, and gray to scaly, thick, and reddish brown.

In the hand: The combination of two-inch-long, stiff, pointed needles, one-inch-long buds, and two-inch-long cone bracts cannot be found anywhere except on Santa Lucia fir.

HABITAT

It occupies steep, rocky slopes above the cool, windswept, foggy coast, usually between 2,000 and 5,000 feet, but with one stand at 600 feet. It grows in mixed-evergreen forests at sites where annual rainfall can exceed 100 inches.

DISTRIBUTION

It is restricted to the Santa Lucia Range on the central California coast in Monterey County and the very northern edge of San Luis Obispo County.

Santa Lucia Fir
Abies bracteata

From Griffin and Critchfield

129

SPRUCES

The name *Picea,* derived from *pix,* the Latin term for pitch, is highly appropriate for this genus that comprises more than 30 species. Spruces produce copious amounts of pitch in their bark, wood, needles, and cones. In this respect they are perhaps exceeded among the conifers only by pines.

Spruces bear their dangling seed cones high in the crown, and the light, winged seeds quickly disperse when the cones open in the fall. Spruce needles are prickle-tipped and attached to woody bases that remain on the branchlet when the needle falls. In combination these characters make spruce branchlets as pleasant to hold as a handful of barbed wire. As though to compensate for this gratuitous inhospitableness, spruces offer comfortable armchairlike seats between the trunk buttresses that lead to their shallow major roots.

Spruces inhabit moist forests from as far south as the Tropic of Cancer in Mexico to northern Siberia, and from sea level to Himalayan peaks nearing 15,000 feet in elevation. Most grow up in the shade and cast a dense shade of their own. Two of California's three spruces form the southern tips of ranges far more extensive further north, and one of them—Brewer spruce—is the rarest spruce in the United States.

Opposite: A Sitka spruce greets the incoming surf from its bluff-top perch. [Samuel H. Boardman S.P., OR] STEVE TERRILL

Sitka Spruce • *Picea sitchensis*

SITKA SPRUCE

No other California conifer so tolerates wet feet—or at least moist roots—as does Sitka spruce, the quintessential tree of the world's greatest temperate rainforest. Its namesake, Sitka, Alaska, has an annual precipitation of nearly 90 inches; and the species' old name, tideland spruce, reminds us that over its 1,800-mile range down the Pacific coast, Sitka spruce is restricted to a narrow, fog-bound belt, which dwindles to a mere 30 miles of width in California.

Precipitation in many Sitka spruce venues approaches 100 inches, and in some it greatly exceeds this figure, such as at Ketchikan, 151 inches, and Quinault, 128 inches. Two-thirds of a Sitka spruce's year is likely to be cloudy, and from Vancouver south spruces usually experience at least seven frost-free months in which to grow.

Sitka spruce is found overseas where similar mild and superhumid conditions occur. Among its new homes are the Scottish Highlands and the blanket bogs of Ireland. In both these lands, slopes are trenched prior to planting to drain off the bog blackwater; seedlings are then planted on the berms of soil along the trenches, where they grow with amazing rapidity. Nevertheless, these rigidly straight trees are not popular with the natives. The geometric blocks in which they are planted are alien to the nearly treeless landscape and the spruces' acidic needles, slowly decomposing upon the sphagnum and among the heath, contaminate the salmon streams downslope.

Sitka spruce is the largest of its genus worldwide, and it is one of only a distinguished handful of forest trees known to have attained 300 feet in height. Apparently, the tallest Sitka spruce is a 320-foot specimen

Sitka spruce often grows at seaside locations where redwood cannot tolerate the salt spray. [Prairie Creek Redwoods S.P.] JIM STIMSON

with narrow but evenly spaced annual rings in golden-hued wood that is stronger—pound for pound—than steel. Craftsmen have utilized this esteemed wood for aircraft and boat construction and to fabricate the soundboards of concert harps, grand pianos, and violins.

Sitka spruces that yield raw material for wood products are usually tall, straight residents of the forest, but this tree exhibits various other forms depending on its habitat. Those that hug the shore where the sea wind blows form dense, low hedges just above the beach. Scattered trees on cliffs, bluffs, and headlands extend long, spare branches that make good sites for bald eagle nests. Trees further inland, out of the wind and in the company of western hemlocks, grand firs, and redwoods, produce long, columnar trunks, swollen or buttressed at the base. Open-grown trees establish long, broad crowns of thick limbs that eventually die in the shade of those above; they are replaced by clusters of thin branches arising from the bases of the original ones. Branches arc gracefully upwards, issuing masses of dangling branchlets. Fallen Sitka spruces become nurse logs for germinating spruce and hemlock seeds, but as bark sloughs off over the

in British Columbia, which is probably larger than the giants that astonished Lewis and Clark upon their arrival at the Pacific coast. Trees with trunks that are 14 to 16 feet in diameter still exist, despite the headlong rush during most of the twentieth century to reduce magnificent stands of Sitka spruce to lumber, plywood, and paper pulp. Old-growth forests produce trees

years, it takes many of the seedlings with it, so their long-term survival is a rare event.

IDENTIFYING SITKA SPRUCE

At a distance: Sitka spruce is a tall, straight tree with a narrowly conical crown of upswept limbs. The trunk, columnar above, is buttressed or swollen at the base.

Standing beneath it: The bark of mature trees is thin, and flakes off large, purplish gray scales.

In the hand: Needles measure up to one inch long and are stiff, sharply pointed, and flat; as new growth they are green, but turn darker, even bluish, with age. Cones are pale yellow to reddish brown and measure to four inches long; the cone scales are thin, papery, and crinkled with a toothed margin.

HABITAT

It is found in wet, mild, coastal localities from beaches and sea cliffs to bogs around river mouths. Western hemlock, grand fir, Douglas-fir, shore pine, and redwood are its common associates in California.

DISTRIBUTION

It is found in California along the coast of Del Norte and Humboldt counties as far south as Ferndale, then in scattered stands between Fort Bragg and Big River in Mendocino County. Elsewhere, it ranges northward along the coasts of Oregon, Washington, British Columbia, and Alaska to Kodiak Island.

Young sitka spruce grow here near the upper tide-line. [Prairie Creek Redwoods S.P.] ROBERT TURNER

Coastal winds often deform Sitka spruce crowns. [Redwood N.P.] ROBERT TURNER

Sitka Spruce
Picea sitchensis

From Griffin and Critchfield

Brewer Spruce • *Picea breweriana*

BREWER SPRUCE

This Weeping Spruce is the most imperfectly known conifer of North America. . . . Already less widely scattered and less multiplied than any other Spruce-tree, it seems destined soon to perish by fire, which has no doubt confined it to the few isolated and inaccessible mountain peaks where it has found its last resting-place. It seems hopeless, therefore, to expect that the few isolated trees of this species can long escape their ravages.

—Charles Sprague Sargent
The Silva of North America

Charles Sprague Sargent's gloomy prediction for weeping, or Brewer, spruce, expressed in 1890, has not come to pass. Although this spruce is the most narrowly distributed member of its genus in America, it is scattered rather widely across five California counties, and two in Oregon, and is hardly an endangered species. The misconception that it is rare probably derives from the fact that Brewer spruce populations are largely restricted to high country where access even by foot is difficult and extensive pure stands unusual.

In the floristically rich Klamath Ranges, Brewer spruce mixes with many coniferous associates, including sugar, foxtail, and western white pines, mountain hemlock, white and Shasta red firs, incense-cedar, and Douglas-fir. Its characteristic drooping branches, often as much as six feet in length, give this darkly somber tree a growth habit that Donald Culross Peattie described as "sorrowful." It has been suggested that the pliant branches shed snow loads, and the flexible stems bend before the

Weeping mutants have been discovered in several spruce species, but only Brewer spruce is a weeping species.
[Kalmiopsis Wilderness, OR] DAVID MUENCH

Brewer spruce is North America's rarest spruce. [Siskiyou Mts.] ROBERT TURNER

weight of a creeping snowpack, allowing the spruce to withstand heavy snow accumulations without suffering undue breakage. Brewer spruce also appears to tolerate deep shade, drought, cold, and infertile soils.

Despite the rigors of its habitat, Brewer spruce is capable of reaching considerable size: it has attained 170 feet in height and four feet in diameter, and it can live at least 900 years. Engelmann spruce grows with Brewer spruce, and Sitka spruce is just a few miles away, but neither is viewed as a close relative of Brewer spruce. Instead, the faraway Chihuahua spruce *(Picea chihuahuana)* of northern Mexico is considered to be its closest kin. Researchers examining needle tissues of Brewer spruce have identified no fewer than four alkaloids that not only have never been found in any other spruces, but which are indeed unknown anywhere else in the entire family Pinaceae.

Brewer spruce has no known commercial value and has apparently resisted domestication as a pampered garden tree. It has therefore received little attention from plant scientists and retains much of its mystery.

IDENTIFYING BREWER SPRUCE

At a distance: No other North American conifer has the long, dark-foliaged, pendulous branches of this spruce.

Standing beneath it: The cones, which dangle from short branchlets, are two to five inches long, turning from purple, or green tinged with purple, to light brown. The bark is broken into thick scales, whitish on the outside, reddish on the inside.

In the hand: This species is distinguishable from all other American spruces by its combination of blunt, flattened needles with whitish rows of stomatal wax on the upper surface and smooth-margined cone scales.

HABITAT

Brewer spruce grows where annual precipitation totals 50 to 100 inches, most of which comes as wet, heavy snow. It can be found on soils derived from a wide variety of rocks, and it occurs in simple or diverse conifer forests.

DISTRIBUTION

In California Brewer spruce grows in Del Norte, Shasta, Siskiyou, Trinity, and Humboldt counties, scattered in the Klamath Ranges at elevations from 3,300 to 9,000 feet. In Oregon it is found in contiguous parts of Josephine and Jackson counties.

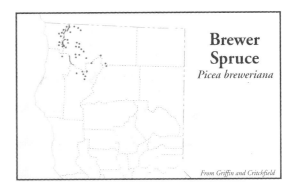

Brewer Spruce
Picea breweriana

From Griffin and Critchfield

Engelmann Spruce • *Picea engelmannii*

ENGELMANN SPRUCE

ngelmann spruce is a mainstay of the subalpine forests of the Rocky Mountains and a lesser member of the Cascade's east-slope forest. After Willis Linn Jepson found some Engelmann spruce near the California border in Oregon in 1909, scientists anticipated its rapid discovery in California. But it wasn't located in the state until 1921 when Southern Pacific forester W. H. Snell reported a two-mile strip of it along Clark Creek in the Pit River drainage of the Cascade Range. Since then more has been found about 65 miles to the northwest, mainly in seven drainages around Russian Peak in the Salmon Mountains, which are part of the Klamath Ranges. Here Engelmann spruce tends to grow on streamside terraces and moist slopes. It does well in these wet habitats and maintains its presence by establishing seedlings on deep humus and rotting logs in the heavy shade of the spruce canopy.

It is not surprising that most of Engelmann spruce's limited California distribution occurs in the Klamath Ranges. This rugged and jumbled mass of mountain peaks, high ridges, and river canyons has managed for many millions of years to escape the decimation of its flora by volcanism, glacial activity, or the incursion of inland seas. With the Pacific Ocean close by, temperatures have probably remained equable over very long periods of time. Thus these ranges seem to have become museums of endemic species; some are refugees from glaciation in the recent past and some became established here long ago and remain trapped, as in amber, unable to find a way out. The result is extreme floristic diversity. For example, in a square mile centering on the Russian Peak area, there are 16 species of conifers (including Engelmann

Dense forests of Engelmann spruce characterize the high Rockies from New Mexico to British Columbia. A thin ribbon comes south into California's Klamath Ranges. [Wasatch-Cache N.P., UT] SCOTT T. SMITH

These Engelmann spruce tower over firs (foreground). [Okanogan N.F., WA] RON LANNER

spruce) and one taxad, which is possibly a world record for such a compact locale.

Engelmann spruces have a varied mien. They may be spire-topped and as pointed at the tip as the subalpine firs with which they often associate; more often, however, they have an acute summit that rounds with old age. Many feature conspicuously drooping branchlets that issue gracefully from gently arched limbs, while others have starkly rigid horizontal branches that carry hardly any branchlets. In its high Rocky Mountain haunts Engelmann spruce often forms the treeline where long winters and strong winds beat it into the shape of a bush. But where conditions are less severe the trunks are tall, columnar, and flare at the base, betraying with low buttresses the major roots spreading widely just beneath the surface. The shallow roots, resinous wood and foliage, and thin bark make Engelmann spruce, like many other spruces, highly sensitive even to light ground fires. But by forming its ribbons of growth in stream bottoms and cool, moist ravines, it can escape most fires and live to a ripe age.

IDENTIFYING ENGELMANN SPRUCE
At a distance: Look for tall, narrow-crowned conifers with horizontal limbs bearing dark

foliage. The columnar trunks are pinkish in places and flare at the base. Numerous bright brown cones hang, open and empty, high in the upper crown.
Standing beneath it: The bark sheds in thin flakes, exposing the pink underbark in patches. The root buttresses make comfortable "armchairs" for lunch breaks.
In the hand: The short, stout needles are thick and easily rolled between thumb and forefinger. They are mounted on peglike woody outgrowths of the twig that make leafless branchlets rasplike to the touch. The cones are 1 to 2 1/2 inches long and have thin, flexible scales with rough edges.

HABITAT
It grows on moist lower slopes and streamside terraces, from about 3,300 to 6,500 feet, often mixing with subalpine, Shasta red, and white firs, sugar pine, incense-cedar, and an occasional Brewer spruce.

DISTRIBUTION
In California it is located in drainages around Russian Peak in Siskiyou County and along Clark Creek in Shasta County. Elsewhere, Engelmann spruce extends up the Cascades in Oregon and Washington, throughout the Coast Mountains and Rockies of British Columbia, and down the Rockies to southern Arizona and New Mexico.

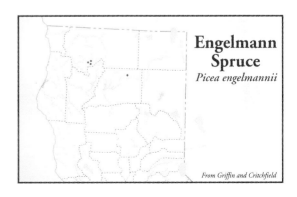

Engelmann Spruce
Picea engelmannii

From Griffin and Critchfield

HEMLOCKS

Hemlocks, or "hemlock spruces" as they were called in the eighteenth and nineteenth centuries, are dark-trunked conifers with dense crowns of short, flat needles. The blunt needles, which often have conspicuously whitened rows of stomates on the lower surface, are narrowly stalklike at the base and fastened to minute, woody outgrowths of the stem. The cones hang downwards in great numbers from the outer limbs, and turn reddish brown as they mature. The hallmark of hemlocks is the drooping leader tip that bends to the prevailing wind.

Hemlocks grow in eastern and western forests of North America, in the Himalayas, and the Far East. Indeed, *Tsuga* is the Japanese name for the hemlock. Two of the four American hemlocks are eastern trees, but the other two species enter California: western hemlock tentatively, staking out its territory in the northern redwood zone; and mountain hemlock more boldly, forming stands along much of the Klamath Ranges and the higher elevations of the Sierra Nevada and Cascades.

Opposite: Groves of mountain hemlock often approach the tree line in the high country of the Sierra Nevada and Cascades. [Lassen Volcanic N.P.] JEFF GNASS

Western Hemlock • *Tsuga heterophylla*

WESTERN HEMLOCK

In the coast region, where this tree delights in the humidity which every breeze brings in from the ocean, the forest floor is so deeply covered with mosses and with many strong growing shrubs that the delicate seeds of the Hemlock often find their only opportunity to germinate on the trunks of fallen trees, which, in consequence, are frequently covered with miniature Hemlock forests.

—Charles Sprague Sargent
Silva of North America

A century ago Charles Sprague Sargent summarized the two basic requirements for healthy western hemlock: moist air and rotten wood. In recent years, it has become increasingly clear that decaying logs play a crucial role in the regeneration of western hemlock. Its seedlings must have decaying logs to grow upon, but not just any log will do. Western hemlock is hostage to the availability of just the right logs—preferably those of Douglas-fir that are still sound enough to provide a surface well above the choking cover of mosses, liverworts, and evergreen shrubs that blanket the forest floor. The ideal log still has some adhering rough bark, and its rotted, moisture-retaining sapwood provides hemlock seedlings a friendly rooting medium that harbors several species of mycorrhizae-forming fungi. When several hemlocks growing on the same "nurse log" succeed in putting down roots into the soil, and the log subsequently decomposes out from under them, they form the "colonnades" of lined-up, stilt-rooted trees common in the northwestern rainforests.

To succeed in its wet habitat, western hemlock has adopted a seed-dispersal strategy apparently shared only with its common associate, Sitka spruce. Its small, winged seeds are wafted on the wind during all months of the year, whenever the warmth of a transient sun-break opens the scales on the masses of pendent cones that ornament the tree's crown. On summer days the cone-scale fibers shrink in the drying air, pulling the cone scales open and releasing more seeds. When the cool, wet weather returns, the cones close up again. Some seeds cannot wait for a warm day and they germinate, with disastrous results, within the tomb of their waterlogged cones.

In the early days of logging in northern California and the Pacific Northwest, western hemlock was regarded as a weed, of little value compared with Douglas-fir and Sitka spruce. As the availability of these species declined, it dawned upon the wood products industry that the fast-growing western hemlock pulped as well as spruce, and the rainforest's most common tree quickly became commercial. Today western hemlock is a major economic asset. Its wood goes into piles and pilings, railroad ties and construction lumber, groundwood and pulp. Growing up through the shade cast by forests of Douglas-fir, hemlock frequently attains heights of 200 feet (maximum about 260 feet) and can live half a millennium.

IDENTIFYING WESTERN HEMLOCK
At a distance: Look for tall, straight trees with drooping leaders and branch tips.
Standing beneath it: The short, flat, blunt needles are shiny, dark green on top, and have two bright white lines below. Bark of old trees forms flat, cinnamon red plates.
In the hand: There are both short ($1/4$ inch) and longer ($3/4$ inch) needles, whose slender stalks attach to minute woody outgrowths of the branchlet and which lie flat to both sides of the branchlet. The cones are no more than one inch long.
HABITAT
Western hemlock is mainly a tree of temperate rainforests, but it also occurs in the northern Rockies.

Once regarded as a forest "weed," western hemlock has become a major industrial asset. [Mt. Rainier N.P.] PAT O'HARA

Western hemlock often takes root on decaying logs, eventually appearing as if propped on stilts. [Prairie Creek Redwoods S.P.] ROBERT TURNER

On the coast, it may experience 150 inches of rain (in Alaska), or less than 40 inches (Eureka, California). Inland it is confined to shady, north slopes and stream bottoms. It tolerates a wide variety of soils and ranges from sea level to 2,000 feet. Western hemlock in California grows mostly among redwood, Sitka spruce, and western redcedar.

DISTRIBUTION

In California it ranges from the Oregon border to the Gualala River in Sonoma County. It is distributed more or less continuously as far south as the lower Mad River and is generally within 20 miles of the shore. Elsewhere it stretches up the Pacific coast to Alaska's Kenai Peninsula and has a separate area of distribution in contiguous Rocky Mountain areas of British Columbia, Washington, Idaho, and Montana.

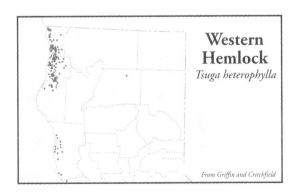

Western Hemlock
Tsuga heterophylla

From Griffin and Critchfield

Mountain Hemlock • *Tsuga mertensiana*

MOUNTAIN HEMLOCK

Mountain hemlock is widely admired for its beauty. Even the taciturn Charles Sprague Sargent, dean of early twentieth century American dendrologists, viewed this tree as "the loveliest cone-bearing tree of the American forest." To John Muir, writing in *The Mountains of California,* it was "the most singularly beautiful of all the California coniferae." After an almost worshipful description of what was then called the hemlock spruce, Muir surrenders: "But the best words only hint its charms. Come to the mountains and see."

Mountain hemlock's seductive beauty is principally derived from its form and color. Like other hemlocks, its tips droop. Thus every tree's leader bends gracefully leeward, like the stalk of a "nodding lily" in Muir's felicitous phrase. And the branches, which leave the trunk at a right angle, droop also at their tips, lending an almost mournful appearance typical too of other hemlocks, but most pronounced in this one. Such leaders and branch tips grace erect, 100-foot trees as well as short ones thrust from thickets of dwarfish shrubs. The larger trees are found at such "low" elevations in the eastside Sierra Nevada as 9,000 to 10,000 feet above sea level. Here specimens with diameters that surpass four feet are still common, though one must look long and hard to find a six-footer such as Muir saw at Lake Hollow. Some of these trees live for more than eight centuries. The dwarfed *krummholz* must be sought at higher elevations, up to 11,500 feet, or somewhat lower on exposed windswept slopes. Branches pinned to the ground by the snowpack often take root there, forming clonal thickets that provide superb cover for the birds and mammals of this rarefied zone.

Mountain hemlock is a tree of many colors. Its needles are deep green, but a waxy surface bloom imparts a bluish cast. The bark—even of young trees—becomes roughened by splits that create deep furrows between narrow ridges, and it ranges in color from a dull purplish brown to a bright, reddish brown. The latter bark color mimics that of California red fir and old western white pines—two of mountain hemlock's neighbors. The hemlock's male cones are blue or purplish blue and shed their pale yellow pollen in early summer. The pendent, cylindrical seed cones measure two to three inches, much longer than those of western hemlock, and turn from purplish blue to purplish red, then reddish brown as they mature and open to shed their small winged seeds. Masses of these empty cones hang in the crowns a year or more. The cone scales bend back towards the cone base, exposing to view the "shadows" of the seeds that earlier reposed there.

In California mountain hemlock inhabits only the high, snowy country. For months, supple young saplings bow beneath the snow until spring thaw releases them. The short summers are brilliantly sunny except for occasional thunderstorms. Here, mountain hemlocks may be scattered among California red fir, lodgepole, western white, and whitebark pines, or they may form small, pure groves among granite boulders.

Mountain hemlock's unusually long cones, its habit of bristling its needles in all directions from the shoot, and the presence of "wings" on its pollen grains are traits most unhemlock-like. Thus some have argued that this species originated as a hybrid of western hemlock and Sitka spruce. The argument has been taken further with the claim that the Sierra Nevada mountain hemlock is a species separate from mountain hemlocks to the north, and that its origin resulted from crossing of the above-mentioned hybrid and Engelmann spruce! Unfortunately for advocates of this prehistory, no crosses between genera of the pine family have ever

Mountain hemlock leaders bend gracefully leeward. [Inyo N.F.] CHRISTOPHER T. FRANK

Rough hemlock bark is often festooned with lichens. [Crater Lake N.P.] JEFF GNASS

Mountain hemlock tolerates thin soils and deep snowpacks. [Lassen Volcanic N.P.] DAVID LANNER

In the hand: The needles are blunt. They are semi-circular in cross-section and can be rolled between thumb and forefinger. Seed cones are two to three inches long, and their scales bend back towards the base of the cone after opening.

HABITAT

It grows in subalpine forests from 4,000 feet in the Siskiyou Mountains to 11,600 feet in the southern Sierra Nevada. It is often found on rocky ridges or in basins where heavy snow-packs accumulate on coarse soils low in organic content.

DISTRIBUTION

In California it occurs in the Klamath Ranges, and in the Cascades near Mount Shasta and the Lassen Peak region. It ranges down the Sierra Nevada to northern Tulare County. Elsewhere it runs from Oregon to Alaska's Kenai region, and then jumps east to the northern Rockies of Idaho and Montana.

been substantiated, and no compelling evidence of the presumed crossing events has been brought forth.

Perhaps in response to Earth's recently warming climate, mountain hemlock is expanding its range by invading subalpine meadows and late-lying snow basins in the Coast Mountains of British Columbia, the Olympic Mountains of Washington, and in the Cascades, including Lassen Volcanic National Park. In the shadow of Lassen Peak, mountain hemlock has colonized meadow sites since the warming trend that followed on the heels of the Little Ice Age, during the middle and late 1800s. In the future, researchers expect further increases of mountain hemlock regeneration, in places where it has not previously grown. This will be welcomed by admirers of mountain hemlock, despite the reduction it will occasion in meadow area.

IDENTIFYING MOUNTAIN HEMLOCK

At a distance: No other western conifer of high elevations has drooping leaders and branch tips.
Standing beneath it: Needles bristle in all directions from the shoot, not in a flat plane. The bark has purplish tones.

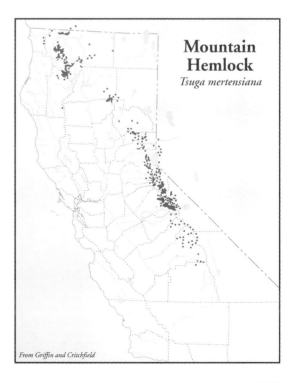

Mountain Hemlock
Tsuga mertensiana

From Griffin and Critchfield

DOUGLAS-FIRS

Pseudotsuga, literally "false hemlock," is one of those genera that has gravitated to the east and west rims of the Pacific basin. Thus we find two species in California—one of them an endemic—and several in China, Japan, and Taiwan. They are large, shade-intolerant trees with soft, blunt, stalked needles attached to shallow depressions on the shoot. The dormant buds are long, shiny, brown, and pointed.

Like their cousins the pines and spruces, Douglas-firs have resinous wood. Their most distinctive character is the seed cone, which has long trident-shaped bracts protruding between the seed-bearing scales. Bark of young *Pseudotsuga* is much like that of the true firs— smooth, gray, and resin-blistered. However, it becomes very thick, fibrous, and furrowed with age. The two California *Pseudotsuga* grow at the environmental extremes inhabited by the genus: one may thrive in virtual rainforests and montane forests, the other tolerates droughty Mediterranean scrub.

Opposite: The South Fork of the Smith River churns through a canyon guarded by old-growth Douglas-firs. [Smith River N.R.A.] LARRY ULRICH

Douglas-Fir • *Pseudotsuga menziesii*

DOUGLAS-FIR

After coast redwood, Douglas-fir is the world's tallest conifer, and one of the most massive. A specimen now standing in Coos County, Oregon rises 329 feet high and has a diameter at breast height of about 11 $1/2$ feet. A tree that once stood in Mineral, Washington was reportedly 385 feet high with a 15-foot diameter. It was the huge volumes of old-growth Douglas-fir that drew the American lumber industry from the cut-out pineries of the Great Lake States to the Pacific Northwest, and it was Douglas-fir plywood and boards that built much of suburbia following World War II.

Douglas-fir is one of the west's most widely distributed trees. It is found from the mountains and coast of British Columbia south into Washington, where it splits into two great population systems: one extends down the Pacific coast and along the west side of the Cascades and Sierra Nevada; the other trends southeast down the chains of the Rockies, breaking up into fragments deep in central Mexico. The western populations comprise the typical variety, *Pseudotsuga menziesii* var. *menziesii,* or coast Douglas-fir. The eastern populations are denoted as *Pseudotsuga menziesii* var. *glauca,* or Rocky Mountain Douglas-fir. Only the coast variety is found in California.

Along the state's north coast, Douglas-fir grows at the southern end of the world's largest temperate rainforest; further south it endures California's long, hot, dry Mediterranean summer. Since Douglas-fir is a pioneer species, it requires nearly full sun for its best development and usually colonizes areas that have been burned, logged, or otherwise cleared of competing vegetation.

Like most other conifers, Douglas-fir shares a mutualistic relationship with so-called mycorrhizal fungi dwelling in the forest soil. The bodies, or mycelia, of these fungi are made up of long filaments, or hyphae, that are one cell in thickness. These wind through the soil like great skeins of yarn, and when conditions are right they form the highly organized, temporary fruiting bodies we call mushrooms. Though the fruiting body is the most conspicuous part of the fungus, the great bulk of its body is underground, in the form of hyphae. Mycorrhizal fungi are not very effective saprophytes; they possess few enzymes capable of breaking down complex organic materials. They solve this problem by forming an intimate association with the roots of higher plants that can provide them with the fruits of photosynthesis. The fungal hyphae associated with Douglas-fir, and with other members of the Pinaceae, envelop tender new roots, forming a feltlike mantle of

A young Douglas-fir takes advantage of a sunny opening in the forest. [Trinity Alps] DAVID MUENCH

woven hyphal material around them. Some of the hyphae penetrate the root and grow between the cells of the root's inner tissues. The fungus produces a hormone that stimulates branching of the root, thus increasing root surface area, and enhancing the tree's ability to absorb soil water and mineral nutrients. The new structure thus formed—part root, part fungus—is called a mycorrhiza, Greek for "fungus root."

A mycorrhiza not only allows a fungus to thrive by providing it with sugars and vitamins made in the tree, but confers benefits on the tree as well. Beyond increasing the root area, for example, mycorrhizal roots are more efficient in absorbing water from the soil, thus safeguarding the tree against drought. They enhance the uptake of dissolved phosphorus, and perhaps nitrogen, and prolong root life. They even have an antibiotic effect on parasitic fungi that attack tree roots. So the mycorrhizal relationship is of immense benefit to both the fungus and the tree. The association may be obligatory for some fungi, and probably for many trees as well. When mushroom hunters prowl California's conifer forests in search of esculent chanterelles, boletes, milky caps, matsutake, and coral fungi, they are indirectly harvesting the fruits of a conifer's labor, for all of these are mycorrhizal fungi.

Not all of Douglas-fir's mycorrhizal fungi form above-ground fruiting bodies for the dispersal of their spores. Some form truffles, fruiting bodies which remain deep underground and do not open to release their spores. Each truffle species creates its own characteristic odor that attracts mice, voles, chipmunks, flying squirrels, and deer. The foraging animals sniff out the truffles, dig them up, and eat them. The truffle's spores are consumed in the process, but they have tough skins and are later excreted, unharmed by digestive juices. Lying on top of the soil, incorporated into fecal matter, they become available for wind or water transport into the soil, where they can germinate and find another cooperative host plant. This arrangement benefits tree, fungus, and mammal. It may also benefit an endangered bird, the northern spotted owl, since flying squirrels and other truffle-eating mammals are their major prey.

IDENTIFYING DOUGLAS-FIR

At a distance: Douglas-fir is a large tree with gracefully drooping limbs and dark gray-brown bark.

Standing beneath it: The bark of young stems and branches is smooth and gray; bark of maturing trees is gray and scaly, while that of old and large trees is deeply furrowed.

In the hand: The seed cones have characteristic three-lobed bracts projecting from between cone scales and pointing up the cone. Needles are flat and joined to the branchlet by a short, thin stalk. Terminal buds are long, shiny, brown, and pointed.

HABITAT

In California Douglas-fir occupies a broad spectrum of habitats, from wet, north coast forests where redwood is dominant to westside Sierra Nevada mixed-conifer forests, where summer drought is severe. In the Klamath Ranges, it is a lower montane species. Douglas-fir seldom forms extensive pure stands, but is usually associated with other conifers. It ranges from sea level to about 4,000 feet in the North Coast Ranges and to 6,000 feet in the Klamath Ranges. In the Sierra Nevada it is generally found from about 2,500 to 6,000 feet, but reaches 7,500 feet near the southern end of its distribution in this range.

Spotted owls and Douglas-fir have an interest in truffles. [Point Reyes N.S.] GALEN ROWELL/MOUNTAIN LIGHT

DISTRIBUTION

Within California it ranges from the Oregon border south through the Klamath and Coast ranges to the Santa Cruz Mountains. It is also found along the Little Sur River in the Santa Lucia Range. It is common in the Cascades and Sierra Nevada, extending south into the Yosemite area. There is an outlying grove in the Purisima Hills of western Santa Barbara County, growing on diatomaceous earth. This site is about 21 miles from the nearest stand of the closely related big-cone-spruce, with which it never quite overlaps.

Douglas-fir
Pseudotsuga menziesii

From Griffin and Critchfield

Bigcone-Spruce • *Pseudotsuga macrocarpa*

BIGCONE-SPRUCE

(ALSO CALLED BIGCONE DOUGLAS-FIR)

Bigcone-spruce is not a spruce. It is a *Pseudotsuga,* whose common name has by government dictate been declared "bigcone Douglas-fir," after its big brother the Douglas-fir, *Pseudotsuga menziesii.* But since there are no binding rules with regard to plant common names, many Californians continue to cling to the old name. Perhaps because this is a tree that successfully defies both the laws of thermodynamics and gravity, calling it a spruce while knowing better seems entirely appropriate under the circumstances.

In youth, a bigcone-spruce looks much like a young Douglas-fir. Its needles are grayer or bluer than those of coastal Douglas-fir and somewhat sharper-tipped, and its buds are a bit shorter. Both trees have young bark that is smooth and gray and sometimes has resin blisters. They both grow at a rapid juvenile rate if unshaded from above, but as a bigcone-spruce matures, it goes its own developmental way and the similarities end. The cones are much larger, heavier, and woodier than those of Douglas-fir and hang like ornaments from the tips of pendent branches. Their three-pointed bracts are shorter than those of Douglas-fir cones, and their scales are much stiffer and more resonant when plucked with a fingernail. The winged seeds of bigcone-spruce are much larger and heavier than those of Douglas-fir, suggesting the possibility of dispersal by small mammals, although nothing is yet known about this facet of the tree's natural history.

The bark of large bigcone-spruces is redder than that of Douglas-fir and more likely to be scorched black by the fires that frequent its habitats. Those fires also modify a bigcone-spruce's appearance in a way most unusual among conifers. Bigcone-spruce develops long, horizontal to gently drooping limbs. When scorched by a passing ground fire, the needles are killed and soon fall. At this point the tree is little more than a rectilinear framework of burned, dead-looking limbs anchored in a blackened trunk. But soon great numbers of buds on the unburned, upper-branch surfaces sprout, producing masses of fresh, green foliage. Other buds, lying dormant beneath the bark of the trunk, also sprout, creating a jacket of foliage. This ability to respond to fire in an adaptive way is what allows bigcone-spruce to occupy its fire-prone habitats, especially those it shares with inflammable chaparral shrubs. There is no question that its response to fire allows bigcone-spruce to live longer than it otherwise would and to continue to reproduce by bearing additional seed crops.

While not notable for great longevity or large size, bigcone-spruce may live nearly 700 years, and trees 300 years of age are capable of sprouting new foliage after fire or other injury. Old trees commonly exceed 80 feet in height, and "Old Glory," a locally famous bigcone-spruce near Mount Baldy village in the San Gabriel Mountains, is reported to be 91 inches

Bigcone-spruce grows only within southern California. [Palomar Mountain S.P.] ROBERT TURNER

in trunk diameter, and was 145 feet tall until it lost its top in a 1950s windstorm.

Bigcone-spruces are usually found not in continuous forest, but as isolated trees, or in small groups or patches. They are scattered along ridgelines, on precipitous slopes, in steep ravines, and even on cliff faces. The species is a California endemic and is found nowhere else, despite old reports of its occurrence south of the border. Within its limited range in southern California, it can occur as low as 900 feet above sea level or as high as nearly 7,400 feet. This broad elevational range makes it at home in both chaparral and mixed-conifer associations and puts it in the company of such varied neighbors as singleleaf pinyon, gray, knobcone, Coulter, ponderosa, Jeffrey, and sugar pines, incense-cedar and California white fir, Fremont

Bigcone-spruce forms islands of biodiversity among chaparral. [Los Padres N.F.] DAVID LANNER

cottonwood, bigleaf maple, white alder, and California walnut. In addition, nearly everywhere bigcone-spruce grows, it is joined by canyon live oak. Some ecologists think that canyon live oak protects bigcone-spruces from high-intensity fires by dampening them. Indeed, a stand of battered old bigcones leaning steeply downhill from their anchorage somewhere within a canyon live oak canopy is a common sight in southern California's mountains. At its lower elevations, bigcone-spruce is the only conifer, and often the only tree, found over large areas. The diversity it adds to the landscape, and the three-dimensionality it imparts to bird, insect, and mammal habitats, give it an ecological significance beyond its mere numbers.

IDENTIFYING BIGCONE-SPRUCE

At a distance: Within its range, what appear to be the masts and spars of old square-riggers, arising from a ravine or a steep mountain slope, can only be an old-growth stand of bigcone-spruces.
Standing beneath it: Bark is reddish brown, often blackened by fire. Limbs are long, straight, horizontal or slightly drooping, often covered on top by masses of short, leaf-bearing branchlets.
In the hand: Cones measure up to seven inches long and are hard and woody when dry. Short, three-pointed bracts emerge from between the cone scales. Its needles are 3/4 to 1 inch long and pointed at the tip. Buds are dark brown, shiny, and pointed.

HABITAT

Bigcone-spruce is found on droughty to moist mountain slopes and canyon bottoms from 900 feet (in chaparral) to 7,400 feet elevation (in mixed-conifer forests in the San Gabriel Mountains). Within its range, precipitation varies from 20 to 50 inches, summers are hot and dry, and winters cool and moist. It grows on a variety of substrates, including sandstone, gneiss, and granite, and usually occupies steep terrain.

DISTRIBUTION

It is mainly found in a broad east-west band, from the San Rafael Mountains in Santa Barbara County through the Transverse Ranges to the San Bernardino Mountains, with its greatest abundance in the San Gabriel Mountains. It is scarce in the Peninsular Ranges, where it is found in the Santa Ana and San Jacinto mountains, and on Mount Palomar and Volcan Mountain in San Diego County.

Despite frequent exposure to fire, bigcone-spruce may live 700 years. [Los Padres N.F.] DAVID LANNER

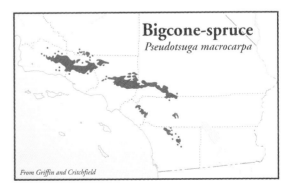

Bigcone-spruce
Pseudotsuga macrocarpa

From Griffin and Critchfield

THE CYPRESS FAMILY

This family is represented in California by cypresses, false cypresses, incense-cedar, junipers, and an arborvitae. With a total of 18 species in this family, California far exceeds any other state. Members of this family have in common scalelike leaves that press closely to the shoot and usually have a gland that produces aromatic oils. The branchlet is often in the form of a flat spray, though in junipers and cypresses it may be clumpy. The wood of cypress family members is infiltrated by organic substances that confer decay resistance and make it very durable, even in contact with the soil. Though trees of this family are often called cedars, they bear no close relationship to the true cedars (the genus *Cedrus*), which are Old World members of the pine family. Some taxonomists contend that members of the Taxodiaceae, or baldcypress family, should be included within the cypress family. See page 235 for information on the relationship of that family to this one.

Opposite: Sierra juniper is the only tree of the cypress family to colonize the high country of its namesake range. [Yosemite N.P.] JEFF GNASS

CYPRESSES

Cypresses are trees or large shrubs with scalelike leaves that over-lap on the branchlet in alternating pairs, much like those of junipers. The branchlet in most species is therefore round or square in section, and only seldom flat. Minute, resin-secreting glands are present on the surface of the scale leaf. If the gland is active, the foliage is aro-matic when crushed and is often sticky to the touch. Some species have inactive glands.

Cones of both sexes are borne on shoot tips on the same tree. Pollen cones in most species mature in winter or early spring and the shedding of their yellow pollen may temporarily stain the tree. Seed cones turn from green to brown and become nearly spherical and very woody as they mature over a period of two years. Each of their 6 to 14 scales usually bears a projection on its surface (called an umbo), which is often spikelike and gives the scale the appearance of a shield. The cones often remain closed for several years, weathering ashy gray and retaining the seeds inside until they are opened by heat. When the cones open, the seeds are released. Thus many of the cypresses are adapted to regen-erating in fire-prone woodlands.

Cypresses grow in North America, southern Europe, Africa, and Asia. There are an estimated 25 species worldwide and more than one-third of them are found in California.

Opposite: The Monterey cypress groves of Point Lobos are among the most-visited conifer stands in California. [Point Lobos S.R.] JEFF GNASS

CALIFORNIA'S PROBLEMATIC CYPRESSES

The cypresses are more numerous in California than any other genus of conifers except the pines. The number of cypress species, however, has long been in dispute among both amateur and professional botanists. There are several reasons for the state of confusion that has come to surround these sturdy trees. One problem is that evolution has dealt us a poor hand. The cypresses simply do not show the clear differences between species that we find in most other conifers. Perhaps too little time has elapsed in their evolution, and a few million more years must pass before they are fully differentiated. Another difficulty stems from their isolation from each other. Cypress species usually grow separately in small groves, often on soils that may induce abnormal growth behavior. We therefore do not have the opportunity to compare the appearance or behavior of two species since they do not occur naturally in the same environment. This makes it hard to judge whether certain characteristics are influenced mainly by genetic or environmental conditions. In addition, most studies of California's cypresses have been fragmentary, and there have not been many of them.

Piute cypresses in the Bodfish grove on Bald Eagle Peak. [Kern Co.] JIM A. BARTEL

Considering the large number of species that grow in California, the cypresses have received remarkably little attention from plant scientists. One result of these factors is that taxonomists have tended to disagree on the basic question of delineating species. For example, in 1948 Carl B. Wolf, an eminent member of this fraternity, carved California's cypresses into 15 species. A few years later, E. L. Little, Jr. found only six! Few better examples can be found of the "splitting" and "lumping" tendencies in plant taxonomy. In recent years taxonomists have published three divergent views. James R. Griffin and William B. Critchfield listed 10 cypress species in *The Distribution of Forest Trees of California* in 1972. Jim A. Bartel reduced these to eight species and two subspecies for *The Jepson Manual* in 1993. That same year James E. Eckenwalder chose a different group of seven species for inclusion among the cypresses in *Flora of North America,* including one species not mentioned in either of the other works. The strategy followed here is to arrange the species listed by Griffin and Critchfield in approximately the order one would encounter them in progressing through the state from north to south and to note in their descriptions how these entities were later viewed in *The Jepson Manual* and in *Flora of North America.* This will allow a diversity of views to be expressed without overtaxing the reader's patience.

More research is needed before taxonomists can come to agreement on the status of California's cypresses. The existing published knowledge base of these

Tecate cypress on a fire-prone site at Guatay. [Cleveland N.F.] JOHN EVARTS

species is insufficient to support firm conclusions on their relationships. Molecular genetic studies would be very helpful; old-fashioned crossability studies, in which all the entities are bred with each other, would also be valuable.

The good news is that there is really no identification problem when one is observing *natural* populations of the California cypresses. With one exception (see page 175), all of the species listed by Griffin and Critchfield occupy exclusive natural ranges. So if a cypress observer knows where she is, she need only consult this book's maps to find out which cypress she is observing.

Monterey Cypress • *Cupressus macrocarpa*

MONTEREY CYPRESS

The strikingly beautiful Monterey cypress is perhaps California's most celebrated tree in the limited areas where it naturally occurs. Surprisingly, it was somehow overlooked by three assiduous searchers-for-new-species who roamed its home range in the nineteenth century. Neither David Douglas, nor his countryman Archibald Menzies, nor even Thomas Nuttall ever collected and named this twisted wraith of the sea fog. Instead, those privileges were claimed in June 1846 by German botanist Karl Theodor Hartweg.

There are only two natural populations of Monterey cypress, both of them on or near the Monterey Peninsula. The larger is at Cypress Point, just north of Carmel; the smaller is three miles to the south at Point Lobos State Reserve. Both grow under the influence of the cool sea breeze, the fog, and the salt spray from ocean swells that crash violently on rugged granite cliffs and headlands. Back from the shore, the trees are tall and relatively straight-boled, with fast-growing, whiplike shoots growing off in all directions. But trees overlooking the surf are severely wind-trained; they lean to lee and form tabular, infinitely-branched crowns bearing masses of foliage so dense they block out skylight. As a result of growing in a prevailing wind, their contorted trunks, clothed in neatly braided gray bark, are out of round, and even planklike in section. The large, $1^1/_2$-inch diameter cones, nut brown and shiny, open slowly without fire, or more rapidly with it. Although this habitat feels soggy-wet most of the time, it can parch in full sun sufficiently to support wildfire, as blackened trunks of Monterey cypress at Point Lobos attest.

Salt-laden sea breezes desiccate foliage, kill windward new growth, and prevent trunks from developing a circular cross-section, thus creating picturesque but crippled living trees. [Point Lobos S.R.] CARR CLIFTON

Though a Monterey County endemic, Monterey cypress has been planted worldwide as a windbreak and an ornamental in wild, dwarfed, columnar, and golden varieties. [Point Lobos S.R.] MARK J. DOLYAK

Due to its fast growth and dense habit, Monterey cypress early became a favorite tree for hedges and windbreaks in places as disparate as New Zealand, Kenya, the south of France, Hawaii, and Ireland's County Galway. A mild and humid climate is required for successful growth, however, and trees planted in dry places seldom persist.

Monterey cypress has always been regarded as a good species without taxonomic entanglements. Dendrologists report specimens with heights of 75 feet and diameters of six feet. The upper age limit is estimated to be about three centuries. Its foliage is bright green, without surface resin, and is not aromatic. The spontaneous hybridization of Monterey cypress and

Alaska-cedar (named *Cupressocyparis* X *leylandii*), which first occurred over a century ago in Britain's Kew Gardens, shows the close relationship of cypresses to the genus *Chamaecyparis*.

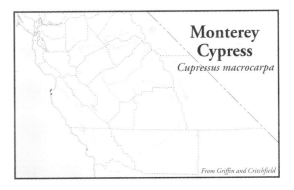

Monterey Cypress

Cupressus macrocarpa

From Griffin and Critchfield

McNab Cypress • *Cupressus macnabiana*

MCNAB CYPRESS

McNab cypress is relatively common on poor soils derived from serpentine, gabbro, greenstone, and basalt in chaparral and foothill woodland areas of the inner North Coast Ranges, Cascades, and westside Sierra Nevada. There are at least 30 groves of McNab cypress, several of which are more than two miles across. They occur at 1,000 to 2,800 feet and are spread across 12 or more counties. More groves probably remain to be discovered.

McNab cypress most often grows as a large shrub, but reports exist of 60-foot-high specimens. Unlike any other California cypress, its foliage is arrayed on relatively flat branchlets, though not as much so as in incense-cedar or western redcedar. When crushed it gives off a pleasant resinous fragrance. Its inch-wide cones have prominent umbos.

There is some evidence that McNab and Sargent cypresses interbreed in their overlap zone in northern Napa County and adjacent Colusa and Lake counties. This is the only overlap zone of two species of cypress in California and the only presumed example of natural hybridization of cypresses anywhere. In the overlap zone, McNab cypress tends to grow on ridges and Sargent cypress on lower slopes, but they do mix. McNab cypress is accepted as a species both in *The Jepson Manual* and *Flora of North America*. (See page 181 for species photo and distribution map.)

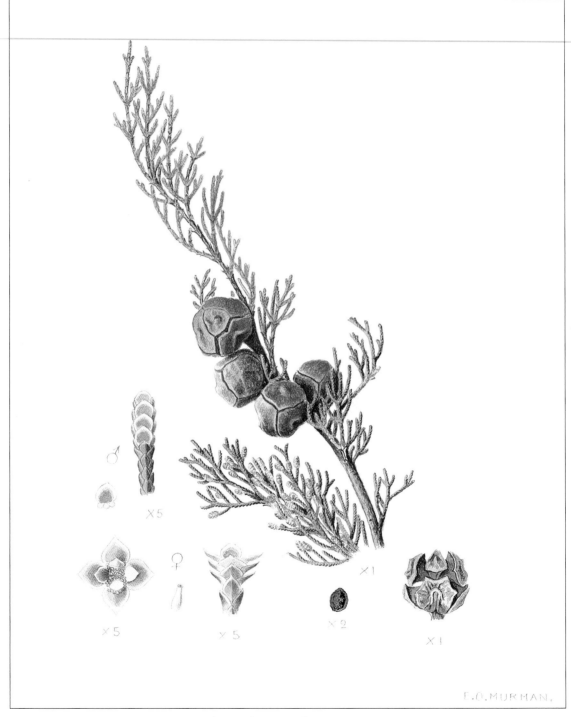

Mendocino Cypress • *Cupressus pigmaea*

$$\textit{Cupressus pigmaea}$$

MENDOCINO CYPRESS

(ALSO CALLED PYGMY CYPRESS)

The Mendocino White Plains are probably the only place in the world where one can find three species of conifers bearing cones on trees no taller than knee-height. Two are pines—Mendocino White Plains lodgepole pine and bishop pine—and the third is the Mendocino, or pygmy, cypress. Like its pine associates at White Plains, Mendocino cypress is not a genetic dwarf: it exhibits the stunted growth known only to plants that develop on very infertile soils.

The White Plains' soil is almost devoid of nutrients, which have been leached away by heavy rainfall and the slow downward percolation of standing water. The soil is also highly acidic, with pH readings as low as 2.8—not far from that of vinegar. In addition, there is an iron hardpan layer just below the surface that prevents tree roots from penetrating into the more fertile subsoil beneath it. Mendocino cypress growing on this substrate may take a century to attain 10 feet of height, while on better soils nearby, these so-called pygmies may reach 100 feet. Such contrasting behavior of a species under different environmental conditions is often referred to as its "phenotypic plasticity." Although Mendocino cypress is well-known for the White Plains' pygmy stands, this species is probably the tallest—and receives the most annual rainfall—of all the cypresses. A 157-foot-high specimen was reported in 1929.

Mendocino cypress occurs mainly between Fort Bragg and Albion. *The Jepson Manual* recognizes Mendocino cypress as a subspecies of Gowen cypress, and *Flora of North America* considers it as merely the undifferentiated northern population of Gowen cypress. (See page 181 for species photo and distribution map.)

Baker Cypress • *Cupressus bakeri*

BAKER CYPRESS

Baker cypress is restricted to several isolated sites in the Siskiyou Mountains, northern Sierra Nevada, Cascades, and Modoc Plateau. The southernmost groves, and the most recently discovered, are several miles east of Greenville in Plumas National Forest. Here, the largest trees of this species, to 84 feet in height, and to 56 inches in diameter, grow at elevations above 6,900 feet. This is the highest elevation reached by any California cypress, though *Cupressus montana*, endemic to Baja California's Sierra San Pedro Mártir, reaches 10,100 feet. Baker cypress reaches its northern limit near Prospect, Oregon. The largest population of the species is found on the Modoc Plateau, around Timbered Crater at 3,500 to 4,000 feet. Naturalist Donald Culross Peattie aptly described these groves as being scattered across a 7,000-acre landscape of "black clinkers, old fumaroles, stacks of jagged rocks, and choppy seas of knife-edged frozen lava."

Baker cypress experiences accumulations of four to six feet of snow at its higher locations, and it is probably the most cold-tolerant cypress species of North America. It often develops a long, straight trunk covered in youth by cherry red, peeling bark, and in maturity by blocky, grayish bark. The gray green to dark green foliage has numerous active resin glands and is pleasingly aromatic when crushed. Seed cones are $^1/_2$ to 1 inch in diameter with four to eight scales, each with a prominent umbo.

Baker cypress may be associated with a variety of other conifers, depending mainly on elevation and aspect. For example, the high groves near Greenville intermingle with red and white firs and Jeffrey and

A young Baker cypress grows in a woodland that burned 10 years earlier. [Siskiyou Mts.] ROBERT TURNER

Baker cypress can exceed 80 feet in height. [Shasta-Trinity N.F.] TODD KEELER-WOLF

Dark-foliaged populations from the Siskiyou Mountains and from Goose Nest Mountain farther east, were placed in subspecies *matthewsii* by Carl B. Wolf in 1948. There is currently no consensus on this matter. *Cupressus bakeri* is accepted in both *The Jepson Manual* and *Flora of North America.*

lodgepole pines while the cypresses at Timbered Crater are neighbored by ponderosa and knobcone pines and western juniper. In fact, cypresses here can easily be mistaken for juniper, as first pointed out by Milo S. Baker, the discoverer and namesake of this tree, who was not shy about admitting his confusion. In Baker's words, quoted by Jepson, "unless one looks carefully at every tree the cypress would be mistaken for juniper, the fruit being about the only character the eye readily distinguishes."

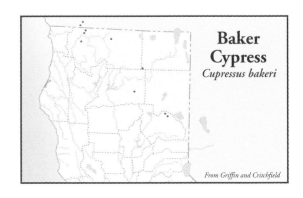

Baker Cypress

Cupressus bakeri

From Griffin and Critchfield

Dwarfed Mendocino cypress forms dense thickets.
[Mendocino Pygmy Forest] JOHN SAWYER

Above, top: Mendocino cypress at the White Plains.
[Mendocino Pygmy Forest] ROBERT TURNER
Above, bottom: This McNab cypress grows on serpen-
tine in the Sierra foothills. [Butte Co.] HASKEL BAZELL

McNab
Cypress
Cupressus
macnabiana

From Griffin and Critchfield

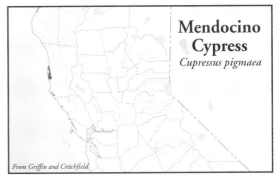

Mendocino
Cypress
Cupressus pigmaea

From Griffin and Critchfield

Santa Cruz Cypress • *Cupressus abramsiana*   ARTWORK: SUSAN BAZELL

SANTA CRUZ CYPRESS

The five small populations of Santa Cruz cypress are found on the foggy, western slopes of the Santa Cruz Mountains northwest of Santa Cruz. There is debate as to whether this tree is regarded as a species in its own right: *The Jepson Manual* says it is, while *Flora of North America* includes it within Gowen cypress. Some taxonomists suggest that Santa Cruz cypress may have arisen through hybridization of Gowen and Sargent cypresses.

Santa Cruz cypress is listed as an endangered species under the federal Endangered Species Act of 1973 (the only other listed tree species grows in Florida.) Its groves are found at the headwaters of Majors Creek, on Butano Ridge, near Eagle Rock, at Brackenbrae in Boulder Creek canyon, and at Bonny Doon. All Santa Cruz cypresses grow with chaparral on sandy soils, but not on serpentine. Where soils are thin, knobcone pine is an associate; deeper soils support ponderosa pine as well. Santa Cruz cypress differs from typical Gowen cypress in having slightly larger cones; they measure to 1 inch or more in diameter compared to Gowen cypress's $^2/_3$ inch. The tree may reach heights of 50 feet, but on thin, nutrient-poor soils it grows into a pygmy tree of 3 feet. (See page 189 for species photos and distribution map.)

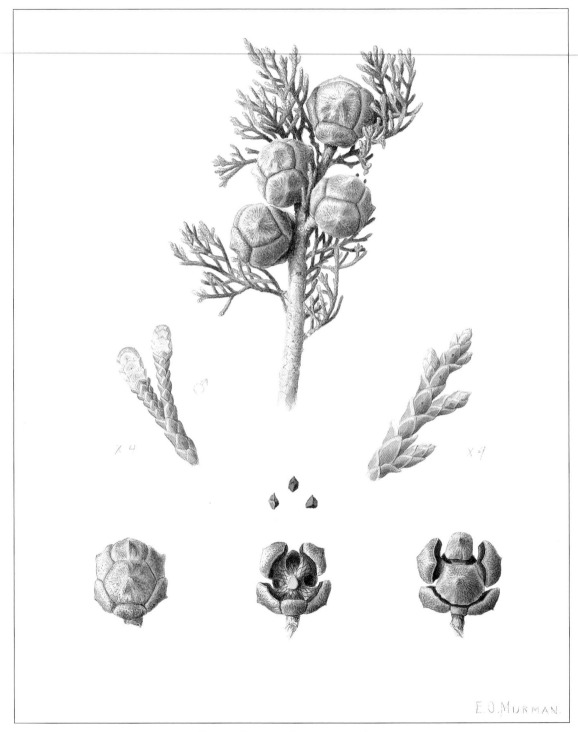

Gowen Cypress • *Cupressus goveniana*

GOWEN CYPRESS

Gowen cypress is found in only two locations, both on the Monterey Peninsula. The smaller stand of the two is located on Gibson Creek in Point Lobos State Reserve. The larger, and more rewarding to visit, is in the S. F. B. Morse Botanical Reserve on Huckleberry Hill in Del Monte Forest. Monterey cypresses approach within one mile of Gowen cypresses at Gibson Creek, and within two miles of those on Huckleberry Hill, but the two species never co-occur.

The two stands of Gowen cypress are both associated with Monterey pine. The Gibson Creek population grows within a forest of Monterey pine. Gowen cypress mixes with both Monterey and bishop pines at Huckleberry Hill, which is the only place where these two pines are found together. Here bishop pine grows on the poorly drained, acidic, old Pleistocene beach terraces favored by the stunted Gowen cypress, while Monterey pine holds the richer, more fertile soils. Due in part to summer fog-drip, the Del Monte Forest can become a soggy place, but forest fuels dry quickly when the sun shines, and intense fires have periodically burned up the old stands, allowing the closed-cone pines and cypress to establish new stands.

Gowen cypress is quite close morphologically to Mendocino and Santa Cruz cypresses. Therefore *Flora of North America* lumps both of those entities with the Monterey Peninsula populations as part of a more broadly constituted *Cupressus goveniana. The Jepson Manual* considers Mendocino cypress to be a subspecies of Gowen cypress. (See page 189 for species photo and distribution map.)

Sargent Cypress • *Cupressus sargentii*

Cupressus sargentii

SARGENT CYPRESS

Sargent cypress is the most widely distributed member of its genus in California. Its range extends nearly 400 miles, from Red Mountain in Mendocino County south to the Manzana Creek drainage in Santa Barbara County. Throughout its broad distribution in the Coast Ranges, Sargent cypress is almost always restricted to soils of serpentine origin. Gray pine and leather oak are its most common associates, but numerous other chaparral and woodland shrubs also grow in its vicinity.

For Sargent cypress, as well as the other California cypresses, fire is the predominant event triggering its regeneration. Sargent cypress often grows in dense stands that can quickly explode into a crown fire when exposed to flames. The heat of the fire melts resin bonds that otherwise keep the serotinous cones tightly closed, and the seeds are liberated upon the ashes. Following such a fire on Cuesta Ridge above San Luis Obispo in 1994, a green carpet of cypress seedlings sprung up below the charred skeletons of fire-killed trees, but not beneath adjacent trees that had escaped the blaze. The reasons for this were probably twofold. First, fewer seeds were blown beneath the unburned trees than were released and fell under the burned ones; second, those seedlings that got started in the shade and organic litter under living cypresses suffered heavier early mortality than those that became established in the sunlight and on the bare mineral soil beneath the dead trees. The close connection between fire and Sargent cypress regeneration is highlighted by the common correlation between stand age and the number of years since the grove last burned. In the absence of a timely fire, cones will eventually and slowly open, releasing their seeds over a longer period. These drop

187

Sargent cypress, seen here on Cuesta Ridge above San Luis Obispo, is California's most widely distributed cypress. [Los Padres N.F.] JOHN EVARTS

to the inhospitable, shady woodland floor, where, if they germinate, few will survive.

Sargent cypress varies widely in stature. It can be a dwarfish bush, described by Griffin and Critchfield as forming "vast dense shrubby thickets on ridges, as on Cedar Roughs in Napa County," or a cypress giant, with dimensions of 90 feet in height and three feet in diameter. Some Sargent cypresses have dense, pyramidal crowns; others are more open and rounded. The foliage is usually not resinous and has little fragrance. Seed cones have 6 to 10 scales, are about one inch in diameter, and have inconspicuous umbos. The species has long been regarded as good and is accepted in *The Jepson Manual* and *Flora of North America*. For a discussion of hybridization between Sargent cypress and McNab cypress, see McNab cypress on page 175.

Sargent Cypress

Cupressus sargentii

From Griffin and Critchfield

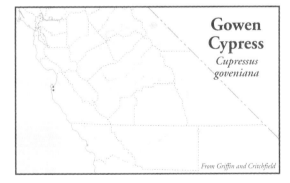

Gowen
Cypress
*Cupressus
goveniana*

From Griffin and Critchfield

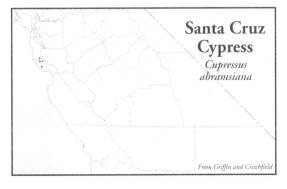

Santa Cruz
Cypress
*Cupressus
abramsiana*

From Griffin and Critchfield

Top, left: Gowen cypress grows with bishop pine in a closed-cone woodland. [Monterey Peninsula]
ROBERT TURNER
Top, right: Santa Cruz cypress grows among knobcone pine at Bonny Doon. [Santa Cruz Co.] ROBERT TURNER
Above: Santa Cruz cypress grows as a pygmy in sandstone near Bonny Doon. [Santa Cruz Co.]
ROBERT TURNER

189

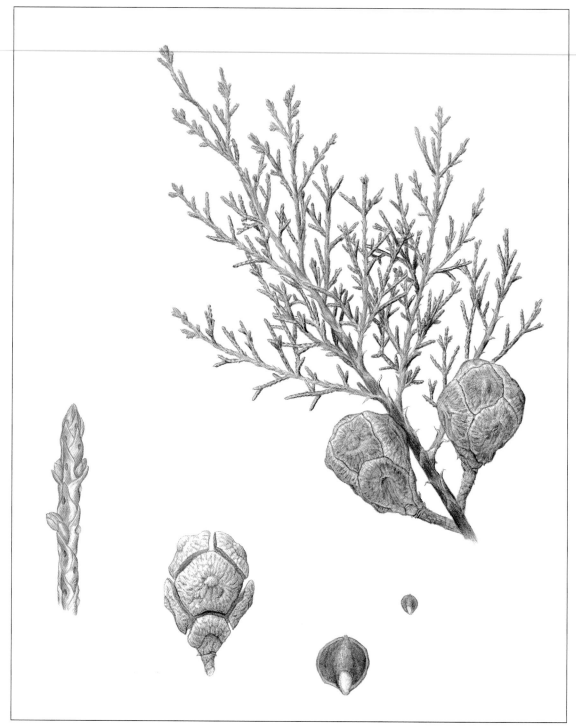

Piute Cypress • *Cupressus nevadensis*　　　ARTWORK: SUSAN BAZELL

PIUTE CYPRESS

Piute cypress occurs in a dozen or more groves in the Piute and Greenhorn mountains north and south of Lake Isabella in the southern Sierra Nevada. The largest grove covers more than 500 acres on the north face of Bald Eagle Peak in northeastern Kern County. It grows at 4,000 to 6,000 feet, where considerable amounts of heavy, wet snow falls in some years. Piute cypress is found on a variety of soils and some trees live over 500 years.

Conifers that associate with Piute cypress are gray pine, singleleaf pinyon, and California juniper; some arid-land shrubs include the gymnosperm *Ephedra.* Piute cypress bears seed at 15 years of age or less, and regenerates after fire-heat opens its serotinous cones. It has gray-green foliage which is very resinous and aromatic. Like all the cypresses, it bears its pollen in small (usually $1/8$ to $1/4$ inch long), oval pollen cones located at the tips of the branchlets. The shedding of the wind-dispersed pollen takes place in February or March and temporarily gives heavily-bearing trees a yellowish cast. Seed cones are to $1 1/2$ inches in diameter, have smooth scales, and weather to a silvery gray.

This cypress is morphologically quite similar to the Arizona cypress, *Cupressus arizonica,* a species widely distributed in the Southwest and Mexico. As a result, some taxonomists lump it into that species, and in *Flora of North America* it is so treated. In *The Jepson Manual* it is given somewhat more distinction by being recognized as subspecies *nevadensis* of Arizona cypress. (See page 197 for species photo and distribution map.)

Cuyamaca Cypress • *Cupressus stephensonii*

CUYAMACA CYPRESS

(ALSO CALLED ARIZONA CYPRESS)

In California Cuyamaca cypress is restricted to the southwestern slopes of Cuyamaca Peak in San Diego County between 4,000 and 5,500 feet. Here, fire-killed snags project from the green of live cypress thickets along the upper drainage of King Creek. The tallest trees are about 30 feet; one old report tells of a 48-footer no longer living. The cypresses grow amid chaparral and scattered Coulter pines. This grove has been reduced in size by fires that burned in 1950 and 1970, and like so many other cypress groves, this one could be lost in a single fire. Cuyamaca cypress was thought to be endemic to this one area until the early 1970s when scattered trees were discovered growing near the village of El Rincón in the Sierra Juárez of Baja California, 100 miles to the south.

Although taxonomists consider Cuyamaca cypress to be quite similar to Tecate cypress (found about seven miles away), the two species differ in several ways. Cuyamaca cypress foliage is more coarse to the touch, and it is resinous and gray-green while Tecate's is non-resinous and bright green. Cuyamaca cypress sheds its pollen in mid-summer, while Tecate and virtually all other cypresses shed in winter to spring.

The cones of Cuyamaca cypress measure up to an inch in diameter and have very conspicuous umbos up to $1/4$ inch long. If brought indoors for a few weeks, the cones readily open, shedding their crop of reddish brown seeds.

In *The Jepson Manual* Cuyamaca cypress is merely the typical subspecies of Arizona cypress, *Cupressus arizonica* ssp. *arizonica*. In *Flora of North America,* Cuyamaca cypress is simply incorporated into Arizona cypress without nomenclatural notice. (See page 197 for species photo and distribution map.)

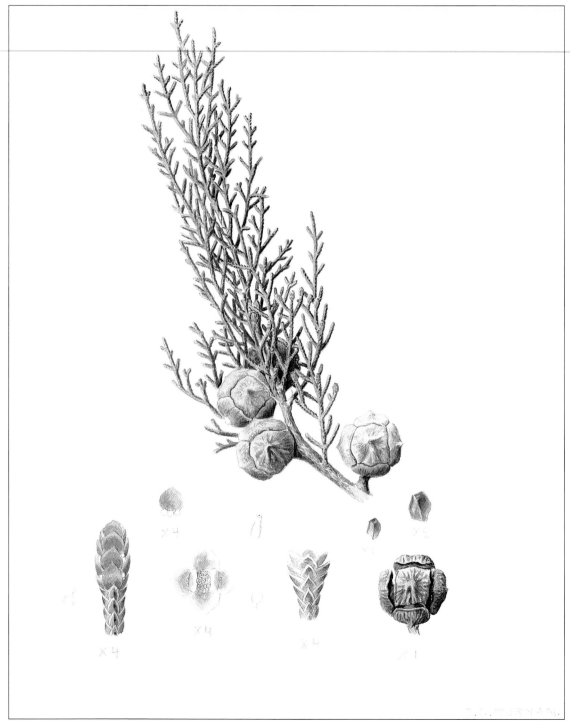

Tecate Cypress • *Cupressus forbesii*

TECATE CYPRESS

(ALSO CALLED FORBES CYPRESS)

Stands of this cypress are scattered across 250 miles of the Peninsular Ranges, with most of the population found in Baja California. It grows mainly on mesic, north-facing chaparral sites underlain by soils derived from gabbro and metavolcanic rocks that are low in nitrogen, phosphorus, calcium, and potassium.

The largest Tecate cypress population in California is southeast of San Diego on Otay Mountain, where it occurs mostly above 2,000 feet. The Otay Mountain groves are associated with no less than six rare and endangered plants. Another significant, border-straddling stand occurs five miles to the east in the Tecate Peak-Potrero Peak area; about 17 miles north of this stand is another smaller population, at about 4,000 feet, near Guatay in Cleveland National Forest. Nearly 100 miles separates these southern San Diego County stands from the other California colonies of Tecate cypress, which are located at the very north end of the Santa Ana Mountains around Sierra Peak. Found in Coal, Gypsum, and Fremont canyons, these northernmost Tecate cypresses together cover about 1,000 acres, much of it in dense stands. They are home to the oldest known Tecate cypresses, estimated at over 200 years, and perhaps the largest native specimen, which measures eight feet in diameter and 35 feet high. In Baja California, where there may be a few hundred groves of Tecate cypress, the species ranges south to Rancho El Ciprés, 170 miles beyond Tijuana.

Tecate cypress stands in California face various threats. Urbanization is pressing ever closer to the populations in the Santa Ana Mountains and on Otay Mountain. The cypresses on Tecate Peak, which covered about 260 acres in the 1920s, have been reduced to about a third of that by the 1990s due to an increased frequency of wildfires.

Tecate cypress tends to form multiple trunks and is often shrubby, but it occasionally reaches 30 feet in height. It has reddish brown bark that peels off in strips and bright green foliage that lacks surface resin. The serotinous seed cones are 1 to 1 1/2 inches in diameter.

In a fire, the resin sealing the cone scales vaporizes and bursts into flame, allowing the scales to immediately begin spreading and liberating the stored seeds. According to one study, the average interval between fires in Tecate cypress stands is 25 years, ranging from 15 to 63 years.

Tecate cypress is accepted as a good species by *The Jepson Manual,* but *Flora of North America* relegates it to variety *forbesii* of *Cupressus guadalupensis,* the Guadalupe cypress, whose typical variety is found only on Guadalupe Island, offshore from Baja California.

Top, left: Tecate cypress trunks display peeling, reddish brown bark. [Cleveland N.F.] JOHN EVARTS
Bottom, left: Tecate cypress at Guatay. [Cleveland N.F.] JOHN EVARTS
Above: Tecate cypress at Otay Mountain, one of the largest U.S. stands. [San Diego Co.] ROBERT TURNER

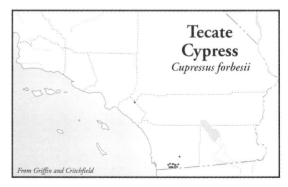

Tecate Cypress
Cupressus forbesii

From Griffin and Critchfield

Cuyamaca cypress is the only California cypress to shed pollen in summer. [San Diego Co.] DAVID LANNER

Piute cypress near Bodfish, California. [Kern Co.]
ROBERT TURNER

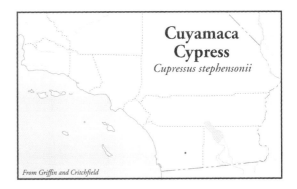

Cuyamaca Cypress
Cupressus stephensonii

From Griffin and Critchfield

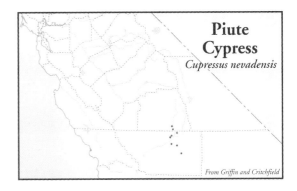

Piute Cypress
Cupressus nevadensis

From Griffin and Critchfield

FALSE CYPRESSES

This small genus, made up of only seven or eight species, boasts some of the most beautiful members of the cypress family. In North America there is one species on the Atlantic coast and two on the Pacific. Both of the latter enter California, though neither is extensively distributed here. Their relatives grow across the Pacific and include one species in Taiwan that is among the largest of Asian trees. The *Shen-mu,* or Sacred Tree, of Taiwan's Alishan Range is reputed to exceed 2,000 years of age.

Like several other cypress family genera, the false cypresses have durable, fine-grained wood, aromatic foliage of scalelike leaves, and fibrous bark. Their cones are globose in shape, and leathery or fleshy, with a little umbo on each scale. They are typically found in moist, shady forests among other conifers.

Chamaecyparis differs from most true cypresses of the genus *Cupressus* in having flattened branchlets and non-woody cones. These characters may not indicate deep-seated evolutionary differences, however, and some taxonomists have lumped the genera together in *Cupressus* (see for example *The Jepson Manual*).

Opposite: Port Orford cedar, the largest, rarest, and most at risk of the New World false cypresses. [Siskiyou N.F., OR] BARBARA ULLIAN

Alaska-Cedar • *Chamaecyparis nootkatensis*

ALASKA-CEDAR

(ALSO CALLED YELLOW CYPRESS)

Alaska-cedar, a tree of coastal mountains from southeast Alaska to southwestern Oregon, is represented in California by a few small groves in the Siskiyou Mountains. These are at Mount Emily, Little Grayback, Preston Peak, Devil's Punchbowl, and Bear Lake. They are on north-facing slopes or cirques from 4,500 to 6,900 feet, and most consist of populations of scattered shrubs of this cedar, which is often dwarfed at high elevations. Alaska-cedars often grow in avalanche chutes and have drooping, yellowish foliage made up of scale leaves with sharp, spreading tips. The cones are similar to those of Port Orford cedar, but have only four to six scales. Canada's oldest known tree, an Alaska-cedar with 1,636 annual rings in its stump, is said to have perished on Vancouver Island in the early 1990s. (See page 205 for species photo and distribution map.)

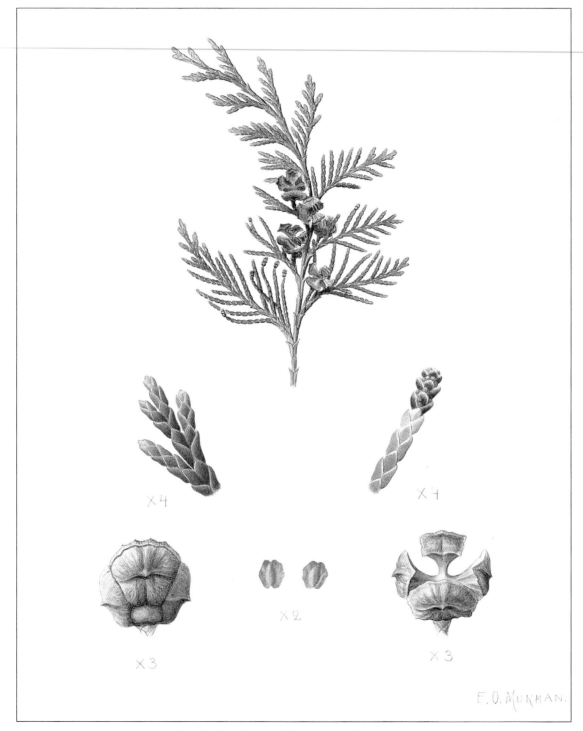

Port Orford Cedar • *Chamaecyparis lawsoniana*

PORT ORFORD CEDAR

When mushroom hunters go afield to pick their prey in the national forests of northwest California where Port Orford cedar grows, they must first and last steam-clean their vehicles, and they may find many roads closed to them. When loggers operate in those same areas, and up the Oregon coast, they too must clean their trucks and heavy equipment before moving it. And when federal foresters depart at the end of a workday from forests where this cedar is found, they scrape the mud from their boots to avoid contaminating the soil of other places. These cleansing rituals are a belated, if well-intentioned, attempt to stem the spread of *Phytophthora lateralis,* a parasitic, root-rotting fungus that kills Port Orford cedar.

The fungus probably originated in a commercial nursery in Oregon and then moved into the natural forest. Within four decades it has spread throughout nearly the whole range of Port Orford cedar. This fungus digests only Port Orford cedar roots, starting at the tender tips and working up the root to the stem base. It kills cedars of all ages and has elicited no signs yet of natural resistance in the cedar population. Its spores are spread naturally by splashing or flowing water, and they are transported when spore-laden soil is moved by man, logging or construction machinery, and animals (elk are high on the list of suspects). First found in the natural forest in the northern part of cedar's range in the 1950s, it had reached Potato Patch Creek in the drainage of the Klamath River by the mid-1990s.

In most forests where Port Orford cedar occurs, the cedars are scattered among several other conifers. Thus when they die—and they will be dying from this root rot for years to come—the gaps they leave will be filled by their neighbors' crowns, much as oaks and hickories filled in behind the blighted American chestnuts of the eastern broad-leaved forest not so many years ago. Just as the chestnut has averted extinction, though narrowly, so too, probably, will Port Orford cedar. As it is further decimated, the fungus that depends upon it will have less and less success in finding the survivors, and eventually an uneasy balance of parasite and host may result.

What will we have lost when we effectively lose Port Orford cedar? We will have lost a large tree with a cylindrical bole supported by a flaring base wrapped in foot-thick bark that fissures into long, stringy-edged plates. Not the biggest of northwestern trees, but one that could occasionally put 200 feet between its tip and its base, Port Orford cedar seems at home among Douglas-fir and other local giants. The species can live for 600 years and is the source for a vast number of varieties, or "cultivars," many of which are patented and cloned from oddities found in nurseries. Port Orford cedar is well known in Europe—especially in Britain and the Netherlands—where approximately

200 different cultivars are found in manicured parks and gardens.

The loss of Port Orford cedar will be felt in trans-Pacific commerce, as well. Japanese buyers have created a robust market for the light, strong, fine-grained, creamy heartwood, which is redolent of volatile ginger-scented oil and toxic to termites. They use it for coffins, temples, and prestigious homes. Having long ago harvested the native populations of their own *Chamaecyparis obtusa,* the hinoki cypress, Japanese buyers of fine woods have looked east for decades, and have paid us handsomely to export our fast-declining supply. Perhaps the most important loss will be the elimination of viable, biologically capable populations of one

Port Orford cedar as an upland species. [Shasta-Trinity N.F.] CONNIE MILLAR

Port Orford cedar as a riparian species. [Siskiyou N.F., OR] BARBARA ULLIAN

Alaska-cedar is often a pioneer species on avalanche chutes in the Cascades. [Cascade Range, OR]
DAVID IMPER

more organism that evolution placed on our territory, and that just by being here, made our territory unique.

IDENTIFYING PORT ORFORD CEDAR

At a distance: Mature, forest-grown trees have narrow crowns of somewhat drooping branches on a tapering trunk covered with deeply fissured, brownish gray bark. The foliage is yellow green to dark green, but occasionally has a bluish cast.

Standing beneath it: The many seed cones in the crown are bluish gray in spring, green in summer, and purplish to reddish brown when they open in the fall. They are 1/3 to 1/2 inch in diameter.

In the hand: Cones have 6 to 10 shieldlike scales bearing two to four seeds each. Each of

the broad "facial" leaves usually has a linear resin gland on its upper surface, unlike the Alaska-cedar with which it can be confused.

HABITAT

It grows on wet coastal sites, such as river terraces, with Douglas-fir. The inland populations are often on drier sites underlain by ultramafic rocks; here it is found in association with Jeffrey, lodgepole, and western white pines, and incense-cedar.

DISTRIBUTION

In California Port Orford cedar is found mainly in Humboldt and Del Norte counties, notably in the Klamath River drainage, south to the area west of the Trinity and Klamath rivers. The inland distribution is in the upper Trinity and Sacramento River systems, where Shasta, Siskiyou, and Trinity counties meet. Elevations range from just above sea level to 5,000 feet. Elsewhere it is found in southwestern Oregon.

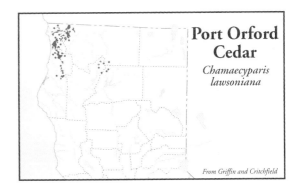

Port Orford Cedar

Chamaecyparis lawsoniana

From Griffin and Critchfield

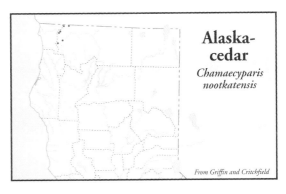

Alaska-cedar

Chamaecyparis nootkatensis

From Griffin and Critchfield

INCENSE-CEDARS

In many older tree books the incense-cedars and a few other species of the Cupressaceae, or cypress family, were lumped together in the genus *Libocedrus.* As a result, our one native incense-cedar was referred to as *Libocedrus decurrens,* the name conferred upon it in 1853, when John Torrey described specimens sent him by explorer John Charles Frémont. Comfortable as foresters and botanists were with that name, there was remarkably little complaining when Rudolf Florin suggested a new generic name based on rather minor technical differences among species. Thus our tree has in recent years become accepted as a member of the new genus *Calocedrus.* The two other species in this genus are native to Taiwan and to southern China and Burma. All have wood so durable in contact with the soil that carpenters have hewn coffin boards from ancient logs dug out of alluvial deposits in China. *Calocedrus* species have aromatic, scalelike leaves, fibrous bark, and cones made up of six leathery scales bearing seeds that have two wings, one long, the other short.

Opposite: Incense-cedar, the only member of its genus found in North America, is one of California's most common forest trees. [Yosemite N.P.] PAT O'HARA

Incense-Cedar • *Calocedrus decurrens*

INCENSE-CEDAR

In his report, *Forest Conditions in the Northern Sierra Nevada,* published by the U.S. Geological Survey in 1902, John Leiberg called attention to a population explosion that even today has escaped general notice: the increase of incense-cedar on the Sierra Nevada west-side. Leiberg, a seasoned observer of western forests, pointed out that this member of the cypress family was rarely cut by the otherwise assiduous lumberers of the late nineteenth century because frequent "worm holes" made its boards practically valueless. Therefore the disproportionate number of incense-cedar seed trees that were left standing seeded disproportionately into the cutovers where pines had previously dominated. The result, once the pines themselves seeded in a new generation and outgrew the slow-paced cedars, was a rich understory of incense-cedar in the mixed-conifer forest. Suppression of forest fires further favored the survival of fire-tender young cedars, allowing them to survive in great numbers.

This forest management history has probably been good for chestnut-backed and mountain chickadees, which overwinter in woods thick with incense-cedars; these birds flake and chip away at the thin bark of branches and young tree-trunks in search of the scale insects that take refuge there. It is also good for those Americans who eschew the use of greasy-inked ballpoint pens, because incense-cedar is the unrivaled champion of available domestic pencilwoods. It may not be so good for those foresters and woodworkers who must pass through thickets of incense-cedar on their way somewhere, for those thin, dead, lower limbs seem always positioned to welt a cheek or poke an unsuspecting eye.

Incense-cedar's relatively fire-resistant bark allows old trees to survive repeated wildfires in California's highly combustible forests. [Mendocino N.F.]. GEORGE WARD

Like most "cedars"—and the name is applied to members of several genera—this one has heartwood that is reddish brown, soft, light, fine-grained, and pleasantly aromatic; sharpen a cedar pencil to prove it. The tannins, phenols, and gums that give the heartwood character also retard decay and repel moths; this is why incense-cedar has been traditionally used for railway ties, posts, greenhouse benches, shingles, mud sills, siding, decking, and cedar chests. Even the pocket-rot-afflicted wood that repelled early loggers now commands a fancy price for interior paneling.

In contrast to the pine family species with which it associates, incense-cedar sheds its dust-like pollen on the wind in time for Christmas and the New Year. Suddenly, trees in the open appear strangely yellow, and gusts of wind drive puffs of yellow cloud from their crowns. The snow beneath them bears a yellow stain until new snow layers cover it.

Young, open-grown incense-cedars can be almost perfect pyramids clothed in their fernlike fronds of scale-leafed foliage. As they get older and larger their rounding crowns are elevated on tapering cinnamon red-barked trunks that flare at the base. Old trees, veterans of centuries, usually carry deep basal fire scars, pitchfork tops, and butts tunneled by carpenter ants.

It would not surprise John Leiberg to know that incense-cedar still reproduces with abandon, or that its population is increasing even where ozone kills other species. Incense-cedar is susceptible to annosus, Armillaria, and black stain root rot; all three of these fungi still bring big, old trees crashing to the forest floor.

IDENTIFYING INCENSE-CEDAR

At a distance: Mature trees have yellowish green crowns of gracefully drooping branchlets and trunks clothed in cinnamon-red bark.

Standing beneath it: The bark is thick, fibrous, and furrowed. Pendent in the crown are many slender, spindle-shaped, inch-long, brown cones, whose two longest scales open like a duck's bill in late summer.

In the hand: The sprays of foliage are made up of elongate, flattened scale-leaves arranged in four rows surrounding the branchlet, giving it a jointed appearance. The leaves are aromatic when crushed.

HABITAT

This species tolerates a wide array of soils—even ultramafic rock—derived from a broad variety of parent rocks, and it experiences annual precipitation that ranges from 15 to 80 inches. It usually occurs between 2,000 and 7,000 feet in the Sierra Nevada, and to 8,000 feet in southern California's mountains.

DISTRIBUTION

It is ubiquitous in the Sierra Nevada, especially on the west slope. In northern California it is also found in the Cascades, North Coast and Klamath ranges, and Modoc Plateau. In southern California it is scattered in the Tehachapis and South Coast, Transverse, and Peninsular ranges, growing as far south as Sierra San Pedro Mártir in Baja California. Elsewhere it extends through Oregon nearly to the Columbia River.

Incense-cedar grows in mid-elevation forests throughout California. [Shasta-Trinity N.F.] RON LANNER

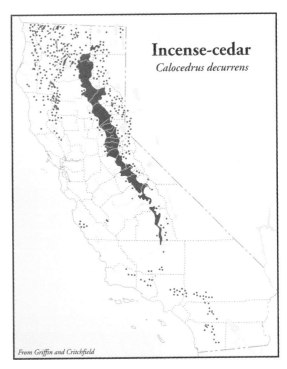

Incense-cedar
Calocedrus decurrens

From Griffin and Critchfield

ARBORVITAES

This is another of those small genera of conifers—similar to Douglas-firs, hemlocks, false-cypresses, and incense-cedars—whose members are distributed in Asia, on the west coast of North America, and often with an eastern North American representative as well. The *Thuja* of the northeastern states and adjacent Canadian provinces is northern white-cedar, while its cousin on the other side of the continent is western redcedar. Both have aromatic foliage of scale-leaves, small, leathery cones that bear tiny, laterally winged seeds, fibrous bark, and durable heartwood that is fine-grained, aromatic, and deeply colored. *Thujas* are trees of moist forests and often grace lakeshores and riverbanks.

Opposite: The nooks and crannies of ancient redcedars gather windborne soil particles and become seedling nurseries. [Olympic N.P., WA] DAVID MUENCH

Western Redcedar • *Thuja plicata*

Thuja plicata

WESTERN REDCEDAR

California's western redcedar stands are a minor southern extension of the species' main distribution. We therefore do not often hear of western redcedar, if we hear of it at all, except in dismissive tones. The great pitchfork-topped giants, common to southeast Alaska, British Columbia, Washington, and even Oregon, have not in historic times been as dominant in California's wet north-coast woods as they have in forests further north.

For Native American tribes who lived in the Northwest's coastal forests, western redcedar was a central resource in their material cultures. The tree's great size, the precise grain, softness, and rot-resistance of its wood, and its proximity to tidewater and riverbanks led to its extensive use for crafting fleets of voyaging and trading canoes and giant totem poles. Entire villages built from huge cedar logs and broad cedar planks dotted the Pacific Northwest coast when Captain Cook sailed into the region in 1778.

To harvest western redcedar, teams of men would assemble scaffolding to elevate themselves above a tree's buttressed base. They then set red-hot stones in a cavity chiseled into the wood, repeating this until they had burned through the trunk and felled the tree. Scores of men would drag the downed tree over log rollers, to the sea or a nearby river, and float it home where wide planks would be split from it with mauls and wedges. Precisely squared and thinned planks were grooved, and the grooves steamed over wet seaweed piled over hot rocks buried in the beach sand. Then the planks were laboriously bent along the softened wood of the grooves to form water-tight boxes. Countless implements

Western redcedar was the most important resource in the material culture of northwestern Native Americans, providing everything from cooking boxes to seafaring canoes. [Olympic N.F., WA] PAT O'HARA

were fashioned from cedar wood, and its bark was used for all things woven.

Today western redcedar is a mainstay of the housing industry, providing hand-split roof shingles, siding, and many other specialty products. Its heartwood, reddish brown and aromatic when first opened up, weathers to a characteristic gray. The popularity of cedar shingles, and their considerable cost, has caused more than a few trees to be spirited out of national forests in the dark of the night. There is a growing awareness, however, of the flammability of cedar shingles, which are often ignited by the windborne embers of advancing wildfires; as a result, a number of California municipalities now prohibit roofing with cedar shingles, treated or not.

IDENTIFYING WESTERN REDCEDAR

At a distance: The trunk is straight and tapered, with a buttressed or swollen base. Upper limbs are horizontal, lower ones droop; but most have upturned tips. Foliage is lighter green than that of associated conifers. In the Pacific Northwest it can exceed 200 feet in height and 10 feet in diameter.
Standing beneath it: The bark is reddish brown to gray and fibrous. Frondlike masses of foliage hang loosely from the branches. Trunks often have deep seams where windborne soil collects and seeds of cedars and hemlocks germinate.
In the hand: The delicate, flattened sprays of scale leaves arranged in opposite pairs are delightfully aromatic when crushed in the fingers. In autumn, masses of oblong, brown cones, to $1/2$ inch long, hang pendent; they are made up of four to six pairs of opposite scales.

HABITAT

In California, western redcedar grows under temperate rainforest conditions alongside redwood, Sitka spruce, western hemlock, and Douglas-fir. Summers are relatively cool, winters are mild, rainfall is heavy and supplemented by ample fog-drip. It is sometimes found in boggy soil.

Western redcedar is scattered in California's temperate rainforests. [Six Rivers N.F.] WILLIAM M. SMITHEY

DISTRIBUTION

Look for western redcedar in the lower Mad River drainage and south of Ferndale, in Humboldt County. It is less common in coastal northern Humboldt County and Del Norte County. Elsewhere it ranges up the coast to Sumner Strait, Alaska through the Coast Ranges and Cascades of Oregon, Washington, and British Columbia. It also has a separate distribution in the Rocky Mountains of Idaho, Montana, and British Columbia.

Western Redcedar
Thuja plicata

From Griffin and Critchfield

JUNIPERS

It is sometimes hard to visualize junipers as members of the cypress family because their frosted, fleshy, berrylike fruits hardly resemble the hard, woody cone of a cypress. But look closely and observe the faint ridges marking the edges of the scales of these "berrycones," where early in their development they have fused and then remained fleshy. Some junipers are shrubby, even prostrate, while others become massive old trees. Their juvenile foliage is needlelike, but later most species develop scale leaves that are closely appressed to the stem. The sexes are usually segregated on separate trees. The aroma of the foliage and cones emanates from the same compounds that flavor gin. The purplish, aromatic, durable heartwood of juniper contrasts sharply with the narrow shell of bone white sapwood that surrounds it.

Junipers grow widely across the Northern Hemisphere and often form open woodlands with various species of pine. California is home to four junipers; one of these, the circumboreal common juniper *(Juniperus communis)*, is a shrub wherever it grows in the mountain West.

Opposite: A ragged old Sierra juniper grows alongside the historic California Trail above Donner Lake. [Tahoe N.F.] JEFF GNASS.

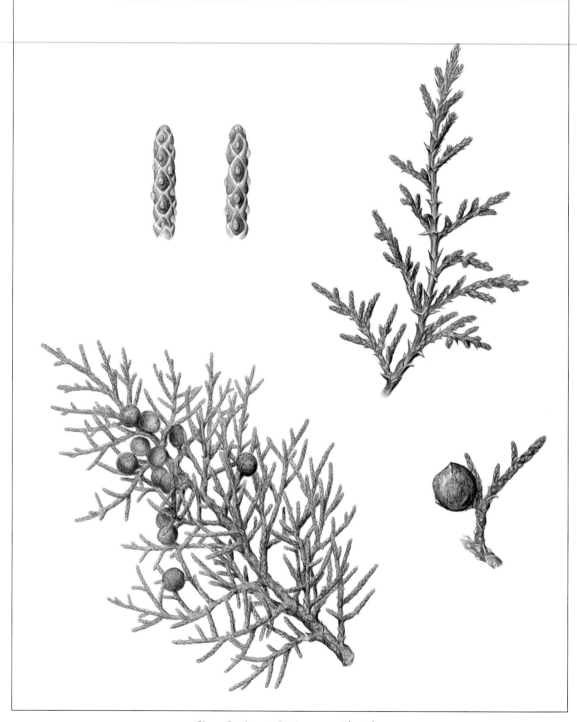

Sierra Juniper • *Juniperus occidentalis*

ARTWORK: SUSAN BAZELL

SIERRA JUNIPER

(ALSO CALLED WESTERN JUNIPER)

This is one of the Sierra Nevada's most striking trees. Many travelers encounter it for the first time in high passes, like Tioga, Sonora, and Carson. Here, at 7,000 to 10,000 feet, one is amazed to see what first appear to be shrunken giant sequoias clinging to vertical faces of white granite. On closer examination, one notices that the enormously thick but very short, cinnamon red trunks support compact, often wind-pruned crowns of scaly, gray-green juniper foliage, liberally peppered with frosty blue berries. A whiff of crushed branchlets and the sight of the little "spikes" found on all juniper fruits settles the issue. This satisfying tree is indeed a juniper, probably the most spectacular of all its far-flung tribe.

In high-elevation habitats, Sierra juniper grows near lodgepole, Jeffrey, and whitebark pines, mountain hemlock, and California red fir. It does not form intimate associations with these other species, but instead occupies rocky habitats among their stands. It survives in places these pine-family trees cannot invade, where only its searching roots can thread themselves into rocky fissures in the quest for water. Such habitats are patchy, so the Sierra junipers are scattered in ones or twos, or in small groves—never, in the Sierra Nevada, in extensive woodlands.

Sierra juniper occupies quite a different landscape on the Modoc Plateau. Here it forms extensive woodlands, growing principally with sagebrush in rolling hill and plateau country. These populations, as well as those in the Cascades, are usually considered the typical subspecies, *occidentalis,* while those to the south, mainly concentrated in the Sierra Nevada, are subspecies *australis.* Their differences are summarized in "Identifying Sierra Juniper," beginning on the next page.

The largest and oldest Sierra juniper is said to be the Bennett Juniper of Deadman Creek. This tree, growing on a private inholding within Stanislaus National Forest, is somewhat over 85 feet tall and almost 13 feet in diameter. Although this champion grows on the west slope of the Sierra, it is found in a patch of mule ears and Jeffrey pine that more resembles an eastern Sierra landscape. Waldo S. Glock, one of the pioneers of dendrochronology, measured this tree in 1937 and estimated its age at 3,000 years. Though Glock was an experienced and careful investigator, he had to base his age estimate on very short increment cores taken

from a massive trunk, with an unavoidably large risk of error. Even today, the Bennett Juniper sports a deep, luxuriant crown supported upon a full-barked, tapering trunk that is surmounted by only a negligible amount of dead wood. This is not how ancient trees ordinarily look, however, and the Bennett Juniper may be an impostor. Enormous Sierra junipers also occur in the locale of Onyx Summit in the San Bernardino Mountains.

IDENTIFYING SIERRA JUNIPER
At a distance: Mature trees are short and broad-crowned and often grow on bare rock. Trunks

Junipers form no buds, so their shoots grow whenever climate permits. Therefore, they do not form reliably annual rings, and exact ages cannot be determined. [Lava Beds N.M.] JEFF GNASS

The Bennett Juniper, shown here, may or may not be 3,000 years old. [Stanislaus N.F.] WHIT BRONAUGH

are strongly tapered, with ascending limbs that bear dense masses of deep gray-green foliage. **Standing beneath it:** Masses of typical juniper "berries" (actually seed cones) litter the ground after falling. Before they drop in the fall, the berries give the tree crown a frosted appearance due to their waxy surface.
In the hand: The scale leaves are often glazed whitish with dried secretions from leaf resin glands. Crushed foliage has a distinct aroma of gin. The leaves are arranged around the stems, mostly in threes in subspecies *australis,* in twos and threes in subspecies *occidentalis.* Trees either have all male or all female cones in subspecies *australis,* while both sexes are found on the same tree in subspecies *occidentalis.*

HABITAT
Subspecies *occidentalis* usually occurs from 4,000 to 5,000 feet in northeastern California, in pure stands or with ponderosa pine.

Subspecies *australis* is found on thin, stony soils or bare rock, usually from 6,500 to over 10,000 feet in the Sierra Nevada, where it is often exposed to severe winds. Its common associates are Jeffrey, whitebark, western white, limber, singleleaf pinyon and lodgepole pines, as well as mountain hemlock and white and red firs.

DISTRIBUTION
In California it ranges from the Scott Mountains in the eastern Klamath Ranges across the Shasta Valley and Cascades and onto the Modoc Plateau. It also occurs throughout the Sierra Nevada, mainly down the crest and east slope to southern Tulare County, with scattered stands on the westside. It is extensively distributed north and east of Big Bear Lake in the San Bernardino Mountains. Outlier populations are common in the San Gabriel Mountains, less so in the Panamint, Inyo, and White mountains. Elsewhere it ranges through eastern Oregon and Washington.

Sierra Juniper
Juniperus occidentalis

ssp. *occidentalis*
ssp. *australis*

From Griffin and Critchfield

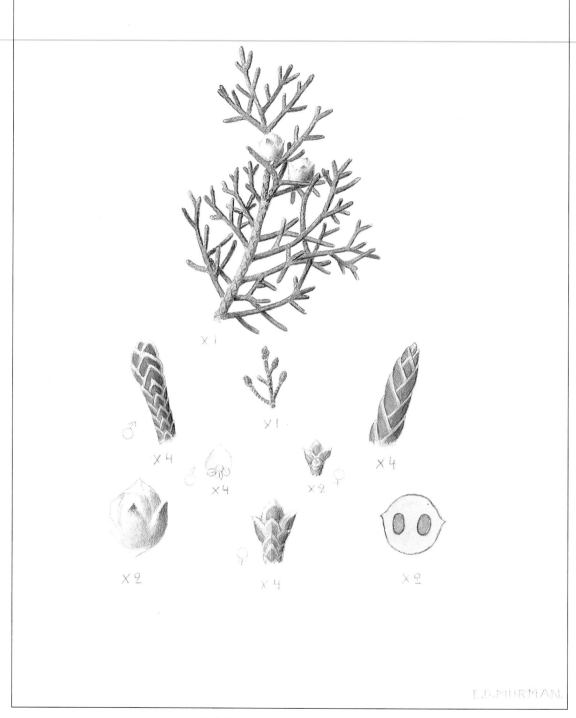

Utah Juniper • *Juniperus osteosperma*

UTAH JUNIPER

The vast coniferous woodland of the Great Basin that carpets much of Nevada and western Utah begins on the Sierra Nevada eastside and in the ranges of the Mojave Desert. These are the westernmost mingling-grounds of singleleaf pinyon and Utah juniper, among the most stress-resistant and drought-hardy trees of the American silva. From here, Utah juniper spreads east to New Mexico and north to Montana. Wherever it is found, it seems to select the harshest of possible habitats, save those of salt flats.

Utah juniper is as rugged in appearance as in character. The coarse foliage of this small, spreading tree is often aggregated into dense, globose clumps, and feels like coral not yet fully hardened. Its branchlets, with their exfoliating sheets of reddish bark, are stiff and stout, and the short, forked trunks are covered with gray-brown bark that sloughs off in shaggy, fibrous strips. The berrylike seed cones are larger than those of most junipers, sometimes exceeding $^1/_2$ inch in diameter, and they mature to a bronze color coated with a whitish frosting. Utah juniper usually produces both male and female cones on the same tree, in contrast to California juniper and most Sierra junipers. Though they are generally round-crowned and spreading, Utah junipers seem to occasionally mimic the form of other conifers: you may find that a fir or pine, high on some forsaken, nearly unclimbable rocky point, was really a Utah juniper. California's largest Utah juniper, said to measure 27 $^1/_2$ feet around at ground level, grows on the Inyo Mountains' crest just north of Waucoba Pass.

Juniper firewood, including that of this species, was a favored cooking fuel of Great Basin Indians. The wood was also used for carving utensils and other objects because it is fine-textured, soft, and easily worked. The berrylike cones of Utah juniper were a Great Basin foodstuff, and the shredded bark found its way into rope, sandals, and other clothing. Birds, too, eat the fruits, as do coyotes and jackrabbits. Excretion of the bony seeds *(osteosperma)* disperses them into new habitats, allowing junipers to become established there.

Juniper's outer sapwood is almost white in color, but the aromatic heartwood contains an accumulation of chemical substances that color it deep red. Thus junipers are often called cedars by people who know woods better than they do botanical nomenclature, and junipers are surely responsible for such inland California place-names as Cedar Glen, Cedar Grove, and Cedarville. Another result of juniper's heartwood compounds is an almost legendary resistance to decay. Millions of Utah junipers have served generations of ranchers in the humble role of fence-post.

Not many pests afflict Utah juniper, perhaps because of the repellent powers of its heartwood compounds and foliage oils. A dwarf-mistletoe parasitizes its limbs, and a gall-forming insect infests its shoot tips, causing purple, budlike

Utah juniper is one of the West's most widespread conifers. It usually forms low woodlands with a pinyon pine species, often with a sagebrush understory. [White Mts.] DAVID LANNER

Utah juniper provided most of the Great Basin's fence posts. [Inyo N.F.] STEPHEN INGRAM

structures to form. These organisms do not kill trees, but fire does, and when the woodland burns, junipers are quickly decimated. Researchers report that Utah juniper hybridizes to a limited extent with Sierra juniper in northwestern Nevada, just east of California's Warner Mountains.

IDENTIFYING UTAH JUNIPER
At a distance: It is a small tree with a single, often forked trunk, covered with grayish brown bark and a spreading crown of yellowish green foliage.
Standing beneath it: The bark peels off in shredded, fibrous strips. The foliage is often clumped in discrete, globose masses.
In the hand: The foliage is rigid and coarse to

the touch. Many of the scale leaves are arranged on the shoot in opposite pairs.

HABITAT
Utah juniper is typically seen in open woodland with singleleaf pinyon. It usually grows between 4,000 and 8,000 feet (to 9,500 feet in the White Mountains) on arid slopes or foothills, on thin, stony, often alkaline soils. In addition to the pinyon, big sagebrush is a common associate.

DISTRIBUTION
In California it occurs along lower slopes of the eastside Sierra Nevada, Great Basin Ranges (Sweetwater, Inyo, and White mountains), in several east Mojave ranges (Mid Hills, New York, and Providence mountains), and on desert-facing slopes of the San Gabriel and San Bernardino mountains. Elsewhere it ranges across Nevada, Utah, Colorado, Arizona, New Mexico, and north through Wyoming to Montana.

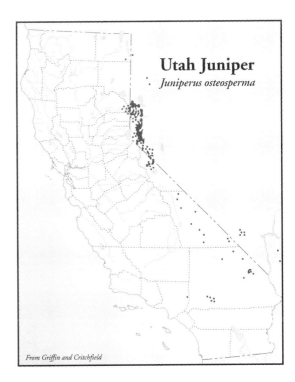

Utah Juniper
Juniperus osteosperma

From Griffin and Critchfield

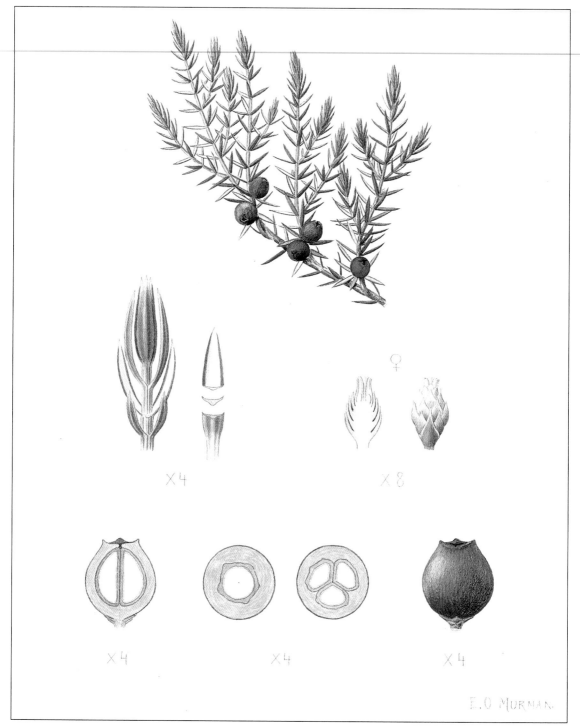

Common Juniper • *Juniperus communis*

COMMON JUNIPER

Common juniper is the world's most widely distributed conifer, spanning all of Europe and northern Asia, as well as North America from coast to coast. In the western United States it is represented by variety *saxatilis,* which is a compact, prostrate shrub found at high elevations. On Wheeler Peak, Nevada, common juniper grows at more than 11,000 feet among ancient Great Basin bristlecone pines. A sectioned, prostrate stem collected here was found to have 208 annual rings along a one-inch radius.

Common juniper foliage is made up entirely of awl-shaped needles that are prickly to the touch and less than an inch in length. Its cones are 1/3 inch in diameter and blue-black when mature. The bark is reddish brown in color and peels off in strips. This is an easily identified conifer and botanists who look for it in alpine and subalpine locations may help extend its known California range beyond the few areas from which it has been reported. It occurs in the Trinity Alps and Salmon Mountains of the Klamath Ranges, in scattered locales of the northern Sierra, and in the eastern Sierra by Ellery Lake and in Lundy Canyon. (See page 233 for species photo and distribution map.)

California Juniper • *Juniperus californica*

CALIFORNIA JUNIPER

This is the shrubby juniper of the inner Coast Ranges, extending from northern California south to the Peninsular Ranges of California and Baja California and eastwards through the Mojave Desert to southern Nevada and northwestern Arizona. The most detailed of the few studies made of this plant found that it usually has 14 to 24 gray-barked stems and averages about 11 feet in height. Its low stature and lack of a single main trunk mark it as a shrub, but an occasional individual has been known to reach 25 feet or more.

When California juniper and Utah juniper intermix, their contrasting sizes and forms allow them to be easily distinguished. In the San Bernardino Mountains, California juniper usually grows in creosote bush scrub just below the woodland of singleleaf pinyon and Utah juniper. In various California locales it occasionally associates with cypresses as well. (See page 232 for species photo and page 233 for distribution map.)

California juniper is usually found as a large shrub among plants of the desert scrub community. This specimen bears a heavy cone crop. [Joshua Tree N.P.] FRED HIRSCHMANN

Above: Common juniper is a low, circumboreal, subalpine shrub, whose California range is poorly known. [Six Rivers N.F.] WILLIAM M. SMITHEY

California Juniper

Juniperus californica

◆ Denotes counties where specimens collected

From *SMASCH Database*

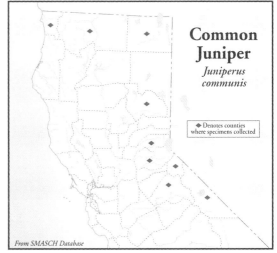

Common Juniper

Juniperus communis

◆ Denotes counties where specimens collected

From *SMASCH Database*

THE BALDCYPRESS FAMILY

From 1824, when English botanist David Don gave redwood the name *Taxodium sempervirens,* until the 1970s, redwood was usually viewed as a member of the baldcypress family, or Taxodiaceae. The closely related giant sequoia, discovered in 1852, was also placed in this family, along with the baldcypress of the southeastern states. But over the last century, and especially since the 1970s, some taxonomists have argued that the "taxodiads" have as much in common with members of the cypress family, or Cupressaceae, as they do with each other, and therefore all of these conifers should be lumped into an expanded cypress family. Biochemical evidence has tended to support that position. *Flora of North America* follows this concept, while *The Jepson Manual* does not. Until more evidence emerges in support of this view, it seems prudent to keep redwood and giant sequoia in their traditional family.

Opposite: The Bull Buck, over 246 feet tall and 99 feet in girth, exemplifies the giant sequoia resource in the national forests. [Sierra N.F.] BILL EVARTS

SEQUOIA & SEQUOIA-DENDRON

These closely related genera each contain only one species. The species descriptions therefore also serve as genus descriptions. Coast redwood and giant sequoia are California's most enormous forest trees. Before examining these famous organisms, it is important to dispel some of the confusion that has been sown by their history of name changes.

Redwood has had a rather stable nomenclature. David Don named it *Taxodium sempervirens* in 1824 because of its general similarity to baldcypress, *Taxodium distichum,* of the southeastern United States. In 1847 Austrian conifer specialist S. F. L. Endlicher transferred redwood into a new genus, *Sequoia,* believing it differed enough from the baldcypresses to warrant a genus of its own. Thus redwood became known as *Sequoia sempervirens* (D. Don) Endl. and has remained so to this day. By contrast, the giant sequoia, also originally described as a species of *Taxodium,* was later placed in genera specially created for it and now all but forgotten: *Wellingtonia* and *Washingtonia.* Then it was classified as another member of the genus *Sequoia,* along with the redwood. Several decades went by without changes, but in 1939 Illinois botanist J. T. Buchholz took giant sequoia out of that genus and into a new one: *Sequoiadendron.*

These changes were based on strong biological arguments. For example, seed development takes one year in redwood, but two in giant

Opposite: From southern Oregon to central California, redwood is a creature of the fog. [Del Norte Coast Redwoods S.P.]. CARR CLIFTON

sequoia. Redwood cones cease their growth at maturity, but giant sequoia cones may continue growing for many years. In total, Buchholz identified nine outstanding differences in the species' patterns of embryo development. Later, it was learned that while giant sequoia has the normal diploid (two sets) chromosome number, redwood is hexaploid (six sets), the only conifer known to have this rare trait. For these reasons most botanists, and eventually foresters as well, accepted the new status of giant sequoia.

The common name of *Sequoia sempervirens* has almost always been redwood, or coast redwood. Its cousin has gone by many names, including bigtree, giant sequoia, Sierra redwood, and Wellingtonia. The last is totally inappropriate, but the others are equally acceptable.

Above, top: Giant Tree at Bull Creek: 363 feet tall, 53 in girth. [Humboldt Redwoods S.P.] WHIT BRONAUGH
Above, bottom: Redwood often bears huge burls. [Big Basin Redwoods S.P.] JOHN EVARTS
Opposite: White fir dominates the understory of unburned sequoia groves. [Yosemite N.P.] LARRY ULRICH

Redwood • *Sequoia sempervirens*

REDWOOD

(ALSO CALLED COAST REDWOOD)

Among California's many remarkable conifers, none is more famous than coast redwood. Its ecological and physical uniqueness, and the never-ending demand for its lumber, have surrounded the redwood in controversy. Indeed, since the birth of the redwood preservation movement in the Santa Cruz Mountains more than a century ago, no other North American forest tree has been more emblematic of environmental activism than this giant of the coastal fogbelt.

Redwood is generally acknowledged to be the world's tallest tree, having reached a verified height of 367.8 feet, according to measurements made in the mid-1970s. One of Australia's many *Eucalyptus* species, the mountain ash, has seriously challenged redwood's reputation; a qualified surveyor measured a 375-foot-high specimen, but the figure was never verified and was not officially accepted. That eucalyptus was cut down decades ago and cannot be remeasured. Every year, hopeful naturalists armed with theodolites, hypsometers, levels, and other devices, prowl the dank old-growth of the national and state redwood parks in hopes of bagging a new contender for world's tallest tree. The situation is dynamic: new growth can create new contenders, while top-kill, breakage, and wind-throw take established giants out of the competition. Trees standing on riverine terraces may have their lower trunks buried in deep silt deposited by floods and forming a new ground level above the original grade. New roots then grow into the freshly-deposited soil, making the tree appear to have originated several feet higher up than it actually has. Measurement of such a tree's height will yield an underestimate.

The Tall Trees Grove harbors some of the world's tallest trees. [Redwood N.P.] WHIT BRONAUGH

In March of 1991 a redwood in Humboldt Redwoods State Park known as the Dyerville Giant, which two decades earlier had been measured at 362 feet in height, slowly tipped and crashed to earth. In 1972 the Dyerville Giant's trunk had measured just over 16 ½ feet in diameter. Redwoods are renowned not only for their height but also for the considerable ages they attain. Trees as old as 1,000 to 1,200 years are not uncommon in protected groves of old-growth forest. A maximum age of about 2,200 years has been recorded, though such old trees are very rare.

Redwood is almost entirely restricted to a narrow strip of fogbelt, about 450 miles long and usually about 5 to 25 miles wide. It is nearly a California endemic, extending just 14 miles north of the California border to Oregon's Chetco River drainage where it occurs in about six small stands. Its southern boundary is located in the Soda Springs Creek area of the Santa Lucia Range, south of Big Sur. Redwood's northern distribution may be restrained by low temperatures, as suggested by high mortality rates of young trees when its northern reaches are inflicted with frost. Nor can it expand to the south, due to the low winter rainfall, or further inland, where the summer fogs do not penetrate. Up north, fog-drip condensed on the surfaces of foliage keeps the soil moist during the dry season, allowing drought-sensitive plants like redwood to function as they would under a higher rainfall regime. But in the south there is insufficient fog to compensate for summer drought, so redwood makes a last stand in moist canyon bottoms, then dwindles and disappears.

The ecological role of fire in redwood forests is somewhat unclear due to inconsistent research findings. On the north coast, lightning ignitions are infrequent, and, according to some studies, fires seem to have burned as rarely as every 500 years on average. Further south and inland, redwoods appear to have been exposed to fire at intervals of about 30 to 50 years. Still other research suggests that fires burned in some redwood forests an average of once per decade, although most researchers attribute such short fire return intervals to Native American burning. Where fires are more frequent, the thick-barked redwood would have the advantage over more fire-tender species like western hemlock and Sitka spruce. Intuitively, it seems likely that fires entering a dripping redwood stand from more combustible grasses or shrubs would be slowed, much as Rocky Mountain aspen stands tend to "snuff out" fires burning into them from sagebrush or coniferous trees. More research is needed to clarify fire behavior and ecology in the redwoods.

If trees could think, redwood would probably be described as having an unquenchable will to live. Even relatively young trees bear abundant crops of tiny, pollen-bearing male cones, and small, semi-woody seed cones. Pollination occurs in the winter, usually before the end of January, and mature seeds are produced the following fall. Vast numbers of minute seeds, the majority of them mysteriously ungerminable, are dispersed by the wind throughout the forest. Those that are viable germinate best on exposed soil and recently deposited silt, but they can also establish seedlings on organic litter and the surfaces of fallen logs. Seedlings tolerate even the deepest shade, and saplings that have been suppressed by a dense canopy as long as 400 years are capable of growing rapidly into newly created light gaps.

Redwood can regenerate itself clonally as well as by seed. Unlike any other North American conifer, redwood harbors basal dormant buds on the large roots that spread from its trunk. When a tree dies, these buds can sprout within months to form a circle of vigorous stems, called "fairy rings," around the parent tree or its stump. They may number as

A mature redwood forest can produce 1,400 metric tons of biomass per acre—much more than tropical rainforests. [Del Norte Coast Redwoods S.P.] LARRY ULRICH

Near the south end of its range on the Big Sur coast, redwood becomes increasingly restricted to moist canyon bottoms. [Monterey Co.] MARK J. DOLYAK

many as a hundred, and can grow six feet in their first year. Many redwoods that appear, by their size, to pre-date settlement, are actually fast-growing sprouts of trees felled in early logging. Genetic analysis of redwoods has shown that clonal members may occasionally form a line of trees up to 100 feet long. These have probably arisen from the rooting of numerous branches of a tree that fell long ago. Further evidence of this blind biological urge to throw out branches is provided by "fire columns," which are trunks damaged in forest fires that sprout heavily; one also sees the sprouting of trees topped beneath utility lines, the fruitless sprouting of cut logs, and the sprouting of burls sold in the tourist trade. In the virgin forest, huge trunks routinely sprout pencil-thin branches to replace their older limbs that have grown too large to be economically supported.

Redwoods produce wood at a phenomenal rate. In 1923 University of California forestry professor Emanuel Fritz and forester Woodbridge Metcalf established the "Wonder Plot" on an acre of second-growth redwood near Fort Bragg; by 1995 it had produced 343,000 board feet of timber. Of all the world's vegetation types, mature redwood forest produces the greatest biomass per unit area—more than 1,400 metric tons per acre according to one study—and far more than the lushest of tropical rainforests. Redwood has long been a mainstay of the West Coast forest products industry. Its strong, decay-resistant, easily worked wood, especially the deep red heartwood, is unexcelled for the manufacture of outdoor furniture and fencing, shakes and shingles, siding, decking, cooling towers, and a host of other uses.

Redwood of all ages grows amid a sprinkling of coniferous neighbors: Sitka spruce, Douglas-fir, western redcedar, grand fir, and western hemlock. Broad-leaved associates include madrone, tanoak, red alder, vine maple, California bay, hazelnut, and bigleaf maple; the lush ground flora consists of such herbs as redwood sorrel, salal, and ferns. Redwood forests are often quiet places, but many animals call them home. Some typical birds include juncos, woodpeckers, Steller's jays, brown creepers, winter wrens, and the marbled murrelet that commutes from its nesting areas in the old-growth to its foraging areas along the seashore. Closer to the ground are the banana slug, red salamander, Coast Range newt, sharp-tailed snake, moles, and shrews.

IDENTIFYING REDWOOD

At a distance: In maturity and old age redwood is an enormously tall tree with fibrous, ridged and fissured, gray to brown bark covering a columnar trunk that is bare of limbs for 100 feet or more. The crown, especially in dense stands, is narrow, pointed to ragged at the top, often spike-topped. Younger trees have reddish brown bark and gracefully downswept lower branches.
Standing beneath it: Looking up the columnar trunk of an old redwood, its crown disappearing into the fog, suggests infinity.
In the hand: The leaves may be scalelike, $1/4$ to $1/2$ inch long, or (most often) linear, flat, to 1 inch long, green above with two whitish stomatal bands below, and lying in flat sprays. Leaves are non-resinous when crushed. Cones are up to one inch long, with 18 to 26 shield-shaped, wrinkled scales.

HABITAT

Stands of redwood are found in a variety of sites. In the north they occupy alluvial flats subject to frequent flooding. They also grow on terraces and range upslope to the tops of ridges separated from damaging salt spray by stands of other species or topography that deflects sea winds. At the southern extremity they are increasingly confined to canyon bottoms and north-facing slopes. They occur from just above sea level to 3,200 feet, but are mostly between 100 and 2,500 feet. Redwood may form almost pure stands in the alluvial flat forests of the north coast, but elsewhere it has a variety of associates, including its frequent companion Douglas-fir, as well as grand fir, western hemlock, Sitka spruce, tanoak, madrone, and California bay.

DISTRIBUTION

It ranges from Little Redwood Creek, a tributary of the Chetco River in Oregon, south to an unnamed drainage between Redwood Gulch and Soda Springs Creek in southernmost Monterey County. Some isolated populations in Napa County are about 42 miles from the Pacific coast, but most redwoods are within 20 miles of the ocean.

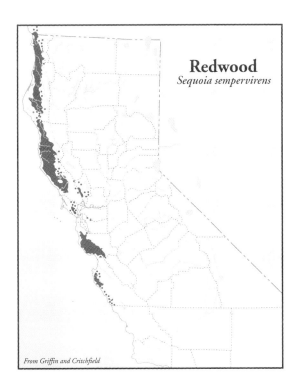

Redwood
Sequoia sempervirens

From Griffin and Critchfield

Giant Sequoia • *Sequoiadendron giganteum*

GIANT SEQUOIA

(ALSO CALLED BIG TREE, SIERRA REDWOOD)

Giant sequoia is world-famous for its massiveness, its rugged appearance, and its ability to live for thousands of years. No other living organism can rival the approximately 2,500 year-old General Sherman tree, for example, of Sequoia National Park. In 1975 it stood about 275 feet tall and had a diameter at breast height of almost 27 feet. In 1981 it contained about 52,500 cubic feet of wood. Its radial growth rate, a mere one millimeter per year, was probably sufficient to make it the world's fastest growing tree, adding about 50 cubic feet of wood annually.

Various maximum heights, ranging from 290 to 360 feet, have been claimed for the giant sequoia. The lower figure is attained by several trees still standing in King's Canyon and Sequoia national parks, and in Calaveras Big Trees State Park; the higher estimates are based on trees felled many years ago and cannot be verified. Giant sequoia's maximum age was thought by John Muir to be about 4,000 years, and indeed for a time it was believed to be the world's longest-lived tree. More accurate study, however, has shown a demonstrated maximum of between 3,200 and 3,300 years, far short of the greatest age attained by Great Basin bristlecone pine.

When comparing giant sequoia and Great Basin bristlecone, there is a peculiar disparity in the apparent causes of their longevity. Bristlecone barely ekes out a precarious living in the high, dry, cold places where it reaches its greatest ages—Nevada's Snake Range and California's White Mountains. Its ability to persist an inordinate number of years seems to be related to the scarcity of murderous pests that

Giant sequoia grows only in scattered groves in the Sierra Nevada, typically on moist sites. It associates with white fir, Douglas-fir, incense-cedar, sugar pine, and ponderosa pine. [Sierra N.F.] BILL EVARTS

can function under those rigorous conditions. Giant sequoia, however, lives where the soils are deep and rich, and the growing season long and mild. It is relatively free of debilitating diseases, has no known serious insect, avian, or mammalian pests, and is covered with very thick and fire-resistant bark. Its long life seems due to the combination of being left alone by most potential enemies, and living the good life among plenty of available resources. In fact, giant sequoia's worst enemy may be its own propensity to grow massive. Given enough time, a very heavy tree will eventually fall. It may become unbalanced due to fire or fungus damage to its base or to a major root or two, or because a massive limb is broken out by heavy snow loads, or because the soil in which it is anchored is incrementally washed out from under it. A young tree can right itself if tipped; an old one has little ability to do so. Once tipped, it is just a matter of time until a gust of wind or the heavy, wet, Sierra snows administer the final push.

Ancestors of giant sequoia were distributed in Nevada and Idaho during the Miocene (about 25 to 5 million years ago), but the growing Sierra Nevada created a rain shadow that made the climate too dry for them to tolerate. By about seven million years ago, giant sequoia had migrated to approximately its current range. It is now found only at middle elevations of the west slope of the Sierra Nevada. It occurs in scattered groves ranging in size from about 3 acres to over 4,100 acres, with the larger groves near the southern end of the species' range. There are between 65 and 75 groves, depending on how they are delineated, and they typically consist of a scattering of giant sequoias within a mixed-conifer forest. About one-tenth of the groves are in private hands, about one-third are in Kings Canyon, Sequoia, and Yosemite national parks, and almost half are in Giant Sequoia National Monument. The 327,769-acre monument was established by proclamation of President Bill Clinton in April,

2000. It is administered by the U.S. Forest Service and encompasses the 34 groves that were previously part of Sequoia National Forest. There are also groves in the Sierra, Stanislaus, and Tahoe national forests and elsewhere in miscellaneous other categories of ownership. The public has come to identify giant sequoia with the national parks, but more trees and a greater grove acreage appear to lie within the national monument.

Huge basal fire scars on these giant sequoias betray a history of frequent ground fires. [Sequoia N.P.]
LARRY ULRICH

Pollination of giant sequoia ovules occurs in April or May, and fertilization follows in August. The fertilized seed cone then overwinters, and by the time the seeds are mature late the next summer, the cone may be up to three inches long. If the cones are left undisturbed, they will remain on the tree, still green and tightly closed, for many years—up to two decades at least—with the cone stalk continually adding narrow annual growth rings. Lichens may grow upon them, forming a thin crust. To disperse the seeds, the cone must open by becoming dried out so the scales can spread apart.

This can happen in several ways, listed here in the apparent order of importance. First, ground fires may convect heat into the tree crowns; second, the larvae of small long-horned beetles of the species *Phymatodes nitidus* may feed within the cone, cutting off its supply of water from the branch; third, Douglas squirrels may feed on the green cone scales, causing them to lose moisture; and finally, storms may tear cones from their limbs or limbs from their trees, severing the vascular tissue supplying water to the cones. By these means there is a year-round rain of seeds beneath a giant sequoia canopy and a reservoir of seeds, preserved in serotinous cones, that can exploit the open habitats provided by wildfire. A huge tree may hold in its crown 30,000 or more cones of various ages, adding several thousand new ones every year. The cones contain a powdery substance, rich in tannins,

Unlike coast redwood, giant sequoia tolerates cold winters. [Yosemite N.P.] FRED HIRSCHMANN

that may function to prevent seeds from germinating within the moist green cone.

For seedlings to become successfully established, seeds must fall on exposed mineral soil supplied with ample moisture. As with other Sierran conifers, first-year drought is the major seedling mortality factor. Fire, therefore, plays a valuable role in the giant sequoia's habitat because it burns off accumulations of organic debris that act as a physical barrier to young taproots seeking soil water. Fire frequency must not be too high, however, because young sequoias are susceptible to fire damage. Older trees develop bark up to about 18 inches thick, and are quite fire-resistant. Eventually, even old trees become deeply fire-scarred at the base and thus structurally weakened. Studies of fire frequency from scars dating back 2,000 years have shown that in several sequoia groves the number of fires varied from none to 50 per century. The suppression of fires during the twentieth century has inhibited regeneration of giant sequoia. As a corrective, controlled burning has become a common management practice in the national parks of the southern Sierra Nevada.

Harvesting of giant sequoia began within a few years of its 1852 discovery and continued sporadically for the next 100 years. The expense of transporting and milling the huge logs, coupled with sequoia's tendency to split or shatter upon felling, kept it from ever competing with coast redwood despite the similarity of their wood. Nonetheless, small milling operations—which often wasted 75% of the felled giants—churned out sequoia grape stakes, fence posts, shakes and other utilitarian items for the towns and farms of the San Joaquin Valley. The peak of logging activity may have occurred in the early 1890s when a 54-mile-long flume connected a mill in Sanger with the immense grove at Converse Basin where all of the mature sequoias were removed, save one—a huge specimen that is the world's third largest tree. Public outrage over logging of giant sequoia along with a fascination with the mammoth trees helped mobilize an unprecedented conservation movement in the nineteenth century. Championed by John Muir and others, a string of sequoia stands were given protected status, beginning with the Mariposa Grove as part of the 1864 Yosemite Grant (precursor to the national park) and followed by Grant Grove in 1880, Sequoia and General Grant National Parks in 1890, and Calaveras Bigtree National Forest in 1909. Although logging of native sequoia groves has nearly ceased, growing sequoia in lowland plantations is relatively new and may become a commercial success in the twenty-first century.

IDENTIFYING GIANT SEQUOIA

At a distance: Old trees may be enormous and seem totally out of scale with their surroundings. They carry dense, deep green crowns on long, tapered trunks covered with deeply furrowed reddish brown bark, and may have huge, curving limbs or dead snag-tops. Young trees are symmetrically pyramidal, and may carry foliage almost to the ground.

Standing beneath it: The bark is fibrous and often charred from past fires.

In the hand: Scale leaves on leading shoots and young trees are bluish green, lance-shaped, widely spaced, and spreading; they measure up to $1/2$ inch long. On lower branches they are crowded, in overlapping spirals, $1/4$ inch long. Cones are egg-shaped and green, with flattened, diamond-shaped scales that have wrinkles radiating from a central fold, to three inches long and two inches wide.

HABITAT

It grows in mixed-conifer forests of the western Sierra Nevada, from about 2,700 to 8,900 feet (but mainly from 5,000 to 7,500 feet), associating with sugar, ponderosa, and Jeffrey pines, red and white fir, Douglas-fir, incense-cedar, and California black oak. The groves are usually around meadows, seeps, or springs where soil

Douglas squirrels cache and feed on green sequoia cones. [Kings Canyon N.P.] RANDI HIRSCHMANN

moisture is available in the summer. Precipitation is about 36 to 56 inches, falling mostly as snow, with infrequent summer rains.

DISTRIBUTION

In the Sierra Nevada only. Mostly in Giant Sequoia National Monument and national parks and forests of Tulare, Fresno, Madera, Mariposa, Tuolumne, Calaveras, and Placer counties.

Giant Sequoia
Sequoiadendron giganteum

From Griffin and Critchfield

THE YEW FAMILY

Trees of this family, which are often referred to as "taxads," are not really conifers at all. Their female reproductive structures are formed singly, rather than aggregated in cones of spirally or oppositely arranged scales. Thus their seeds are not borne on the surface of scales, as are those of conifers, but within fleshy structures that may be open at one end, as in yews, or fully closed, as in torreyas. The yews of genus *Taxus,* and the torreyas, or nutmegs, of *Torreya,* are the only North American taxads, though several other genera are represented by species in the Far East and southwest Pacific areas. Both of our native genera consist of species that have male trees and female trees. Taxads are often included in books about conifers because both groups are classified as gymnosperms, and because their evergreen needles are similar in general appearance to those of firs and hemlocks.

Opposite: Pacific yew achieved fame when its bark was found to contain the extract taxol, an effective cancer treatment. [Six Rivers N.F.] WILLIAM M. SMITHEY

Pacific Yew • *Taxus brevifolia*

PACIFIC YEW

Surprisingly, in his *Mountains of California* all John Muir had to say about our native yew was this: "In shady dells and on cool stream banks of the northern Sierra we also find the yew." The always-utilitarian Willis Lynn Jepson went Muir one better by pointing out that the hard, heavy, fine-grained wood of the yew had been the stuff of fish-hooks and spear handles, and was so durable in contact with the soil that Eel River settlers made use of centuries-old drift logs exhumed from riparian sediments. Perhaps the high-water mark of distinction for the wood of Pacific yew was achieved in 1989, when logs sent to Taiwan for religious ceremonial use fetched over $6,000 per thousand board feet. But Pacific yew's greatest and most recent notoriety stems from the discovery that its extract, the diterpene taxol, is an effective treatment for ovarian cancer. No other North American tree has entered the pharmacopoeia so dramatically or with so much fanfare.

Taxol's highly complex molecule has for many years defied attempts to synthesize it economically, so taxol has been supplied by extraction from the bark of yews harvested expressly for that purpose or from trees destroyed in the course of logging the old-growth Douglas-fir forests in which yew is an inconspicuous understory member. That has created a difficult situation for medicine as well as for forest conservation. About 20,000 American women are diagnosed with ovarian cancer annually, and about half of them ultimately die of the disease. Yet the available supply of taxol has been enough for only 200 to 300 patients per year. It takes about 7,000 pounds of dried yew bark to make one pound of taxol, and to get that much bark, up to 2,000 fair-sized trees

Many Pacific yew trees originate as sprouts from cut or broken stumps. [Mt. Hood N.F., OR] STEVE TERRILL

known. Pacific yew can be a painfully slow grower, therefore many years must pass for today's seedlings to yield bark of medicinal quality. The upshot of all this is that by producing enough taxol to meet current demand, the limited pool of useable trees becomes rapidly depleted, thus threatening future use. Attempts are being made to grow yew in high-yielding orchards, to select rapid-growing genotypes of high yield, and to grow taxol-producing cells in culture. In addition, attempts at the laboratory synthesis of taxol continue. In the meantime, "semisynthesis"—the conversion of a closely related compound from domesticated ornamental yews—has become the major source of the drug.

Pacific yew can attain 50 feet in height, with a trunk diameter of two feet or more, or it can grow as a large shrub. It is known to reach at least 500 years of age and perhaps lives much longer. The sexes are on separate trees. Male trees form large numbers of stalked little pollen cones on the undersides of limbs. The wind-dispersed pollen issues cloud-like in early spring. Female trees produce crops of 1/4-inch long, black, elliptical seeds, each contained within a cuplike, fleshy, sweet, edible, scarlet aril. The aril, which is about 1/2 inch in diameter, is attractive to fruit-eating birds which disperse the seeds by excreting them back into the landscape after eating the aril. The apparently common occurrence of small seedling clumps suggests that seeds are also dispersed and cached by rodents. Yews sprout from cut stumps and

must be sacrificed. Unfortunately, yews have extremely thin bark, and trees less than 10 inches in diameter yield negligible amounts of it.

Pacific yew almost never grows in pure stands, and it is usually scattered as individuals, or in small groups among Douglas-fir, redwood, western hemlock, white fir, and other trees of moist forest environments. Yew harvesters must therefore cover large expanses of territory to accumulate sufficient quanities of bark. Adding to the supply problem is the fact that much of the prime yew-growing areas were clearcut before the pharmaceutical value of yew bark was

Pacific yew can be identified by its papery curls of peeling bark. [Siskiyou Co.] MARK GIBSON

can replace felled trees in this way. Limbs in contact with moist soil can layer, striking roots of their own. A layer can become an independent tree if it is detached from its parent. Yew foliage is reported to be poisonous to livestock, but not to moose, elk, or deer, all of which browse the species.

IDENTIFYING PACIFIC YEW

At a distance: Pacific yew has a low, broad crown of slender, horizontal branches supported by a sometimes twisted or fluted trunk.

Standing beneath it: The bark is composed of red or purple brown scales that, according to Donald Culross Peattie, are "always curling and sloughing away to reveal the flowerlike clear rose of the inner bark." In late summer and fall of a flowering year the bright red arils are conspicuous on female trees.

In the hand: The short, flat, pointed needles

spread in two rows from twigs that are green in their first year. They are attached to the twig by short, yellow stalks that run a short distance along the twig.

HABITAT

Pacific yew grows on deep, moist soils under the canopy of old-growth redwood, white fir, and Douglas-fir-tanoak forests in the Klamath, Shasta-Trinity, and Six Rivers national forests. In the northern Sierra Nevada it occurs in ravines or on north slopes beneath mixed-conifer canopies. In both areas, it also inhabits streambanks. It ranges from sea level in the North Coast Ranges to about 8,000 feet on the Sierra Nevada westside and grows as a shrub high in the Klamath Mountains.

DISTRIBUTION

In California it is common in parts of the Klamath and Cascade ranges and extends down the North Coast Ranges to Marin County. It is also distributed south down the Sierra Nevada as far as the North Grove of Calaveras Big Trees State Park. It extends north to islands near Ketchikan, Alaska and east through British Columbia to Alberta, eastern Washington and Oregon, northern Idaho, and western Montana.

Pacific Yew
Taxus brevifolia

From Griffin and Critchfield

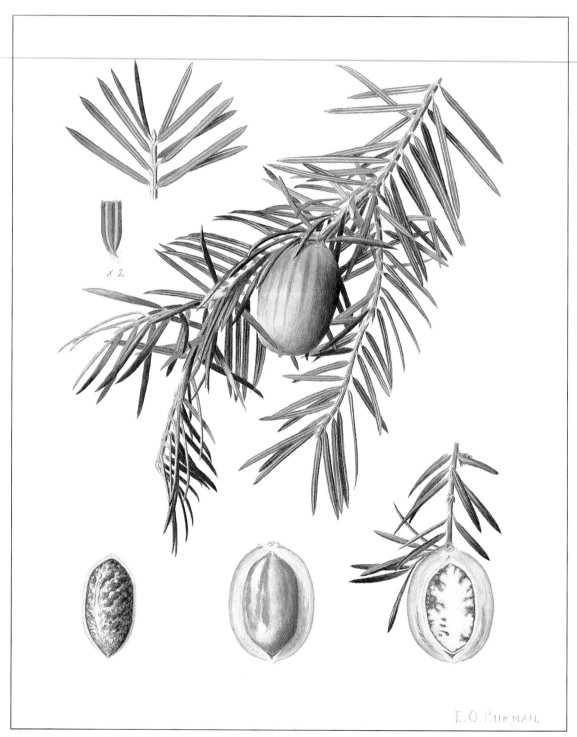

_x 2._

E.O. MURMAN.

California Nutmeg • *Torreya californica*

CALIFORNIA NUTMEG

(ALSO CALLED STINKING CEDAR)

The "interesting Nutmeg Tree," as John Muir called it, is an evergreen widely but sparsely scattered up and down the Coast Ranges and along the westside of the Sierra Nevada and Cascades. Never forming a continuous forest, but found rather as isolated trees or in small groups, the nutmeg or "stinking cedar" is usually seen tucked into shaded ravines or rocky gorges, beneath a canopy of pines or other conifers. Where it is stunted by growth on serpentine soil, it is a shrub of the chaparral; but throughout most of its range it grows as a modest-sized forest tree, 20 to 50 feet tall. One giant near Fort Bragg in Mendocino County reached a height of 141 feet before it was illegally felled.

The genus *Torreya* is closely related to *Taxus,* the yews. Its fruits differ in having closed arils, rather than the open ones seen in yews. It is these structures, shaped like small plums, that were likened by botanists to the tropical, and completely unrelated, nutmegs.

All *Torreya* stink, thanks to an unfortunate and unidentified substance located in the leaves and fresh shoots. But in other respects, California nutmeg is an attractive tree. Its wood, for example, is close-grained, soft, durable, and creamy yellow in color. Its elasticity commended it for use in bows by California Indians, and its decay resistance persuaded early white settlers to build bridges of its timbers. Native Americans also harvested and roasted its rich, oily seeds, which are reputed to taste like peanuts. The Pomo people utilized its roots in the weaving of baskets. And, according to a paper written by V. K. Chesnut in 1900, Native Americans used the long, flat needles "to prick pitch soot into the skin in tattooing."

Though the "stinking cedar" is not a large tree nor a common one, its stiff, prickly needles can make many instant impressions on the hapless visitor who stumbles upon it. [Butte Co.] HASKEL BAZELL

Its fleshy arils give the California nutmeg its name. [Stanislaus N.F.] JENNIE HAAS

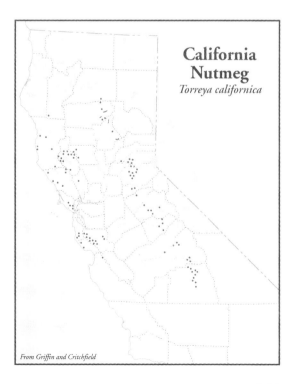

California nutmeg is usually found in moist, shady places. [Stanislaus N.F.] JENNIE HAAS

IDENTIFYING CALIFORNIA NUTMEG

At a distance: Look for a small to medium-sized understory tree with deep green, glossy foliage growing in moist areas like ravines.

Standing beneath it: In the fall, female trees bear elliptical green fruits about one to two inches long. The bark is pale reddish or grayish brown, with narrow ridges separated by shallow furrows.

In the hand: Needles are glossy green on top, spread flat, sharply pointed (like cactus spines, according to one writer), and almost two inches long. The current year's shoot is green, but turns reddish brown by the third year. The green "nutmeg" matures with purple streaks.

HABITAT

California nutmeg is found on moist, rocky microsites within the shade of tall, coniferous forests; it grows as a shrub on serpentine substrate. It has a wide array of associates and ranges from about 2,000 to 7,000 feet.

DISTRIBUTION

It grows in the Coast Ranges from southwest Trinity County to Fremont Peak in Monterey County. It is also found in the Cascades and Sierra Nevada, ranging from Shasta County south to Tulare County.

California Nutmeg

Torreya californica

From Griffin and Critchfield

APPENDIX A: CALIFORNIA'S SOFT PINES AND HARD PINES

The pines are divided into two major subgenera: the soft, or white, pines *(Strobus)* and the hard, or yellow, pines *(Pinus).* Both the soft and hard pines are well-represented in California.

The soft pines have whiter and softer wood due to a reduced proportion of summerwood in the annual ring (which may make the rings difficult to count). Their cone-scale outgrowths (apophyses) may resemble those of hard pines by being thick; they are located on the scale's outer surface in the pinyon pine and foxtail pine groups and at the scale tip in sugar, limber, and western white pines. They are often lacking in weaponry. The needles of soft pines are usually in bundles of five, but there are lots of exceptions, including singleleaf pinyon. The soft pines' fascicle sheaths are flimsy and fall off in a year or two.

The hard pines have harder, yellower wood, due to a higher proportion of summerwood in the annual ring. The scales of their seed cones usually have a much-thickened outgrowth (apophysis) on the outer surface near the scale tip, which bears a scar (umbo) that is often armed with a spine, prickle, or even a hook. The needles of hard pines are usually in bundles of two or three, but there are exceptions, one of which is Torrey pine, a five-needled California endemic. The hard pines' needles are bound together at their base by a permanent sheath.

As the table below shows, a consistent difference between soft and hard pines is the number of vascular bundles, or veins, that run the length of the needle: soft pines have one vascular bundle per needle, while hard pines have two.

COMPARISON OF NEEDLE AND CONE CHARACTERS IN CALIFORNIA SOFT PINES AND HARD PINES

GROUP AND SPECIES	NEEDLE NUMBER	VASCULAR BUNDLES PER NEEDLE	PERMANENT FASCICLE SHEATH	CONE SCALE THICKENING (APOPHYSIS)
SOFT PINES				
Sugar pine	5	1	No	Terminal
Western white pine	5	1	No	Terminal
Singleleaf pinyon	1	1	No	Dorsal
Sierra Juárez pinyon	5	1	No	Dorsal
Whitebark pine	5	1	No	Terminal
Limber pine	5	1	No	Terminal
Foxtail pine	5	1	No	Dorsal
Great Basin bristlecone pine	5	1	No	Dorsal
HARD PINES				
Ponderosa pine	2 - 3	2	Yes	Dorsal
Jeffrey pine	3	2	Yes	Dorsal
Washoe pine	3	2	Yes	Dorsal
Gray pine	3	2	Yes	Dorsal
Coulter pine	3	2	Yes	Dorsal
Torrey pine	5	2	Yes	Dorsal
Lodgepole pine	2	2	Yes	Dorsal
Bishop pine	2	2	Yes	Dorsal
Monterey pine	2 - 3	2	Yes	Dorsal
Knobcone pine	3	2	Yes	Dorsal

APPENDIX B: CONIFER HYBRIDS IN CALIFORNIA

Hybridization between members of different species within a genus is fairly common among conifers. It occurs most often in the pine family, but species in the cypress family frequently hybridize as well. Hybrids between members of two different conifer genera are very rare, however, and have not been documented in California's forests and woodlands.

Three requirements must be met for hybrids to form in nature. First, members of the hybridizing species must be close enough to each other geographically to transfer pollen from one to the other. All our conifers have wind-carried pollen, so such transfers can occur even across gaps of several miles. If ranges overlap, however, cross-pollination is much more likely to occur. Second, there must be a period when one of the species' pollen is in the wind and the other has exposed conelets with receptive ovules. The two- to three-week period when one conifer species sheds pollen and the other has ovules able to receive pollen must coincide. Finally, the hybridizing species must be closely related to each other; otherwise they are likely to have differing numbers, sizes, or shapes of chromosomes in the nuclei of their sex cells and will therefore be unable to produce viable hybrid seeds. If all goes well and viable hybrid seeds are produced, the resulting seedlings can mature and take their place in the breeding population.

First-generation hybrids, or F-1s, are usually inter-mediate to their parents in identification characters (like the number of needles per bundle in pinyon pines, or cone size in Jeffrey X Coulter pine crosses) and physiological characteristics (like frost resistance and growth rate in knobcone X Monterey pine crosses). Conifer hybrids are typically fertile. They can cross with each other and they can backcross into either parent species. Widespread crossing among hybrids of several generations and their parent species can lead to a hybrid swarm bewildering in its variability. The long-term result of natural hybridization can be the incorporation of genes of one species into another. This phenomenon, called introgression, brings new genetic information into a species and can be important to that species' further evolution. Its effects are often very subtle and detectable only through statistical or genetic analysis.

California has more pairs of naturally hybridizing conifers than any other state. They are:

Monterey pine X knobcone pine
Ponderosa pine X Jeffrey pine
Coulter pine X Jeffrey pine
Sierra Juárez pinyon X singleleaf pinyon
white fir X grand fir
red fir X noble fir
McNab cypress X Sargent cypress

There are hybrids of Sierra juniper X Utah juniper in western Nevada, and it is possible that such crosses may eventually be detected in eastern California.

APPENDIX C: A KEY TO THE GENERA BASED ON CHARACTERS OF MATURE SEED CONES OR ANALOGOUS SEED-BEARING ORGANS

1. The female reproductive structure is made up of woody or sub-woody scales that are separable from each other at or after maturity (cones) . . . . .go to 2
1. The female reproductive structure has an outer surface of fleshy material and does not have separable parts (berries and arils) . . . . .go to 13
   2. The cone is spherical or nearly so; the scales are attached by stalks that appear to radiate from a central point in the cone and bear a raised knob which may be sharply pointed . . . . .go to 3
   2. The cone is oblong, cylindrical, globose, or ovoid; the scales are attached in spirals or in opposite pairs to an elongate axis in the cone . . .go to 4
3. The cone is woody, rigid, and tightly closed until

heating, aging, or drying cause the scales to separate along their seams . . . . .Cypresses, page 167
3. The cone is sub-woody, squeezable, and opens at maturity . . . . .False cypresses, page 199
   4. The cone scales are arranged in opposite pairs . . . . .go to 5
   4. The cone scales are arranged in spirals . . .go to 6
5. The outermost pair of cone scales are up to one inch long and spread like a duck's bill . . . . .Incense-cedars, page 207
5. The outermost pair of cone scales are up to 1/2 inch long, and do not spread . . . . . . .Arborvitaes, page 213
   6. The scale tips are expanded in a plane perpendicular to the scale stalk, presenting a puckered shield-

shaped surface . . . . .go to 7

    6. Not as above . . . . .go to 8

7. The cone is woody, rigid, up to three or more inches long, and often remains green and closed on the tree for many years . . . . .Giant sequoia, page 247

7. The cone is sub-woody, up to 1 $1/2$ inches long, and opens at maturity on the tree . . . . . Redwood, page 241

    8. The scale has at or near its tip a lighter-colored area that may be conspicuously thickened (apophysis). The apophysis has a scar (umbo) which may be armed with a bristle or prickle . . . . Pines, page 9

    8. Not as above .go to 9

9. The scales are deciduous and are shed from the cone axis following maturity, leaving a bare vertical axis attached to the branchlet . . . . .Firs, page 101

9. Not as above . . . . .go to 10

    10. Three-pointed bracts project from between scales, pointing towards the tip of the cone . . . . .Douglas-firs, page 155

    10. Not as above . . . . .go to 11

11. The scales are tapered towards both ends, and their margins are noticeably toothed . . . .Spruces, page 131

11. The scales are rectangular to fan-shaped (broadest at tip), and their margins are smooth to slightly roughened . . . . .go to 12

    12. The cone-bearing branchlet has needles set on prominent woody pegs that make the leafless stem rasplike . . . . .Brewer spruce, page 137

    12. Not as above . . . . .Hemlocks, page 145

13. The fruiting structure is bright red at maturity and open at its free end . . . . .Pacific yew, page 255

13. The fruiting structure is entirely closed . . .go to 14

    14. The fruiting structure is spherical, up to $1/2$ inch in diameter, resinous, aromatic, and frosted bluish white .Junipers, page 219

    14. The fruiting structure is plum-like, up to 1 $1/2$ inches long, and green to purple in color . . . . .California nutmeg, page 259

APPENDIX D: A KEY TO THE GENERA BASED ON LEAF CHARACTERS FROM LOWER CROWN BRANCHES

(A hand-lens of 10X or more is recommended)

1. The foliage consists mainly or entirely of short scales arranged on the stem in spirals, opposite pairs, threes, or fours, pressed against and obscuring the stem . . . . .go to 2

1. The foliage consists mainly or entirely of linear needles spreading from the stem . . . . .go to 7

    2. The foliage-covered branchlet, or spray, lies flat in one plane, and its individual stems are flat in cross-section . . . . .go to 3

    2. The branchlet does not lie in one plane, but is clumpy, and its individual stems are rounded or square in cross-section . . . . .go to 5

3. Facial and marginal (lateral) scale leaves are in groups of four of the same length (tips are in line), about $1/3$ inch long, have a gland on outer surface, and are aromatic when crushed; the leaf-covered shoot looks oddly jointed . . . . .Incense-cedars, page 207

3. The tips of the facial leaves extend beyond those of the marginal leaves (tips not in line) . . . . .go to 4

    4. A deposit of white wax on the underside of the branchlets is in broad bands forming a butterfly or bow-tie pattern . . . . .Arborvitaes, page 213

    4. The waxy deposit on the branchlet's underside is

either completely absent (Alaska-cedar) or in narrow bands forming an X pattern (Port Orford cedar) . . . . .False cypresses, page 199

5. The leaves are spirally arranged with long, sharp tips, and are up to $1/2$ inch long . . . . .Giant sequoia, page 247

5. The leaves are not in spirals, and are only $1/16$ to $1/8$ inch long . . . . .go to 6

    6. The edges of the leaves are minutely toothed; foliage is entirely of scale leaves; and crushed foliage does not have the aroma of gin Cypresses, page 167

    6. The edges of the leaves are smooth; upright vigorous shoots or sprout shoots associated with wounds may have needle-like leaves $1/3$ to $3/4$ inch long with waxy white bands on the upper surface; and crushed foliage has the aroma of gin . . . . .Junipers, page 219

7. The needles are no more than $1/2$ inch long, pointed, with broad silvery white bands of wax on upper surface; shrubby growth form . . . .Common juniper, page 229

7. Not as above . . . . .go to 8

    8. The needles are pie-shaped to semi-circular in cross-section, 1 $1/2$ to 14 inches long, and attached to the stem in bundles of two to five bound at the base by a sheath of short scales (in singleleaf pinyon

the needle is single and circular in cross-section) Pines, page 9

8. The needles are flat to thickened, usually less than three inches long, and attached singly to the stem . . . . .go to 9

9. The needles completely lack whitish bands of wax and their tips are pointed; leaf stalks run down the stem, and the leaves lie flat in two ranks . . . . .Pacific yew, page 255

9. The needles have whitish bands of wax . . . .go to 10

10. The needles are about two inches long, rigid, and taper to a spiny tip; the underside has two longitudinal grooves whitened with deposits of wax . . . . .California nutmeg, page 259

10. Not as above . . . . .go to 11

11. The needles are flat, 1/2 to 1 inch long, with pointed tips and two whitish bands of wax on the underside. Needles do not fall from the stem singly, but in branchlet-units. Therefore, a plucked needle does not separate cleanly from the stem, but takes some bark with it. Leading shoots bear incurved, 1/4 inch-long scale leaves . . . . .Redwood, page 241

11. Not as above, needles drop from the shoot as individuals, leaving on the stem tiny scars that are covered

with a corky surface .go to 12

12. Dropped needles reveal a flat or concave, circular scar on the stem. Lower-branch needles are usually flat and blunt, and spread in two horizontal ranks. Upper-branch needles are usually thickened and pointed, and sweep upwards. The needles of leading shoots are usually pressed to the stem, rigid, and pointed . . . . .Firs, page 101

12. Dropped needles reveal a minute to prominent, raised woody peg (leaf base) on the stem . .go to 13

13. The raised woody pegs are so prominent that they roughen leafless shoots and make them rasplike to the touch. The needles are rigid and pointed . . . . .Spruces, page 131

13. Woody pegs are only slightly raised and do not noticeably roughen the leafless stem . . . . . . .go to 14

14. The needles are up to 1 1/4 inches long, narrowed at the base, and blunt to sharply pointed. Terminal buds are up to 1/2 inch long, pointed, shiny, and reddish-brown . . . . .Douglas-firs, page 155

14. The needles are blunt and 1/4 to 3/4 inch long. The terminal buds are less than 3/16 inch long and inconspicuous . . . . .Hemlocks, page 145

APPENDIX E: ALPHABETICAL LIST OF CONIFERS GROWING NATURALLY WITHIN CALIFORNIA

Author names follow E. L. Little's Checklist of United States Trees (Native and Naturalized) *(1979) where applicable. Species or subspecies that are endemic to California are followed by an asterisk (*).*

SPECIES, SUBSPECIES, AND VARIETIES

Abies amabilis Douglas ex Forbes
PACIFIC SILVER FIR

Abies bracteata D. Don ex Poiteau*
SANTA LUCIA FIR, BRISTLECONE FIR

Abies concolor (Gordon & Glendinning) Lindley ex Hildebrand
WHITE FIR

    Abies concolor var. *concolor*
    ROCKY MOUNTAIN WHITE FIR

    Abies concolor var. *lowiana* (Gordon) Lemmon
    CALIFORNIA WHITE FIR

Abies grandis (Douglas ex D. Don) Lindley
GRAND FIR

Abies lasiocarpa (Hooker) Nuttall
ALPINE FIR, SUBALPINE FIR, BALSAM

    Abies lasiocarpa var. *lasiocarpa*
    ALPINE FIR, SUBALPINE FIR

Abies magnifica A. Murray
RED FIR

    Abies magnifica var. *magnifica*
    CALIFORNIA RED FIR

    Abies magnifica var. *shastensis* Lemmon
    SHASTA RED FIR, SHASTA FIR

Abies procera Rehder
NOBLE FIR

Calocedrus decurrens (Torrey) Florin
INCENSE-CEDAR

Chamaecyparis lawsoniana (A. Murray) Parlatore
PORT ORFORD CEDAR

Chamaecyparis nootkatensis (D. Don) Spach
ALASKA-CEDAR, YELLOW CEDAR

Cupressus abramsiana C. B. Wolf*
SANTA CRUZ CYPRESS

Cupressus bakeri Jepson
BAKER CYPRESS

    Cupressus bakeri ssp. *bakeri*
    BAKER CYPRESS

    Cupressus bakeri ssp. *matthewsii* C. B. Wolf*
    BAKER CYPRESS

Cupressus forbesii Jepson
TECATE CYPRESS, FORBES CYPRESS

Cupressus goveniana Gordon*
GOWEN CYPRESS

Cupressus macnabiana A. Murray*
MCNAB CYPRESS

Cupressus macrocarpa Hartweg*
MONTEREY CYPRESS

Cupressus nevadensis Abrams*
PIUTE CYPRESS

Cupressus pigmaea Lemmon*
MENDOCINO CYPRESS, PYGMY CYPRESS

Cupressus sargentii Jepson*
SARGENT CYPRESS

Cupressus stephensonii C. B. Wolf
CUYAMACA CYPRESS, ARIZONA CYPRESS

Juniperus californica Carrière
CALIFORNIA JUNIPER

Juniperus communis Linnaeus
COMMON JUNIPER

    Juniperus communis var. *saxatilis* Pallas
    COMMON JUNIPER

Juniperus occidentalis Hooker
SIERRA JUNIPER, WESTERN JUNIPER

    Juniperus occidentalis ssp. *occidentalis*
    SIERRA JUNIPER, WESTERN JUNIPER

    Juniperus occidentalis ssp. *australis* Vasek
    SIERRA JUNIPER, WESTERN JUNIPER

Juniperus osteosperma (Torrey) Little
UTAH JUNIPER

Picea breweriana S. Watson
BREWER SPRUCE

Picea engelmannii Parry ex Engelmann
ENGELMANN SPRUCE

Picea sitchensis (Bongard) Carrière
SITKA SPRUCE

Pinus albicaulis Engelmann
WHITEBARK PINE

Pinus attenuata Lemmon
KNOBCONE PINE

Pinus balfouriana Greville & Balfour*
FOXTAIL PINE

    Pinus balfouriana ssp. *balfouriana**
    FOXTAIL PINE

    Pinus balfouriana ssp. *austrina* R. Mastrogiuseppe*
    & J. Mastrogiuseppe, FOXTAIL PINE

Pinus contorta Douglas ex Loudon
LODGEPOLE PINE

    Pinus contorta ssp. *contorta*
    COASTAL LODGEPOLE PINE, SHORE PINE

    Pinus contorta ssp. *bolanderi* (Parlatore) Critchfield*
    MENDOCINO WHITE PLAINS LODGEPOLE PINE

    Pinus contorta ssp. *murrayana* (Balfour) Critchfield
    SIERRA-CASCADE LODGEPOLE PINE

Pinus coulteri D. Don
COULTER PINE

Pinus flexilis James
LIMBER PINE

Pinus jeffreyi Greville & Balfour
JEFFREY PINE

Pinus juarezensis Lanner
SIERRA JUÁREZ PINYON

Pinus lambertiana Douglas
SUGAR PINE

Pinus longaeva D. K. Bailey
GREAT BASIN BRISTLECONE PINE

Pinus monophylla Torrey & Frémont
SINGLELEAF PINYON

    Pinus monophylla var. *monophylla*
    GREAT BASIN SINGLELEAF PINYON

    Pinus monophylla var. *californiarum* (D. K. Bailey) Silba
    CALIFORNIA SINGLELEAF PINYON

Pinus monticola Douglas ex D. Don
WESTERN WHITE PINE

Pinus muricata D. Don
BISHOP PINE

    Pinus muricata var. *muricata*
    BISHOP PINE

    Pinus muricata var. *borealis* Axelrod
    BISHOP PINE

Pinus ponderosa Douglas ex Lawson & C. Lawson
PONDEROSA PINE

    Pinus ponderosa var. *ponderosa*
    PACIFIC PONDEROSA PINE

Pinus radiata D. Don
MONTEREY PINE, RADIATA PINE

    Pinus radiata var. *radiata**
    MONTEREY PINE

Pinus sabiniana Douglas ex D. Don*
GRAY PINE, DIGGER PINE, FOOTHILL PINE

Pinus torreyana Parry ex Carrière*
TORREY PINE

    Pinus torreyana ssp. *torreyana**
    TORREY PINE

    Pinus torreyana ssp. *insularis* Haller*
    SANTA ROSA ISLAND TORREY PINE

Pinus washoensis Mason & Stockwell
WASHOE PINE

Pseudotsuga macrocarpa (Vasey) Mayr*
BIGCONE-SPRUCE, BIGCONE DOUGLAS-FIR

Pseudotsuga menziesii (Mirbel) Franco
DOUGLAS-FIR

    Pseudotsuga menziesii var. *menziesii*
    COAST DOUGLAS-FIR

Sequoia sempervirens (D. Don) Endlicher
REDWOOD

Sequoiadendron giganteum (Lindley) Buchholz*
GIANT SEQUOIA, BIGTREE, SIERRA REDWOOD

Taxus brevifolia Nuttall
PACIFIC YEW

Thuja plicata Donn ex D. Don
WESTERN REDCEDAR

Torreya californica Torrey*
CALIFONIA NUTMEG, STINKING CEDAR

Tsuga heterophylla (Rafinesque) Sargent
WESTERN HEMLOCK

Tsuga mertensiana (Bongard) Carrière
MOUNTAIN HEMLOCK

NATURAL HYBRIDS

(order of parent species is arbitrary)

Abies concolor X *Abies grandis*

Abies magnifica X *Abies procera* (= *Abies magnifica* var. *shastensis* in part)

Cupressus macnabiana X *Cupressus sargentii*

Pinus attenuata X *Pinus radiata* (= *Pinus* X *attenuradiata* Stockwell & Righter)

Pinus coulteri X *Pinus jeffreyi*

Pinus jeffreyi X *Pinus ponderosa*

Pinus juárezensis X *Pinus monophylla* (= *Pinus quadrifolia* Parlatore ex Sudworth [in part], and *Pinus* X *quadrifolia*) PARRY PINYON

ANNOTATED BIBLIOGRAPHY

Information about the conifers described in this book is widely scattered throughout thousands of technical and popular books and articles on vegetation, flora, trees, conifers, and *Californiana*. The purpose of this listing is to facilitate the serious reader's search for further knowledge by bringing together good sources, old and new, comprehensive and specialized.

WORKS CITED OR REFERRED TO IN THE TEXT

Bailey, D. K. 1987. "A study of *Pinus* subsection *Cembroides* I: The single-needle pinyons of the Californias and the Great Basin." *Notes, Royal Botanical Garden Edinburgh* 44, pgs. 275-310.

Bartel, J. A. 1993. "Cupressus, cypress." In: Hickman, J. C. (editor). *The Jepson Manual: Higher Plants of California.* Berkeley: University of California Press, pgs. 111-114.

Buchholz, J. T. 1939. "The generic segregation of the Sequoias." *American Journal of Botany* 26, pgs. 535-538.

Eckenwalder, J. A. 1993. "Cupressus." In: Flora of North America Editorial Committee, *Flora of North America North of Mexico: Volume 2, Pteridophytes and Gymnosperms.* New York: Oxford University Press.

Frémont, J. C. 1845. *Report of the Exploring Expedition to the Rocky Mountains in the Year 1842, and to Oregon and North California in the Years 1843-44.* Washington: United States House of Representatives.

Griffin, J. R. and W. B. Critchfield. 1972. *The Distribution of Forest Trees in California.* Research Paper PSW-82. Berkeley: USDA Forest Service. (Reprint with supplement, 1976.)

Jepson, W. L. 1910. *The Silva of California, Volume 2.* Berkeley: University of California Press.

Lanner, R. M. 1974. "Natural hybridization between *Pinus edulis* and *Pinus monophylla* in the American southwest." *Silvae Genetica* 23, pgs. 108-116.

Lanner, R. M. 1974. "A new pine from Baja California and the hybrid origin of *Pinus quadrifolia*." *Southwestern Naturalist* 19, pgs. 75-95.

Leiberg, J. B. 1902. *Forest Conditions in the Northern Sierra Nevada, California.* Washington, D.C.: Government Printing Office.

Lemmon, J. G. 1895. *Handbook of West-American Cone-Bearers.* 3rd ed. Oakland.

Little, E. L., Jr. 1979. *Checklist of United States Trees (Native and Naturalized).* USDA Forest Service Agriculture Handbook No. 541. Washington, D.C.: USDA Forest Service.

Mason, H. L. and W. P. Stockwell. 1945. "A new pine from Mount Rose, Nevada." *Madroño* 8, pgs. 61-63.

Muir, J. 1894. *The Mountains of California.* Garden City, NY: Doubleday Anchor. (1961 reprint).

Newberry, J. S. 1857. "Report upon the botany of the route." In *Reports of Explorations and Surveys to Ascertain the Most Practicable and Economic Route for a Railroad from the Mississippi River to the Pacific Ocean.* Washington, D.C.: 33rd Congress, 2nd Session Executive Document.

Peattie, D. C. 1953. *A Natural History of Western Trees.* Boston: Houghton Mifflin Company.

Sargent, C. S. 1890. *The Silva of North America: A Description of the Trees Which Grow Naturally in North America Exclusive of Mexico. Vol. XII, Coniferae (Abietineae after Pinus).* Boston: Houghton Mifflin Company.

Schulman, E. 1958. "Bristlecone pine, oldest known living thing." *National Geographic* 111, pgs. 354-372.

Sudworth, G. B. 1908. *Forest Trees of the Pacific Slope.* Washington, D.C.: Government Printing Office. (Reprint by Dover Publications, New York, 1967.)

Vogl, R. J. 1973. "The ecology of the knobcone pine in the Santa Ana Mountains, California." *Ecological Monographs* 43, pgs. 125-143.

Wolf, C. B. 1938. "California Plant Notes II." *Rancho Santa Ana Botanic Garden Occasional Paper Series* 1 (2), pgs. 44-90.

Wolf, C. B. 1948. "Taxonomic and distributional studies of the New World cypresses." *El Aliso* 1, pgs. 1-250.

Zavarin, E. 1988. "Taxonomy of pinyon pines." In: Passini, M. F., D. Cibrian-Tovar, and T. Eguiluz-Piedra (compilers), *II Simposio Nacional sobre Pinos Piñoneros.* Mexico, D.F.: CEMCA, pgs. 29-39.

FIELD GUIDES FOR IDENTIFYING CALIFORNIA TREES

Bever, D. N. 1981. *Northwest Conifers: A Photographic Key.* Portland, OR: Binford & Mort. Despite the inconveniently large format, this soft-covered book contains lots of good, practical information and useful close-up color photos.

Bowers, N. A. 1956. *Cone-Bearing Trees of the Pacific Coast.* Palo Alto: Pacific Books.

Brockman, C. F. 1968. *Trees of North America: A Field Guide to the Major Native and Introduced Species North of Mexico.* New York: Golden Press. Minimal information for the beginner.

Chase, J. S. 1911. *Cone-Bearing Trees of the California*

Mountains. Chicago: A. C. McClurg & Company. This pocket-sized book "by a tree-lover for tree-lovers" is surely one of the earliest field guides to American trees. Its brief descriptions are complemented by fine photos and Carl Eytel's elegant drawings.

Elias, T. S. 1980. *The Complete Trees of North America: Field Guide and Natural History.* New York: Van Nostrand Reinhold Company. A one-volume updated version of Sargent's Manual (see below), using many of the same illustrations. Too bulky for packing in the field.

Jepson, W. L. 1923. *The Trees of California.* 2nd ed. Berkeley: Associated Students Store. Jepson was an astute student of California's trees, and much can still be learned from this hard-to-find little book illustrated with many of Jepson's nice line drawings.

Lemmon, J. G. 1895. *Handbook of West-American Cone-Bearers.* 3rd ed. Oakland. Perhaps the earliest American tree field guide by an important figure in California botanical history.

Little, E. L., Jr. 1980. *The Audubon Society Field Guide to North American Trees: Western Region.* New York: Alfred A. Knopf. The best-illustrated and most technically competent field guide currently available for western trees.

McMinn, H. E. and E. Maino. 1963. *An Illustrated Manual of Pacific Coast Trees.* Berkeley: University of California Press.

Peterson, P. V. 1970. *Native Trees of Southern California.* Berkeley: University of California Press. Pocket-sized, convenient, with some of Eugene Murman's illustrations in color.

Peterson, P. V. and P. V. Peterson, Jr. 1975. *Native Trees of the Sierra Nevada.* Berkeley: University of California Press. A companion volume to Peterson, 1970.

Petrides, G. A. 1992. *A Field Guide to Western Trees.* Boston: Houghton Mifflin Company. Competent text, fine illustrations.

Sargent, C. S. 1922. *Manual of the Trees of North America.* 2nd ed., 2 vols. Boston: Houghton Mifflin Compnay. (Reprint by Dover Publications, New York, 1965.) More useful at the desk than in the field, this classic is a summarization of Sargent's monumental 14-volume Silva.

BOOKS WITH IN-DEPTH INFORMATION ON CALIFORNIA'S CONIFERS

Arno, S. F. 1973. *Discovering Sierra Trees.* Yosemite: Yosemite and Sequoia Natural History Associations.

Solid natural histories of Sierra Nevada trees with fine drawings by Jane Gyer.

Arno, S. F. 1977. *Northwest Trees.* Seattle: The Mountaineers. Comprehensive natural histories of several trees extending into California. Excellently illustrated by Ramona Hammerly.

Arno, S. F. 1984. *Timberline, Mountain and Arctic Frontiers.* Seattle: The Mountaineers. Absorbing story of the ecology of high-elevation forests worldwide, including California.

Barbour, M. S., S. Lydon, M. Borchert, M. Popper, and V. Whitworth. 1999. *The Coast Redwood: A Natural and Cultural History.* Los Olivos, CA: Cachuma Press.

Burns, R. M. and B. H. Honkala (editors). 1990. *Silvics of North America, Volume 1, Conifers.* Agriculture Handbook No. 654. Washington, D.C.: USDA Forest Service. A detailed technical treatment of conifers important to forestry in the U.S.

Coffman, T. 1995. *The Cambria Forest.* Cambria: Coastal Heritage Press. An elegant little book on the history of Cambria and the biology of its Monterey pines.

Critchfield, W. B. and E. L. Little, Jr. 1966. *Geographic Distribution of the Pines of the World.* Misc. Pub. 991. Washington, D.C.: USDA Forest Service. Taxonomy and atlas of the world's pines.

Dallimore, W. and A. B. Jackson. 1967. *A Handbook of Coniferae and Ginkgoaceae.* New York: St. Martin's Press. One of several standard conifer references.

Engbeck, J. H., Jr. 1973. *The Enduring Giants.* Berkeley: University of California Press.

Evarts, B. 1994. *Torrey Pines: Landscape and Legacy.* La Jolla, CA: Torrey Pines Association.

Farrar, J. L. 1995. *Trees of the Northern United States and Canada.* Ames: Iowa State University Press. An authoritative dendrology book that includes numerous California species.

Flora of North America Editorial Committee. 1993. *Flora of North America North of Mexico.* Volume 2, Pteridophytes and Gymnosperms. New York: Oxford University Press. A generally authoritative treatment of most conifer genera, but with some questionable taxonomic choices.

Griffin, J. R. and W. B. Critchfield. 1972. *The Distribution of Forest Trees in California.* Research Paper PSW-82. Berkeley: USDA Forest Service. (Reprint with supplement, 1976.) Descriptions and precise maps of all California tree ranges.

Hartesveldt, R. J., H. T. Harvey, H. E. Shellhammer, and

R. E. Stecker. 1975. *The Giant Sequoia of the Sierra Nevada.* Washington, D.C.: National Park Service. Historical and biological overview of giant sequoia.

Harvey, H. T., H. E. Shellhammer, and R. E. Stecker. 1980. *Giant Sequoia Ecology, Fire and Reproduction.* Washington, D.C.: National Park Service. Detailed research reports on the effects of wildfire on giant sequoia regeneration.

Hewes, J. J. 1984. *Redwoods, the World's Largest Trees.* New York: Gallery Books. Well-illustrated history and natural history of redwood and giant sequoia.

Hickman, J. C. (editor). 1993. *The Jepson Manual: Higher Plants of California.* Berkeley: University of California Press. The most recent California flora, including conifer descriptions and keys.

Jepson, W. L. 1910. *The Silva of California.* 2 vols. Berkeley: University of California Press. The classic turn-of-the-century authority on California's trees.

Johnston, V. R. 1994. *California Forests and Woodlands. A Natural History.* Berkeley: University of California Press. An engagingly written popular ecology of the forests and their inhabitants.

Krüssman, G. 1985. *Manual of Cultivated Conifers.* Portland, OR: Timber Press. The English translation of an authoritative German conifer reference.

Lanner, R. M. 1981. *The Piñon Pine: A Natural and Cultural History.* Reno: University of Nevada Press. Historical, biological, and ethnological overview of an important group of pines, including species native to California.

Lanner, R. M. 1984. *Trees of the Great Basin: A Natural History.* Reno: University of Nevada Press. A natural history extending to trees of the eastern Sierra Nevada.

Lanner, R. M. 1996. *Made For Each Other: A Symbiosis of Birds and Pines.* New York: Oxford University Press. Ecology and evolution of corvid-pine seed dispersal symbioses typified by that of Clark's nutcracker and whitebark pine in the Sierra Nevada.

Mirov, N. T. 1967. *The Genus* Pinus. New York: Ronald Press. A technical monograph on pine biology, chemistry, paleobotany, and geography by the transplanted Siberian forester who became a well-known California forest scientist.

Muir, J. 1894. *The Mountains of California.* Garden City, NY: Doubleday Anchor. (1961 reprint). Sensual descriptions of the major Sierra Nevada trees, as only John Muir could write them.

Peattie, D. 1953. *A Natural History of Western Trees.* New York: Houghton Mifflin. Beautifully written, botanically accurate in its day, and elegantly illus-

trated with woodcuts by Paul Landacre, this is a model of natural-history writing.

Peterson, E. B., N. M. Peterson, G. E. Weetman, and P. J. Martin. 1997. *Ecology and Management of Sitka Spruce: Emphasizing its Natural Range in British Columbia.* Vancouver: University of British Columbia Press.

Richardson, D. M. (editor). 1998. *Ecology and Biogeography of* Pinus. Cambridge: Cambridge University Press. A worldwide view of the pines by an international group of specialists.

Sargent, C. S. 1891-1902. *The Silva of North America: A Description of the Trees Which Grow Naturally in North America Exclusive of Mexico.* 14 vols. Boston: Houghton Mifflin. The authoritative turn-of-the-century work on all of America's trees known to that time. Illustrated with C.E. Faxon's highly regarded steel engravings.

Stewart, H. 1984. *Cedar.* Vancouver: Douglas & McIntyre. A stunning book documenting the use of western redcedar by northwest coast Indians. Many fine sketches and photos by the author.

Sudworth, G B. 1908. *Forest Trees of the Pacific Slope.* Washington, D.C.: Government Printing Office. (Reprinted by Dover Publications, New York, 1967.) Detailed descriptions and ranges by the dean of western American dendrologists, with incomparable drawings in pen and ink by C. L. Taylor, A. E. Hoyle, and N. Brenizer.

Vidakovic, M. 1991. *Conifers, Morphology and Variation.* Zagreb: Graficki Zavod Hrvatske. The English translation of a recent technical monograph of the world's conifers.

Willard, D. 1994. *Giant Sequoia Groves of the Sierra Nevada.* Berkeley: Dwight Willard. Descriptions and location data for all the giant sequoia groves, in unprecedented detail.

IMPORTANT WORKS ON CALIFORNIA VEGETATION INCLUDING CONIFER COMMUNITIES

Bakker, E. 1971. *An Island Called California: An Ecological Introduction to its Natural Communities.* Berkeley: University of California Press.

Barbour, M., B. Pavlik, F. Drysdale, and S. Linstrom. 1993. *California's Changing Landscapes: Diversity and Conservation of California Vegetation.* Sacramento: California Native Plant Society.

Barbour, M. G. and J. Major. 1988. *Terrestrial Vegetation of California.* New expanded edition. Special Publication No. 9. Sacramento: California Native Plant Society.

Critchfield, W. B. 1971. *Profiles of California Vegetation.* Research Paper PSW-76. Berkeley: USDA Forest Service. Topographic diagrams showing the altitudinal assortment of tree species on mountains throughout California.

Henson, P. and D. J. Unser. 1993. *The Natural History of Big Sur.* Berkeley: University of California Press.

Mayer, K. E. and W. F. Laudenslayer, Jr. (eds.) 1988. *A Guide to Wildlife Habitats in California.* Sacramento: California Dept. of Forestry and Fire Protection.

Sawyer, J. O. and T. Keeler-Wolf. 1995. *A Manual of California Vegetation.* Sacramento: California Native Plant Society.

Schoenherr, A. 1992. *A Natural History of California.* Berkeley: University of California Press.

SOME PERIODICALS WHERE ARTICLES ON CALIFORNIA CONIFERS FREQUENTLY APPEAR

Popular: *American Forests, Audubon, Arnoldia, California Native Plant Society Chapter Newsletters, California Wild, Four Seasons, Fremontia, Natural History, Sierra, Sunset.*

Technical: *Aliso, American Journal of Botany, American Midland Naturalist, Annals of the Missouri Botanical Garden, BioScience, Canadian Journal of Botany, Canadian Journal of Forest Research, Conservation Biology, Ecology, Evolution, Forest Genetics, Forest Science, Great Basin Naturalist, International Journal of Plant Science, Journal of the Arnold Arboretum, Madroño, Northwest Science, Silvae Genetica, Southwestern Naturalist, Western Journal of Applied Forestry.*

SELECTED CONFERENCE PROCEEDINGS

Aune, P. S. (editor). 1994. *Proceedings of the Symposium on Giant Sequoias: Their Place in the Ecosystem and Society, June 23-25, 1992, Visalia, CA.* USDA Forest Service Gen. Tech. Rep. PSW-GTR-151. Albany, CA: PSW Research Station.

Kinloch, B. B., Jr., M. Marosy, and M. E. Huddleston (editors). 1996. *Sugar Pine: Status, Values, and Roles in Ecosystems.* Proceedings of a Symposium presented by the California Sugar Pine Management Committee. Publication 3362. Davis, CA: University of California, Division of Agriculture and Natural Resources.

LeBlanc, J. (editor). 1996. *Proceedings of the Conference on Coast Redwood Forest Ecology and Management, June 18-20, 1996.* Arcata, CA: Humboldt State University.

Miller, P. R. (tech. coordinator). 1980. *Effects of Air Pollutants on Mediterranean and Temperate Forest Ecosystems; June 22-27, 1980. Riverside, CA.* Gen. Tech. Rep. PSW-43. Berkeley: USDA Forest Service.

North American Forest Biology Workshop (Proceedings issued in even-numbered years from 1970-1998).

Oliver, C. D. and R. M. Kenady (editors). 1981. *Proceedings of the Biology and Management of True Fir in the Pacific Northwest Symposium.* Contrib. No. 45. Seattle: University of Washington, Institute of Forest Resources.

Philbrick, R. N (editor). 1967. *Proceedings of the Symposium on the Biology of the California Islands.* Santa Barbara: Santa Barbara Botanic Garden.

Schmidt, W. C. and K. J. McDonald (compilers). 1990. *Proceedings—Symposium on Whitebark Pine Ecosystems: Ecology and Management of a High-Mountain Resource; March 29-31, 1989, Bozeman, MT.* Gen. Tech. Rep. INT—270. Ogden: USDA Forest Service.

INDEX